THE LIFE
OF MIKEY

A MEMOIR

MICHAEL K. WILLIS

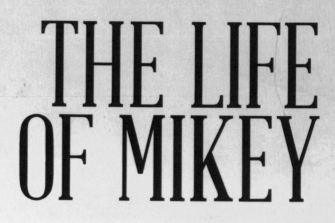

AUTOGRAPHED
COPY

THE LIFE OF MIKEY

A Memoir

Michael K. Willis

Publisher's Cataloging-In-Publication Data
(Prepared by The Donohue Group, Inc.)

Names: Willis, Michael K., 1952-
Title: The life of Mikey : a memoir / Michael K. Willis.
Description: Asheville, NC : Liber Libri Publishing, [2017] | Includes bibliographical
references.
Identifiers: LCCN 2017907352 | ISBN 978-0-9990064-0-5 (paperback) |
ISBN 0-9990064-0-1 (paperback) | ISBN 978-0-9990064-2-9 (hardcover) |
ISBN 0-9990064-2-8 (hardcover) | ISBN 978-0-9990064-1-2 (ebook)
Subjects: LCSH: Willis, Michael K. | Teenage boys--North Carolina--Biography.
| Coming of age--North Carolina. | North Carolina--Biography. | LCGFT:
Autobiographies. | BISAC: BIOGRAPHY & AUTOBIOGRAPHY / Personal Memoirs. |
BIOGRAPHY & AUTOBIOGRAPHY / Cultural Heritage.
Classification: LCC HQ799.72.N8 W55 2017 (print) | LCC HQ799.72.N8 (ebook) |
DDC 305.235/1092--dc23

ISBN: 0999006401
ISBN 13: 9780999006405
Library of Congress Control Number: 2017907352

PO Box 7233, Asheville, NC 28802
http://liberlibripublishing.com

TABLE OF CONTENTS

PREFACE

In 1960, when I was eight, Mrs. Cabe, my second-grade teacher at Cartoogechaye Elementary School, introduced my classmates and me to a book that she read to us over the course of the next several weeks. The book was entitled *The Thread That Runs So True*. It was the tale of a young teacher who chronicled events that took place during his first year of teaching in a one-room schoolhouse in the mountains of eastern Kentucky during the early part of the twentieth century. Even though it was a different era and the writer was much older than I was, I was captivated by the stories and associated my experiences in the mountains of western North Carolina and at Cartoogechaye Elementary School with those of the author's.

When Mrs. Cabe was through with the book, I pledged someday to write about my life. Throughout the years I never forgot that promise. A few years ago, I became curious about the book that had been read to me a half century earlier. I went to the local library and found a copy. The writer was Jesse Stuart, a noted Kentuckian who wrote both prose and verse and became the poet laureate of his state.

Rereading *The Thread That Runs So True* rekindled my old desire to write, which had lain dormant since the second grade. The result is the memoir you hold in your hands. My book chronicles the struggles of my childhood and teenage years growing up in the 1950s and the 1960s. However, it is more than just a tale about my life. Through it, I have also endeavored to convey the essence of time and place; of institutions and economy; of history, politics, and religion; of pop culture; and of the great societal transformations that took place during that era—all of which profoundly affected my life.

I wish to acknowledge my editors, Wanda Griffith and Karen Ackerson, for the superb work they did in transforming my book into a polished product. I also wish to acknowledge my good friend Tommie Jeanne Davis, whose steadfast support during the months it took to write this book and critical review of the material along the way were invaluable. Further, I acknowledge the help of my siblings, Elaine, Gloria, Johnny, Randy, Deborah, Dawn, and Phillip, each of whom contributed to the development of my story in various ways. Finally, I must acknowledge the help of many Franklin High School classmates whose stories of our time at that school were helpful as I wrote of my experiences there.

PROLOGUE

"Mikey, I'm going to beat the shit out of you if you don't stop running and causing all that commotion!" Mother said as I went racing past her. We lived in a tiny rental house in Maggie Valley, North Carolina, where my father pastored Olivet Baptist Church. In my child's world, I was oblivious to the disturbance I was causing in my moment of play. Mother had no sooner gotten these words out of her mouth than Daddy caught me.

"I'll take care of it now!" Daddy said as he unleashed a torrent of lashes with his belt. As his anger rose, he dispensed with the belt and began hitting, punching, and kicking me. Bruised, battered, and crying, I was finally allowed to retreat to my room and away from the anger of Mother and Daddy. Such was life as the child of a Baptist preacher.

When reflecting on my time living in the parsonages and in the churches where my father pastored, I have often thought, *What if these walls could talk?* The walls that surrounded me would speak of both sad memories and humorous tales.

I heard this story from the walls of Mount Hope Baptist Church, where my father pastored when I was four. I arrived at the church with my family. Daddy always wanted to make a good impression when it was church time.

"None of you young'uns had better be doing or saying anything this morning that will embarrass me. Do you understand?" Daddy said as we entered the sanctuary.

"Yes!" we all replied.

As we walked into the church, I encountered the prettiest young woman I had ever seen. In fact, she was probably the first I had ever noticed in my entire life. But then, I was only four years old. Taken off guard and enraptured by the woman's beauty, I quickly forgot Daddy's admonition not to cause him humiliation.

Her form was very shapely, as I gazed up at her. She was standing tall and straight in a tight red dress. Her dark-brown eyes and brunet hair matched perfectly, and her bright-red lipstick accentuated her appearance. Something else about this young woman captured my attention. Pointing upward, I asked, "Mother, what are those sharp things?" I was referring to the girl's breasts, which were held high by her form-shaping bra.

"Mikey!" Mother screeched as she put her hand over my mouth and dragged me over to a pew. "I'm going to beat the hell out of you when we get home," she hissed.

The young woman smiled. From then on, she showered me with attention every time we came to church, which was well worth the whipping Mother gave me after we got home that day.

As far as Grandmother Willis was concerned, my father, John Ralph Willis Jr., was predestined to be a preacher. My mother said that Dad was a "mama's boy"—that he would do anything to please her, even if that meant preaching. Whether it was because of this prediction or because he had a real calling to the ministry, no one will ever know. What is certain is that Dad was preaching tent revivals in Haywood County, North Carolina, by the age of sixteen.

Mother also had another theory about my father's preaching. She believed Dad was lazy and had found the perfect way to make a living in the preaching profession without having to exert much effort. Perhaps her opinion biased my view, but it became my observation too that Dad had an aversion to hard work.

Perhaps it wasn't laziness that drove my father but rather a quest for religious knowledge and truth. He was an intelligent man who enjoyed studying theology and biblical archeology. My early years are filled with memories of Dad's absences as he first attended Fruitland Baptist Bible Institute in Hendersonville, North Carolina, and then Southeastern Baptist Theological Seminary in Wake Forest, North Carolina. During these years he came home only on weekends. When Dad was in the pulpit, he seemed to have a genuine thirst for God and the Bible. He also appeared to be able to express this passion beyond the church and into the community. It was at home that his words and deeds never seemed to match up with his profession.

I never understood my father, and we were never close. He was charming and charismatic in public and before his congregation, but his mood quickly changed when he stepped inside the walls of our home. While he took young men under his wing to nurture them, especially those who aspired to be ministers, he was cold, hard, and brutal at home. In all the sixty-nine years of his life, my father never expressed his love for me. For the most part, he did provide financially for our family, and when he returned from revivals, he often brought us gifts. But these were temporary signs of affection, usually lost in an instant when an outburst brought back his wrath. That was the hectic atmosphere of our home.

Dad had a ruddy complexion and dark hair. He wore glasses and a hearing aid in his right ear. Perhaps Dad was handsome. Many women, it seemed, thought he was. Dad certainly acted as if he thought he was Clark Gable. The confidence Dad displayed won him many followers. He exhibited a unique charm, and his confident walk, or swagger, attracted people to him. In the culture of the southern Appalachians, preachers were highly esteemed. The position of pastor's wife was a coveted position, especially among Baptists. Many women would have gladly traded places with my mother.

My earliest memory of Dad was of a tall, red-faced man who towered over me. A strong man, my father could throw me across the room in one quick motion. His whippings and beatings were so terrible that most, thankfully, have been erased from my memory. By the time I was in high school, I had begun to see him for what he was: five feet seven inches tall, 160 pounds... and just plain mean. I had grown physically to the point where my dad could no longer dominate me. As I matured, we reached a standoff in our relationship, where it stayed until his death many years later.

Mother was five feet four inches tall with extremely fair skin and sandy-brown hair. She was brilliant, probably smarter than my father. I always remember Mother as overweight, but I know now this wasn't a valid description. A picture of Mother holding her sixth child while almost certainly pregnant with her seventh depicts a woman who was young and full-figured but not overweight. Dad said that my mother was "plump," just the way he liked a woman. After she had birthed eight children, it is no wonder that the weight eventually "stayed on her hips," as people in Appalachia described it.

My mother had issues that contributed to the chaos of our home. She often whipped us without the slightest provocation. Unlike my father, Mother wasn't robust enough to inflict lasting injury and enlisted the assistance of my dad, who was all too willing to oblige.

She didn't like anything about being a preacher's wife. In fact, she loathed it. And unlike my dad, who always was invoking Jesus's teachings as the way we should live our lives, Mother seemed mostly ambivalent. Her cursing, too, was contrary to what one would expect of a preacher's wife. Since it was all I had heard as a child,

I didn't realize until later that there was something odd about having a mother who cursed like a sailor.

Mother was emotionally fragile and full of worry and doubt. She must have felt trapped, rearing eight children with her husband gone much of the time. Mother was also the unhappiest person I had ever known. I believe she was almost certainly mentally ill. In modern-day terminology, she may have had bipolar disorder, although I have no expertise in mental health to make that judgment. What I do know is that the affliction occurs on Mother's side of our family. Free from it myself, I do have family members who have the diagnosis. Because of this unhappiness, Mother had abusive tendencies that included attacks on my self-worth. She ridiculed me and said I would never have enough "gumption" to make something out of my life. I wasn't close to my mother and felt uncomfortable any time she touched me, even when she gave me a bath. I never once heard Mother say she loved me, and I cannot recall a single tender moment with her.

The relationship between my parents was complicated, but I am confident that they loved each other. They argued and fought at times, but not too often. One thing they agreed on was the discipline of their children. My parents were a team who worked in concert, dividing and conquering all the siblings in the process. I never recall one time when either one interfered with the other's disciplinary actions. Rather, one defended the other if an attempt was made to appeal the disciplinary measure.

When my eldest sister was old enough to babysit, Mother and Dad would leave the rest of us in her care and take the time to be together. Usually, they never left for more than half a day, but this ritual became symbolic in my mind of their affection for one another. It wasn't unusual, however, for them to criticize each other when the other wasn't around. Mother's disparagement centered on Dad's prolonged absences from home, his laziness, and the fact that he gave his mother too much attention. Dad denounced Mother for nagging him all the time and not being sensitive to his needs. In short, Dad's criticism of Mother was centered in his selfishness, while Mother's criticism of Dad focused on his lack of attention to the household.

Financial conflicts also were frequent. Such disagreements focused on not having enough to supply both needs and wants for such a large family. It is evident, looking back, that we were poor, although my siblings and I never thought of our situation that way. Neither Mother nor Dad had a "poor" mentality and didn't pass one on to their children either.

In my younger years, my red hair was clipped crew-cut style by my father. Fair skinned, I developed a mass of freckles because of the sun. For a time, I wore "husky" jeans, which today many find difficult to believe because of my slight, thin frame. As I age, I am told by those who knew my dad that I look more and more like him.

As I grew from child to adolescent, my stature changed. My red hair still stood out as my most prominent feature, but it was longer, and I could comb it. My dad finally allowed me to go to the barbershop, freeing me from his homemade crew cuts. I was stronger than many of my friends, a key factor in my success as a fighter at school and in the streets. While I could stand up to my peers, the big gap between my two front teeth affected my self-esteem. To me, the gap was unsightly and made me feel ugly. I didn't believe girls thought I was handsome. My small self-image would have consequences in the future when it came to female relationships and dating, although I think my dismal relationship with my mother may have played a bigger role.

Other than these preconceived notions in my head, I had a good opinion of myself. In many ways, I was unflappable. Since I was always high-minded, strong willed, and self-determined, it is no wonder I had many conflicts with both of my parents. Inquisitive, smart, and curious, I took my intelligence from both my parents. Mostly, I viewed life through the filter of humor. Pranks and good-natured ribbing became a way of life. My siblings did not always appreciate my comedy since they were often at the receiving end of my jokes. I viewed life in the most positive light possible, always believing that something better was awaiting me just around the corner. Like the classic optimist, whenever I came to a pile of manure, I picked up a shovel and started digging, convinced that a pony was underneath the pile. I also viewed my life from an "otherworldly" perspective. I believed I was among the people of Appalachia but not of them. I was a character out of place, an oddity among the people of the mountains, and a soul no one understood. Left alone in my thoughts, I created a stable world in my mind filled with the beauty of nature that surrounded me.

My father's ability to whip and abuse me ended when I entered my teenage years. He must have been frustrated because no matter how hard he tried, he was never able to break my strong will. I never understood why he felt it important to do so—we never discussed it. He always wanted me to be a preacher, like him. Perhaps he thought that by beating the perceived demons out of me, it would make me willing to accept the "call." I was never interested.

Four boys and four girls were born to John and Mildred Willis during their marriage. I was the fourth child and second-oldest boy. My seven siblings dealt with the consequences of their upbringing, just as I have, but in different ways. Thus, I have struggled with how to tell this account while being sensitive to them. My effort is meant to tell *my* story and not theirs, while still recognizing that this narrative covers much of their lives too.

The phrase "if these walls could talk" generally alludes to memories of the past. It often conjures up real feelings and emotions, precious memories of family, friends, and fun. The expression is also used to convey the opposite: tears and bitterness, trials and tragedy, sadness and betrayal. My use of the phrase refers to both. Through the years, I have preferred to remember the former while trying to forget the latter, but it has been a futile exercise. Both memories are alive, indelibly written in my heart, in my mind, and in my emotions.

This book is full of reflections played over and over in my mind of walls that not only talk but shout out the hurtful words of degradation and reproach. They also resonate with the fun and laughter I managed to hold on to despite my difficulties. I once believed that over time these memories would fade, but that has not happened. In fact, the opposite is true. They seem more vivid today than ever before, prompting me finally to write them down. These memories have roamed in my head long enough. It is time to set them free.

CHAPTER 1

THE BEGINNING

My father, John Ralph Willis Jr., was the son of John Ralph Willis and Tymah Desdimona Williams. Ralph and Tymah married in 1906; she was fifteen, and he was twenty. Ralph and his brothers farmed in Haywood County, North Carolina, in a cove acquired by their father, William Volney Willis.

Throughout the early twentieth century, Ralph and Tymah raised a family of nine in the Willis Cove, the same farmland on which Ralph and his brothers had grown up. The Willis Cove was located five miles northeast of Canton, North Carolina, and north of Newfound Gap in the North Hominy Community along Willis Cove Road.

By the mid-1930s, the Great Depression had taken its toll on Ralph and his brothers. One by one, over the next decade, each sold his share of the Willis Cove, as many of the brothers' children grew to adulthood and left to seek livelihoods in places other than the mountains of western North Carolina.

The Willises, realizing farming had become increasingly difficult as each child moved on, cashed in, sold their land, and used the money to buy homes closer to town, taking jobs where they could find them. They moved from the cove that had borne the Willis family name for nearly a century.

Ralph went to work at Sluder Furniture Company on Main Street in Canton, an incorporated town within the borders of Haywood County. Ralph and Tymah also bought a small two-story, white wood-framed house at 198 Newfound Street in Canton.

John Ralph Jr., their youngest child, was still an adolescent, having been born July 3, 1923. Settling into town life meant Ralph and Tymah rarely visited Plains Methodist Church, where they were members and where they had had John Ralph Jr. baptized when he was an infant. From the time of her youngest son's birth, Tymah had said that someday John Ralph Jr. was to be a minister of the gospel. Bouncing him upon her knee when he was a toddler, Tymah often said, "This one is my little preacher."

After moving to Newfound Street, Tymah attended Calvary Baptist Church, located just down the street. John Ralph Jr. went with her and became a Baptist. Dropping his middle name, John began preaching when he was sixteen years old. He was formally ordained at Calvary Baptist Church several years later. He and his older brother, Floyd, went around with a tent, preaching all over Haywood County. They also conducted church revival services. He developed an exceptional reputation among the Baptists for his charming personality and fiery sermons. Revival preaching was his gift, his specialty.

During one of these church revivals, John met my mother, Mildred Grace Parks, born July 19, 1928. Her parents were Jesse Harley Parks and Nova Alice Chapman. Jesse and Alice had reared seven children in Haywood and surrounding counties; Mildred was the youngest.

Like his father, Tom Parks, Jesse was a blacksmith, which meant moving the family throughout western North Carolina to find work. Eventually, he ended these itinerant jobs and moved the family back to his native Haywood County. Jesse took a job as a janitor at the Enka Plant, a rayon mill in adjoining Buncombe County, riding a bus back and forth from Canton daily. Mildred, the youngest child, grew up during these years.

Mildred fell in love with John shortly after they met. John was smitten too, but he had other young women who vied for his hand over the next several years. Still, as each relationship ran its course, John returned to Mildred. In 1945, Mildred graduated from Canton High School. John, who was five years older, had also attended Canton High but dropped out to concentrate on his preaching. World War II might have changed things for John and Mildred, but fate intervened. John enlisted in the marines on September 12, 1942, and was shipped off to the Marine Corps Recruitment Depot, Parris Island, South Carolina, for boot camp. While there, he discovered he was nearly deaf in his right ear. The marines honorably discharged John due to this medical disability on October 17, 1942. He returned home to Canton. John, twenty-two, and Mildred, seventeen, married right after her high school graduation on July 23, 1945. They eloped to Georgia.

In the early morning hours of February 6, 1952, Mildred Willis was in labor with her fourth child at Marion General Hospital in Marion, North Carolina. John and Mildred had moved there in 1950. Marion was a small town, the county seat of McDowell County. At the time of the move, John and Mildred had two children: Elaine, born in 1946, and Gloria, born in 1948. Johnny was born in Marion in 1951. Preacher Willis had first come to McDowell County to pastor Woodlawn Baptist Church, but by the time of my birth, he was the pastor at Yancy Street.

Nestled in the foothills of western North Carolina, shielded to the west by the Black Mountains, McDowell County's scenery was magnificent, with the Catawba River flowing through the heart of the county, emptying into Lake James. The Pisgah National Forest covered nearly half the county.

McDowell County was a place many proudly called home, but my parents weren't happy there. They missed Canton, their hometown in Haywood County. In contrast to the foothills of McDowell County, Haywood County contained some of the most rugged mountains in all the Blue Ridge. The Pisgah National Forest continued its broad reach along the northeastern and southern parts of Haywood County. At 6,030 feet, Cold Mountain, located in the southeast, was located within Pisgah's borders. Haywood County also contained a portion of the Qualla Boundary, the tribal reservation for the Eastern Band of the Cherokee Indians. In the northwestern section of Haywood County was nestled a part of the Great Smoky Mountains National Park. The county was believed to be one of the highest counties by elevation in all the Appalachian chain. Its height produced winters that were sometimes harsh, while summers were mild. The ancient Appalachians spread wide open here atop a plateau uplifted millions of years before. Majestic in their beauty, on a clear day these mountains seemed to float in the distance along the horizon. When cloud covered, they appeared foreboding, dark, and haunting. The only blemish on the otherwise beauteous Haywood County was the Champion Pulp Mill, located in Canton.

Since 1906, the pulp operation had provided much-needed employment for many of the residents. These jobs came with a price—the environment suffered greatly in exchange for the above-average wages the mill paid. The plant's smokestack polluted the air, and its processing operations ruined the Pigeon River. The problems, ignored in the early twentieth century, became a rallying cry for environmentalists by century's end. This issue stirred a rare dispute between Tennessee and North Carolina as the brownish, white-foamed, foul-smelling water flowed downstream into Cocke County, Tennessee. The malodorous smoke wafted through the air from the time of the mill's opening. The smog in downtown Canton was at times so thick it clouded the air, choked the throat, and burned the eyes.

"Mother, what's that smell?" my siblings and I would invariably ask when we came to visit Grandmother and Granddaddy Willis. "It tastes awful!"

"It's that damn Champion mill!" Mother said. "I've never gotten used to that rotten egg smell. It's one of the nastiest smells I know!"

"My eyes are burning," I said. "I can't breathe."

"The fog is hanging low over Canton today," Daddy said. "Sometimes that happens when the wind is just right. That's what makes you cough and causes your eyes to burn."

Most residents defended the mill and dismissed the environmental issues as minor inconveniences. They referred to the odor from the smokestack as "the smell of money." With new ownership in 1999, aggressive steps were undertaken to clean up the pollution. Over time, the smell from the plant also lessened.

Just before daylight at Marion General Hospital, Dr. Paul McBee, Mildred's doctor, greeted John in the waiting room. "Preacher Willis, you have a beautiful, healthy, seven-pound-and-two-ounce baby boy, born at 6:32 a.m. Mildred's doing fine too. Once we get the baby cleaned up, we'll let you see him."

Following my uneventful arrival, Mother named me Michael Keith but called me "Mikey." I was brought home to my parents' home on Yancy Street, where I joined my brother and two sisters.

Within a few weeks, I attended my first church service at Yancy Street Baptist Church. A few months later, Mother and Daddy moved us back to their beloved Haywood County.

CHAPTER 2
HAYWOOD COUNTY

M y earliest memory was of Mother holding me in her arms outside Olivet Baptist Church one bright, sunny Sunday. A woman touched me under the chin, which made me yelp. This stranger's touch raised my fiery temper, a trait that became a prominent feature of my personality. It also matched my red hair. I was very young at the time, too young to walk.

Olivet, located in Maggie Valley and within Haywood County, was the church Daddy had come to be the pastor of. It was a small gable-front church covered with plain weatherboards painted white. In the summer the windows were raised to allow the cooling breezes to flow inside. In the winter, it was warmed by a large stove that sat halfway down the length of the auditorium. The small building had unfinished wood flooring. There were many churches like it throughout western North Carolina.

On Sundays, the church members complimented Mother and Daddy on how well behaved their children were. We were always well groomed and dressed in our best clothing. We sat on one row with Mother, while Daddy sat up front at the podium. Not a peep emanated from our lips even if the hardwood bench became uncomfortable. All the Willis children were a picture of perfection. On Sunday afternoons Daddy also preached at a newly established church, Victory Baptist, which met at Peachtree Methodist because Victory had not yet acquired a permanent meeting place.

Haywood County was home to all my relatives and ancestors. Even though I was born in Marion, my heritage rested within this rural county. In the 1950s, its population was approximately thirty-eight thousand, larger than that of neighboring counties. The Maggie Valley area, where we lived, was a little-known rural community. The rest of western North Carolina in the 1950s was also primarily rural, except for Asheville and Buncombe County, the economic center of the region. Farming, tourism, lumber, textile mills, mining, and retailing made up the bulk of the business. Tobacco was a chief cash crop, but livestock production was also an important aspect of farming. We lived around farmers who raised cows, chickens, pigs, tobacco, and other cash crops. Many were part-time farmers who held down other full-time jobs.

One unique feature of the agricultural industry in western North Carolina was the growing of the mountain balsam, also known as the Fraser fir, on Christmas tree farms. These were traditional Christmas trees for those who could afford them. For our Christmas, Daddy always got a cedar tree for free from one of the nearby farms or wooded areas.

The growing season for crops was short. Harvests consisted of hardy varieties of fruits and vegetables that grew quickly in the short summer season. Apples were a cash crop, while corn was grown primarily for cattle feed. Church members gave us a wide variety of fruits and vegetables, which we ate all summer long. What we didn't eat, Mother canned and kept for the winter.

Western North Carolina, with its mountain resorts, recreational trails, ruby mines, and music festivals, drew visitors from across the nation. I only saw glimpses of these as we passed by along the rugged mountain roadways. We never stopped.

The logging industry thrived, as clear-cutting on both national and private land was a standard practice, with lumber mills a common fixture in many rural communities. The furniture and wood products businesses were spin-offs of this logging enterprise. In the winter, I rode along with Daddy as he went to lumber mills in search of free kindling to start our coal stove. Occasionally he asked for two-by-fours or other boards to use at home or the church. Sometimes he got them free; other times he got the "preacher's discount."

Textile mills were common in many rural counties of western North Carolina, and they provided needed jobs for many locals. The railroads and mining operations also provided employment. The mining industry in western North Carolina consisted of mica and feldspar. Quarrying of granite was also common. Many of Daddy's church members held down full-time jobs at the Champion Pulp Mill or other local enterprises. Daddy was averse to taking a job, as it would have interfered with his preaching responsibilities and his attendance at Fruitland Baptist Bible Institute.

Things had changed dramatically in America. By the 1950s, World War II had ended, and the country had emerged as a supreme world power. An opposing power had also developed—the Soviet Union. These two clashing giants defined global politics for the next forty years. Mother and Daddy followed the world and national events in the newspaper and on the radio until 1956, when Daddy got our first TV. With its arrival, Mother and Daddy also watched TV news, something I became attracted to at an early age.

America had emerged from the Great Depression, which had devastated people's lives before the war. Things were looking up. People were working, and families were settling down. The country had returned to normal, except for the new Cold War threat that loomed large in people's minds, along with another war that had begun in Korea. This new world order had a vivid impact not only on Daddy's preaching but also on the sermons of all his Baptist preacher friends. Daddy intoned dramatic end time addresses at most of his revivals and other church gatherings.

Harry S. Truman was president. He ended World War II in 1945 by dropping atomic bombs on the Japanese cities of Hiroshima and Nagasaki. Daddy said we were safe under Truman. Mother liked him too.

Dwight D. Eisenhower, the great general who led our troops to victory over Germany and the Axis powers, followed Truman as president in 1953. Daddy liked Eisenhower because of his military success and believed he was just what we needed after Truman.

In America, hysteria over Communism burned white hot. Beginning in 1950, Senator Joseph McCarthy led the charge against it—Communists were spying, plotting to turn Americans into Communists. He held hearings in 1954, falsely accused many, and ruined their lives. But by 1957, both McCarthy and his McCarthyism had died. The evil of godless Communism was also a big topic for Daddy's end time preaching. As the nuclear arms race advanced, the Soviets launched Sputnik in 1957, the first satellite to orbit the earth. America started its program, and the Space Race was born. Daddy believed the Soviet Union came "from the pit of hell."

The US Supreme Court ruled in 1954 that segregated schools were unconstitutional. In 1955, Rosa Parks, an African American woman in Birmingham, Alabama, declined to give up her bus seat to a white passenger. She was arrested and jailed. Martin Luther King Jr. led a boycott of Birmingham's bus system to protest the city's discriminatory policies, beginning the civil rights movement. Mother was concerned about this movement, arguing, "They're trying to ruin our way of life."

Daddy was worried by the civil disobedience but otherwise was a little more sympathetic. "God made every man equal, but I don't think the coloreds should disobey the law," he said. I was oblivious to all these things. Growing up was my singular purpose. For me, the evil and injustice in the world were problems for others.

⊷ ⊶

During the years that Daddy pastored Olivet Baptist Church, we lived in three different rental houses. When we arrived in Haywood County, we lived in a small house located along Jonathan Creek. It was fifteen miles west of Canton. Jonathan Creek was a community near Maggie Valley. This unincorporated township derived its name from the creek that ran through it. We lived right next to the creek. To get to our house, you had to turn off the main road and cross Jonathan Creek on an old, handmade wooden bridge. This bridge was just barely wide enough to allow our old Dodge Desoto to pass. A graveled driveway led to the house, which we usually entered through the back door and into the kitchen. A cornfield, enclosed by a deer fence, was visible across the driveway. Beyond the cornfield were woods.

The small wood-framed house was painted white and had a front porch where my brother, Johnny, and I often played. The elements had weathered the unpainted wooden floor. The home had a small living room, a kitchen, three bedrooms, and a bathroom that had hot and cold running water. Mother gave us daily "dab baths" through the week and a tub bath every Saturday evening.

Several of my earliest memories involve Jonathan Creek and the bridge that crossed over it.

When I was eighteen months old, we were coming home from church one night, and Mother said to Daddy, "John, stop the car at the bridge and let me go across the road to borrow a cup of sugar from Mrs. Cagle." Daddy complied.

I wanted to go, but Mother said sternly, "No, Mikey, you can't go! I'll only be a minute. I'll see you at the house." As she departed and Daddy began driving the car across the bridge, I opened the back door and bolted out. My siblings started to scream as I left the car. I fell, face down, on the edge of the bridge, which had no railing. As I clung to the side, I peered into the water below. The waves were passing by swiftly. I could see the smooth, rounded rocks beneath the flowing water.

Daddy stopped the car, jumped out to pick me off the side of the bridge, and threw me back into the car. It was a miracle I hadn't plunged into the creek that evening. Everyone was crying, and I was mad. At home, I refused to get out of the car and go into the house. Daddy said, "Fine, son, stay in the car then," and he took the others and went inside. As dusk settled in and I began to get scared, Daddy returned and carried me into the house. Mother returned shortly with her cup of sugar.

The creek also played a starring role in an incident that occurred after my older sisters took in a stray cat and fed it against Mother's wishes. Still, she tolerated the cat until it had a litter of kittens. Mother found these kittens too much to bear and their care excessively burdensome. One day she got an old burlap sack or "tow sack," as she called it, put heavy rocks in it, placed the kittens in the bag, and tied the mouth.

"What are you doing with that tow sack, Mother?" I asked.

"I'm getting rid of these damn cats."

I followed her to the old wooden bridge at the top of the driveway where I had almost drowned earlier. With a sudden heave, she tossed the burlap sack with the rocks and the kittens into the creek. The bag immediately sank to the bottom. "Where are the kittens?" I asked.

"Never mind; they're gone now," Mother said. Her harsh practice of animal euthanasia was common. Many in the Blue Ridge Mountains employed this method of animal control.

My sister Elaine was baptized in Jonathan Creek one Sunday afternoon when she was eight and I was three. The entire Olivet Baptist Church congregation gathered along the edge of the creek for this event. Dad baptized Elaine, several children, and a few adults that day. In the car on the way home, Daddy said, "When I was a boy, Old Lady Snider drowned while being baptized. As the preacher put her into that watery grave, the current from the bottom of the creek swept her all the way to glory!"

"Then I don't ever want to be baptized!" I said. Daddy just laughed.

One day we were playing in the front yard when a chain gang came by the house. They were working on Jonathan Creek Road. A man in a uniform was standing over the prisoners with a double-barrel shotgun as they worked. I had never seen people linked together by a chain being forced to work. Many were African Americans. About the time I became curious, Mother came out of the front door screaming, "Get in the house! All you young'uns get in the house, now!" Shocked and frightened, we ran into the house.

"Mother, what's wrong?" I asked.

"That's a chain gang—prisoners! You stay away from those niggers! They'll eat you alive." After that incident, I went inside every time I saw the chain gang coming, for I certainly didn't want to be eaten.

During the time we lived at Jonathan Creek, Daddy went back to school. Having dropped out of high school, he felt the need to complete his education to advance in the preaching profession. He attended Fruitland Baptist Bible Institute in Hendersonville, North Carolina. The school, located fifty miles southeast of

Maggie Valley, was a logical choice for someone like Daddy, as applicants could attend without regard to previous academic achievement. Daddy pursued his diploma in earnest, spending most of the week in Hendersonville and returning to preach on weekends. We didn't see him very much during those years. Finally, on March 26, 1954, he received his diploma in theology.

In the 1950s, Maggie Valley was a sleepy little place. Situated within Haywood County's rugged mountains, it was destined to become a popular tourist attraction in the years to come. When I lived in this small town, it was just a hidden rural valley where life was simple—at least for a child.

Our second home in Maggie Valley was on Evans Cove Road, just off US Highway 19, which ran through the little town. It was a small wood-framed house with beige slate siding. The interior was laid out much like the house on Jonathan Creek with a small living room, a kitchen, three bedrooms, and a bathroom with hot and cold running water. My brother and I occupied the back bedroom of the house, down the hallway to the right. The front of the home had no porch but only a small covered stoop at the entrance. The milkman delivered milk by the quart in glass bottles. A hard waxed-paper stopper sealed the bottle top. The iceman came by every few days to provide a new block of ice for the icebox.

The children, now five—Randy was born in June 1953—played and helped Mother with the chores. Mother was a meticulous cleaner. When she waxed the old hardwood floors, she allowed us to buff them. Johnny and I took turns pulling each other down the hallway and over the boards on old rags.

When we became unruly, which was often, we got whippings. If we were lucky, we only got a switching. Usually, Mother used a razor strap she kept hanging in the kitchen or one of Daddy's leather belts. Only at church did we gather ourselves long enough to behave for an extended period. The consequences for embarrassing

Daddy as the preacher or Mother as the pastor's wife were too severe. It was much better to comply at church.

At home, it was a different matter. Mother dispensed whippings liberally among all the children, as we were inclined to fuss and fight much of the time. Mother swore at us, which wasn't typical behavior for a Baptist preacher's wife, but we didn't know this fact—it was something we considered normal. Since swearing came naturally for Mother, I assumed every mother cursed at her children. While Mother's coarse language was prolific, it was never profane. She didn't use the more vulgar words I learned later. Daddy disapproved of Mother's swearing, but there was little he could do to stop it.

"Now Mildred, you shouldn't be talking that way around the young'uns," he'd say. These words fell on deaf ears, as Mother's swearing was set off by an endless array of circumstances. Daddy didn't swear. In fact, I never heard him utter a curse word his entire life. Still, we feared his whippings the most since he scared us with his anger, which usually boiled into a rage and then provoked severe poundings. These whippings often occurred when Daddy came home tired and exhausted.

Christmas at Olivet Baptist Church was memorable in 1954, as my sister Gloria let out a blood-curdling scream when the back door of the church was flung open and a big man in a red suit and white beard appeared in the doorway shouting, "Ho, ho, ho!" The noise scared me too until I saw Santa Claus giving out gifts to all the children. I calmed down and took the gift passed to me, while Gloria stayed hidden under the church bench.

We stayed at the Evans Cove Road house for only a short time, leaving there to live in a house rent-free. By the spring of 1955, we had moved to Waynesville. Sam Bradley's old place was a small wood-framed house, eight miles south of Maggie Valley. It had weathered natural-wood siding, but the window frames were painted white. To enter, we used the home's narrow and steep wooden stairs, which my siblings and I sat on to have our Easter pictures taken. The house had one large room with the front portion serving as the living room. The back part was the kitchen. There was one large bedroom to the left of the living room, where Mother, Daddy, Johnny, Randy, and I slept. Elaine and Gloria slept in a pantry room near the kitchen, which Daddy made into a tiny bedroom. There was a small back porch where my brothers and I usually came and went while playing.

The house in Waynesville was the only home I lived in that had no indoor toilet. Mother cried when we moved into the house because of the outhouse and because it only had cold running water. It was also filthy, but my mother meticulously scrubbed the black soot off the walls before we moved into the home. For our baths, Mother boiled hot water on the stove and poured it into a large galvanized steel tub.

I turned three years old while we lived at Sam Bradley's. By this time, I was potty trained. Occasionally, I was still accident-prone. One day while playing in the house, I had the urge to urinate. Forgetting I only had on a pair of underwear, I let it go, right in the middle of the worn living room floor. As the urine trickled down my legs, forming a puddle, I became curious about the yellow liquid and how it might taste. When I bent down and took a slurp, the taste was bitter and awful. I vowed to myself not to ever do it again.

Mother found me in the middle of the puddle. "You little shit hook! Don't you ever do that again—do you understand me?" she said as she changed my underwear.

Once I was potty trained, I had to use the outhouse just as everyone else did. As one faced Sam Bradley's old place, the outhouse was to the left and up a small hill. Finding one day it had no toilet paper, I proceeded to carry a roll up the hill. As I got near the top, I dropped it and watched as it unrolled all the way down. Mother rewound the toilet paper. "Son, you do some of the damndest things."

In fact, I did do the damndest things, and one involved the cow pasture at the rear of the house. Johnny and I didn't go into the field when the cows were present, because we feared them. Sometimes when the cows were not around, we climbed through the barbed-wire fence and played in the pasture. Johnny and I always tried to avoid the cow patties—especially the fresh ones. On one occasion, I slipped and fell while running. Like a baseball player at home plate, I slid right through a fresh cow pile, which covered me from head to toe in green manure. "You little bastard," Mother yelled as she retrieved me from the field and threw me into the washtub, scrubbing me thoroughly. "Mikey, I'll beat the hell out of you if you ever do anything like that again. You even got cow shit in your ears!"

That spring, Daddy got Johnny, Randy, and me toy rakes, shovels, and hoes. We had a great time raking, digging, and hoeing every-thing in sight. We even helped Daddy as he was making a garden. I was working alongside Daddy when he said, "Mikey, stay in the row." I looked around, but all I could see was dirt everywhere. I didn't understand Daddy, so I just kept on with what I was doing. In a few minutes, Daddy said again, "Son, hoe in the row like I'm doing."

When I gave him a puzzled look, he said, "Oh, just forget it."

I was confused, I knew what a hot dog roll was, but I didn't see one in the garden. "Daddy, where's the hot dog rolls?" I asked.

"Son, I didn't say *roll*; I said *row*. Don't you see the rows I've plowed?" I finally saw the rows where Daddy was working and be-gan working in them too.

Mother made all the children Kool-Aid to drink and, occasionally, as an extra treat, gave us a packet of the tart mixture, which we opened and ate. It was a favorite we all enjoyed immensely. One day after finishing my Kool-Aid packet, I scooped red clay into the empty package and started eating it. I decided it wasn't good for Mother to see me eating this new Kool-Aid concoction. I went inside and hid behind a door. Elaine saw what I had done and said to Mother, "Look, Mikey is eating dirt!"

"Mikey, what are you doing behind that door?"

"I'm eating Kool-Aid."

"Kool-Aid, my ass—that's dirt!" Mother said. She took the package away from me and returned shortly with a washcloth to clean my mouth and gave me a new packet of Kool-Aid.

Throughout the 1950s Daddy listened to a steady diet of southern gospel music at home and in the car. On the road, no shortage of AM radio stations played this genre of music. When one station faded as we topped a mountain, another was picked up by the time we reached the bottom. We regularly heard the screech and crackle of the radio as Daddy searched for his favorite music while we drove along the winding mountain roads and highways.

He especially liked the Mull Singing Convention—a radio program aired every Sunday evening. As the program progressed, Reverend Mull would say, "This is your Mull," leaving off the rest of the program's name as he introduced the next song selection. Throughout the evening, he repeated, in his raspy voice, "This is your Mull!" His announcement always set off a cascade of laughter from us. Daddy liked Mull's Singing Convention, but he didn't like Mull himself. The animosity had developed several years earlier when Daddy and Preacher Mull had competed to pastor the same church. Mull won the competition, leaving Daddy resentful. While the story of the rivalry between Mull and Daddy was interesting, I was fascinated much more by the fact that Daddy knew someone who was on the radio.

Mother liked country music, which Daddy also listened to if he couldn't find a gospel station. Famous country singers included

Hank Snow, Porter Wagoner, Tennessee Ernie Ford, Elvis Presley, Johnny Cash, and Marty Robbins. For me, country music—not southern gospel—attracted my ear. A top country music hit in 1955 was Faron Young's "Live Fast, Love Hard, Die Young." The song captures the feeling of a young man who wanted a hot-rod car, a cowboy suit, and a lot of women thinking lovely thoughts of him. The song's refrain ended with Faron Young singing that he wanted to live fast, love hard, die young, and leave a beautiful memory.

I heard this song all the time and loved it. One day I announced to Mother and Daddy, "When I grow up, I'm going to live fast, love hard, die young, and leave a beautiful memory!" They laughed, but I was serious.

"You want to die young, do you? You're only three years old!" Daddy stated. Embarrassed by their laughter, I soon decided dying young wasn't too appealing after all. Still, I decided to live fast and love hard.

One day at Sam Bradley's, a storm blew up with high winds, thunder, and lightning. Mother was afraid of storms. She made every child get on the bed or under the bed as the rain poured down and the thunder and lightning flashed. Feeling somewhat stubborn and curious about the storm, I went to look out the front door. "Mikey, damnation, get back over here on this bed *now*, before you get struck by lightning!"

I ignored her. "I'm not afraid of the storm!" I said as I continued to watch. Mother was too scared to come and get me, and after the storm had passed, she didn't whip me for disobeying.

Deborah was born in September 1955. Mother and Daddy now had three boys and three girls. Six weeks after Deborah's birth, we moved to Macon County, North Carolina.

CHAPTER 3

MACON COUNTY

D addy decided it was time to advance his preaching career. He wanted to make something of his life. That was the only reason he pulled up stakes and moved from Haywood County, his childhood home and the place where his parents still lived. A bigger church and better opportunity awaited him in Macon County, where Franklin was the county seat. Mother didn't like moving, but what could she do? There were six children to feed, and Mother depended on Daddy to provide for this growing brood. Besides, Mother's parents were dead now, so she didn't have much reason to stay on in Haywood County. Grandmother Parks had died in 1951, just a few months before my birth, while Granddaddy Parks had died in 1953, just after Randy's birth.

No interstate highways existed, and there were few four-lane roads in the Blue Ridge Mountains in the 1950s. Travel was slow, as all the main roads inevitably led into the downtown traffic of each small town along the route. Traffic also backed up as tractor-trailer rigs struggled to make it over the mountains. Some of these highways, such as the one crossing Cowee, were scary—especially in spots where you could look to the side of the road and into what appeared to be a bottomless pit.

We moved into the Dalrymples' house near Franklin in 1955. This house was a half mile from Mount Hope Baptist Church, where Daddy was called to preach.

⇥ ⇤

Macon was another picturesque county situated within the Blue Ridge Mountains. It was approximately forty miles southwest of Haywood County. Rabun County, Georgia, was to its south. The Nantahala National Forest comprised 46 percent of the county's total land area, and the Cullasaja River was its largest natural water supply.

Cullasaja Falls was a long cascade over the course of two-tenths of a mile, dropping 250 feet as it plunged to form a pool at its base. Seen from US Highway 64, southeast of Franklin and northwest of Highlands, it was located near a series of blind curves with sheer rock cliffs both above and below. There was a very dangerous and small pull-off area located there for viewing, but it was best to be cautious. From the highway, there was also a tough hiking trail that led down to Cullasaja Falls for those adventurous enough to try.

Dry Falls was a sixty-five-foot waterfall also situated in the Nantahala National Forest. It flowed over an overhanging bluff, allowing visitors to walk under the falls when the water flow was low and remain relatively dry, which brought about its name. If the water flow was high, visitors were likely to get wet. The hike down to Dry Falls was a pleasurable trip our family often made, even though we got wet at times.

Bridal Veil Falls was a forty-five-foot waterfall that had a short curve of roadway located behind it, making it the only falls in the state of North Carolina where a vehicle could drive underneath the water. It flowed from a tributary of the Cullasaja River. Anytime we traveled along this section of highway, we had to stop under Bridal Veil Falls.

Quarry Falls had a large, deep pool at the bottom, making it a favorite place to swim during warm weather. We went there to swim, just as did many of the locals. The water was always freezing, even during the hottest part of the summer.

✠ ✠

As the county seat, Franklin was at the center of Macon County geographically, politically, economically, and socially. Geographically, Macon County was a large landmass encompassing 519 square miles, much of which was forest and farmland. The population was about fifteen thousand residents. Approximately two thousand lived within the city limits of Franklin.

A drive through downtown Franklin revealed a wide variety of businesses, including the post office, courthouse, banks, and jail. Besides the local five-and-dime stores, there were several department stores and pharmacies. There was a taxi stand located next to the courthouse. Burrell Chevrolet was one of the first businesses you saw when driving up Town Hill. It was located just at the top, on the right as you drove west.

The Macon Theater was next to the automobile dealership. It was a very popular place with the locals, who came to enjoy the latest movies from Hollywood. There were also two hardware stores in downtown Franklin—Western Auto and Macon County Supply.

My earliest memories of downtown Franklin consisted of waiting in the car for what seemed to be endless hours while Mother and Daddy went to the Winn-Dixie for groceries or shopped in the various department stores for clothing. During these stops, more than a few arguments and fights broke out among my siblings and me.

One day Daddy parked at the post office to mail some letters. Afterward, he went down the street and purchased a baseball for Johnny, Randy, and me. He handed it to me as I reached out the window. I lost my grip, and the ball rolled all the way down Town Hill, out of sight. At first, I feared a whipping for losing the base-ball. Instead, Daddy said, "Golly-bum! I'll be tom-thunder." He walked back to the hardware store and purchased another one rather than chase the ball I had dropped.

⇥ ⇤

After we had arrived at the Dalrymples' house, men from the church came to help with the unpacking. I had aspired to help with this job, but Daddy told me I was too little. Instead, Johnny and I went exploring and found a small stream, or "branch," in the backyard. Farther away, we found a tractor trail leading into an open field.

It was cold that day. Mother had little red-haired Deborah wrapped tightly in a thick blanket. Elaine, my oldest sister, watched over her carefully while Mother helped direct the un-packing. Gloria and Randy stayed nearby. The family lived at the Dalrymples' house for only a few months. It was too small and too close to the road.

Johnny and I played along the branch, the tractor trail, and in the field. An old rusted automobile was parked there that Mother insisted we not go near. Randy found the edge of the branch slip-pery. He fell in more than once. He got into trouble for throwing his clothes into an old rain barrel that was full of water next to the house.

The Dalrymples' house was old and made of hewn timbers. It somewhat resembled a log cabin but was much larger and had two stories. The home had a well-pump in the kitchen. We drew cold water from it. But the house did have an indoor toilet. Bath water was heated on the stove and then poured into the galvanized steel tub, the one we had used at Sam Bradley's old place. There were bedrooms both upstairs and downstairs. Mine was upstairs. A potbellied stove heated the house. One night Randy was sleepwalking and walked right into it. He screamed and cried and scared us all. Mother applied a yellow salve. Randy had a few blisters the next day, but he healed up nicely.

At the Dalrymples' house, we got our first dog, a little tan mutt we named Fido. A few days later, he was killed by a car as he tried to run across the highway. My father retrieved his little dead body from the middle of the road. All of us mourned the loss of Fido. Daddy buried him in the woods behind the house.

One morning I discovered a large bug in my bed. "Mother, Mother!" I screamed. Both Mother and Daddy came upstairs to the bedroom.

"Look! What is it?" I cried.

"It's just a bed bug. You'll be fine!" Mother said.

To me, it was a big, green monster. After that, I looked very carefully before getting into my bed. It was years later before I found out real bed bugs were tiny creatures.

CHAPTER 4

MOUNT HOPE

Mount Hope Baptist Church was much larger than Olivet. The church building was in the shape of a cross, a standard design, and situated on a small hill in the Cartoogechaye Valley. The exterior prominently featured a steeple that was shaped much like a bell tower. The block walls were of stucco, painted white. Next to the road on a small grassy island stood a black sign with white letters that had "Mt. Hope" at the top, followed by information regarding service times and the name of the pastor. The church had already added Daddy's name by the time we arrived for our first Sunday meeting.

To the east and west of Mount Hope were cornfields. To the north, positioned on the side of a mountain across the highway, was a hay field with woods beginning at the top of the ridge. There were woods located to the south, behind the church. Cartoogechaye Creek flowed beyond these trees. Behind the church at the edge of the woods, partially hidden by trees but accessible by pebbled paths, were two outhouses. The men's was to the east; the women's to the west.

Mount Hope had running water and toilets installed a few years after our arrival, using water from the well that was dug to service the new parsonage. Until then, the congregation used these out-houses. The front doors of the church opened directly into the sanctuary, which contained wooden oak pews, smooth but hard, and set on hardwood floors. All the furnishings were of oak. A communion table sat in front of an altar that stretched along the length of the podium.

There were four rooms, two on each side of the sanctuary. They were closed off by accordion-style dividers during Sunday school but opened to become part of the sanctuary for services. These sections had smaller pews that faced the podium at ninety-degree angles. The podium contained a large pulpit. Behind the pulpit were two large oak chairs, one for the pastor and one for the song leader or a guest preacher. Daddy sat in the chair to the right as he faced the congregation. Behind these chairs was a railing that divided the podium from the choir. The choir sat on wooden, theater-style seats that folded up when the choir members stood.

The building was cooled in the summer by large windows without screens that opened to allow the cross breezes to blow through. In the winter, the sanctuary was heated by a propane furnace. At night, during the summer months, these open windows attracted a torrent of moths and other insects that were attracted by the light. I spent many Sunday evenings watching these critters as they flew around the light fixtures.

To the right of the sanctuary, as one faced the pulpit, was a door that led to more Sunday school rooms behind the choir, located on two levels. I learned much about the Baptist faith in these chambers. Roll-up windows, again lacking screens, cooled these classrooms in summer. Individual propane heaters heated them in winter. When I got older and moved downstairs to the junior boys' class, I discovered that these unscreened windows served as a means of escape for some of the boys from the boring Sunday school classes. I knew better than to try, for I didn't want to incur the wrath of Daddy.

Within a few weeks after our arrival, Johnny and I asked Mother if we could use the outhouse. It was the time between the end of Sunday school and the start of the worship service. She allowed us to go. The toilet smelled bad, but it was a great adventure.

Johnny said, "Mikey, look down in there at that turd!" I held my nose and looked down. There were feces and toilet paper littering the bottom of the privy. Still, I saw what Johnny saw, a new deposit, long and dark.

"Wow, that's the biggest turd I've ever seen." We laughed as we exited the outhouse and started back toward the church. We discovered several men had taken smoke breaks between Sunday school and worship but had departed for the church by the time we arrived. Cigarette butts were still smoldering. "Let's smoke one," Johnny said. I agreed as Johnny picked up a butt.

We took turns puffing. Just then Mother came around the corner and caught us. "You boys put that cigarette down and get back in the church right now," she demanded. "I'll beat the shit out of you when we get home!" Frightened, we complied. She said nothing more until we got home, but upon our arrival, Johnny and I both got whippings.

"I can't believe I've got three- and four-year-old sons smoking! You little hoodlums! Don't ever let me catch you smoking again!"

That night while getting me ready for bed, Mother asked, "Son, aren't you ashamed of yourself?"

"No," I said, not knowing what *ashamed* meant but thinking it had to be something awful.

"You ought to be," she said. From that time forward, on numerous occasions and for various reasons, Mother asked me if I was ashamed of myself. I always said, "No." She then countered, "You ought to be!"

CHAPTER 5

MOORE'S OLD PLACE

We had moved to Moore's old place before I turned four. This house was closer to town. It was a white, wood-framed house set back on a wooded lot with a detached garage that we used for storage. A small barn was next to the house. A paved driveway, unusual for the 1950s, ascended from the graveled road and came around to the back of the house, where Daddy parked the car. It continued beyond our house to where Moore's large brick home stood. On the far side, a white wooden rail fence followed this driveway from the road all the way to the brick house, separating it from a field in front. On the near side, the rail fence attached to the barn and stretched from that point to the brick house. On the other end of the barn, a barbed-wire fence stretched around a back lot to enclose an area that was more woods than a field.

On February 6, 1956, Mother announced, "Son, today's your fourth birthday. From now on, you're old enough to put on your clothes. I'll lay them out, but you dress. You're a big boy now." From that time on, I put on my clothes except for tying my shoes. I didn't learn that skill until I was six. Learning to tie shoes was a challenge for a lefty.

At the Moore's place, I got the chicken pox. Almost all my siblings got the disease at the same time. The sores on my body were runny and itchy. I ran a fever. In the night, I saw dancing skeletons, and I screamed. Daddy came. "I saw skeletons dancing all over the room!"

Daddy said, "No, it was only a nightmare. You were dreaming."

"No, I saw skeletons!"

"Son, just go back to sleep; it'll be all right," he assured me. For years afterward, I believed skeletons had danced in my bedroom that night. I was glad when we moved, for this meant the creatures stayed there to scare someone other than me.

⊷⊶

Almost every night we had potatoes for supper. Johnny loved mashed potatoes with ketchup. He poured it on heavily and mixed it all up. It looked like a bloody mess to me. I preferred mine with butter. If I could, I sneaked and ate a whole stick at a time. Mother said, "Mikey, don't be eating butter like that; it's not good for you." I ate it anyway.

That summer we played in the yard, the woods, and in the barn. One day Elaine wanted us to play house with her. Thinking this was fun, Gloria, Johnny, Randy, and I agreed. Elaine pretended to make and serve our meals and to boss us around, just like Mother. We scattered when she pretended to whip us, for there was no pretending to it. Elaine beat us thoroughly. We got her back, though, as we ran and told Mother what Elaine had done. Mother promptly whipped Elaine for whipping us. It was one of the few times I took pleasure in seeing one of my siblings whipped instead of me. Another time, Elaine wanted to play church. We sang hymns, Elaine preached, and we all confessed our sins and got saved. Gloria shouted, "Hallelujah," just like Daddy. The service ended well.

One day when Gloria, Johnny, Randy, and I went to the rail fence about halfway up the driveway, I decided it was time to use one of the adult words I had heard. "Shit," I said.

Before I could finish my sentence, Gloria screamed, "Mikey said a cuss word; Mikey said a cuss word—I'm telling Mother!" With that, she was off to the house. Even though I heard Mother say this word a dozen times a day, I knew I was in big trouble. When I got back to the house, Mother was waiting for me.

"Son, did you say a bad word?"

"Yes, I did, but I didn't mean to," I said, assuming I was going to get a whipping.

"Stick out your tongue." I saw a large white bar of soap in her hand. With it, she slathered my tongue. "Now don't spit that out until I tell you to," she said as she returned inside. The bitter taste of the soap was too much. I turned on the nearby spigot and washed out my mouth. That day I learned it was best to be careful when cussing, especially around my brothers and sisters.

Another day Johnny, Randy, and I were playing in the old barn next to the house. It was a hay barn that mostly stood empty. We loved to play there. Randy noticed a knothole in the back side of the barn about shoulder high. He went over. "What're you going to do, Randy?" I asked.

"I'm going to stick my head in this knothole and see what's outside." With that, he stuck his head in the hole. The plan went well until he tried to pull his head out. It was stuck. "Help, help!" he screamed until Daddy came running.

"What's wrong?" Daddy shouted.

"Randy's head's stuck," I cried.

Johnny was screaming, "Get him out, get him out!"

Randy continued to scream, rattling the whole barn as he tried to free himself.

"Randy, calm down, or I'll never be able to get you out," Daddy said.

He finally cooled enough for Daddy to examine the situation. The board with the knothole was loose enough for Daddy to pull it back far enough to free Randy's head. "I'll be tom-thunder," Daddy said. "How in the world did you get your head into that hole?"

"Like this," said Johnny as he stuck his head into the knothole. He tried to get his head out, but Johnny was stuck too. "Help, help! I can't get out!" Johnny cried. Daddy pulled back the board and released Johnny. Upon closer examination of the knothole, Daddy discovered it was elongated to the left, and to get through the hole, the head first had to be cocked about ten degrees in the same direction. Once the head was through the hole and straightened, it took the same reverse motion to get it out.

⚒ ⚒

Every afternoon I noticed the mailman deliver the mail. Mother always got the mail. Sometimes she took mail back to the box and raised the flag. I said to myself, "If Mother can put out mail, so can I." I found mail Mother had put in the trash, took it to the box, and raised the flag. I did this for three days. On the third day, the mailman walked up the driveway and knocked on the back door.

"Mrs. Willis, do you know your children are putting old mail in your mailbox?"

"No sir, but I'll take care of it," Mother said. "Which one of you dipshits did that?" No one answered. "Mikey, did you do it?"

"Yes, I did it, but I didn't mean to."

"Mean to, my ass. Don't let me catch you doing that again," Mother said. I was glad to get by without getting whipped.

⚒ ⚒

In 1956 while we lived at Moore's old place, we got our first television, one we had for the next twelve years. It was an RCA black and white, an entirely square box. It sat on a four-legged metal stand. I had never seen anything like it. I looked at the little people on the screen and wondered how they got so small. I looked in the back of the set to find them, but I only saw white glowing tubes. Daddy explained to me it was television and came out of the air to an antenna from a signal, and no one was in the square box. I didn't understand, but that didn't keep me from watching.

The children's shows were fantastic entertainment, especially *Howdy Doody, Bozo the Clown, Captain Kangaroo,* and the *Mickey Mouse Club.* That year Elvis Presley appeared on television for the first time. He was booked on various variety shows, the first of which was *Stage Show.* Then he appeared on *The Milton Berle Show, The Steve Allen Show,* and, finally, on *The Ed Sullivan Show.* On these programs, Elvis Presley sang "Hound Dog," "Blue Suede Shoes," "Ready Teddy," "Don't Be Cruel," and "Heartbreak Hotel." I was amazed at how he could dance and sing. While Daddy had listened to Elvis on country radio, he didn't like what he saw on television. From 1956 onward, Daddy cited Elvis Presley as a singer who corrupted America.

We also had a telephone for the first time. One evening I was watching a TV show in which a man picked up the phone and said, "Hello, Operator, get me the police!"

I said to myself, "I think I'll try that." The next day, while playing in the house, I saw the telephone and picked up the receiver.

The operator said, "May I help you?"

"Yes, Operator, get me the police!" I heard a chuckle from her, got scared, and hung up the phone. I waited, fearing the outcome, but thankfully the police didn't arrive.

While living at the Moore's, Daddy gave the boys nicknames. "Johnny, you're Atomic Johnny; Mikey, you're Cyclone Mike; and Randy, you're Dynamite Randy." Mine was the only one that stuck. Daddy called me Cyclone until the day he died.

In October 1956, Mother got all six children cleaned up and dressed, and Daddy drove us to Canton for Grandmother and

Granddaddy Willis' fiftieth wedding anniversary. It was the first time I met many of my uncles, aunts, and first cousins since most of them lived in other places such as California, Maryland, and Virginia. We held the event on the grounds of Plains Methodist Church, where my grandparents had been married. Daddy's brothers and sisters complimented him on how well behaved his children were. It didn't take me long to figure out that Mother didn't like Grandmother Willis very much. "Your Daddy goes to Canton every week to see his parents. He's just a Mama's boy! He leaves me here every week with all you young'uns while he's off to Canton to see his folks. Is he never going to grow up?" she said.

The attention Daddy paid to Grandmother and Granddaddy was a constant source of trouble between Mother and Daddy throughout their marriage. It didn't help when Daddy loaded us all up for the weekly trip to Canton, for Mother resented these trips too. "I've got better things to do than staying all day in Canton with your parents," she said.

Mother didn't seem to mind the trips when we visited her sister, Aunt Winifred, who lived in Canton with her sons, Phillip, P. H., and Gedwin. Nor did she complain when we stopped in Sylva on our way to or from Canton to see her other sister, Aunt Dorcas, and our cousins.

I found my grandparents to be somewhat amusing. When we visited, Granddaddy always sat in a large overstuffed chair and watched television. During warm weather, he sat on the porch and watched as cars and people passed. Besides an occasional grunt, I hardly ever heard him speak. Grandmother was a little airheaded. She babbled on and on about things I didn't understand. When we visited, she was always lying in a chaise lounge chair in the living room, where she stayed for most of our visit. On the occasions we visited for dinner, she eventually made it to the kitchen to cook a meal on an old wood-burning stove.

I liked Grandmother's biscuits because they looked very different from Mother's. Grandmother whipped up a batch in a bowl and with a spoon, plopped them right onto a cooking sheet. This method produced a biscuit that was odd shaped. No two were the same. Each had pointed spines all over the top that, when baked, were very crunchy and appetizing. Mother's were much different. They were all perfectly round, all the same size. Mother always took great care to make them just right. She made them daily. They were light, layered, fluffy, and enjoyable. Biscuits, along with cornbread, were staples at our house.

"Mother, why don't you make biscuits like Grandmother's?" I asked one day after our return from Canton.

"Hellfire, no! You'll never catch me making biscuits like that. That's the way a lazy woman makes them! Your Grandmother Willis is lazy—just simply lazy!" she said. That was the first and last time I ever asked Mother to make biscuits like Grandmother's batch.

⇥ ⇤

Dawn, the seventh child, was born in March 1957 while we lived at Moore's old place. When Mother brought her home, Dawn cried all the time, making my life miserable. Nothing could stop her infernal crying. I wished Mother had not gotten her from the hospital.

CHAPTER 6

SAINT JOHN'S

In the spring, after Dawn's birth, we moved again—this time to a small house next to Saint John's Episcopal Church, a few miles from Mount Hope. The road, as was the case with all graveled roads in Macon County, was cut into the sides of the hills, exposing large red-clay banks that eroded with torrential rains. Red clay was common throughout much of western North Carolina. There was a shared entrance to the church's graveled parking lot and to our home's long graveled driveway, which came right up to the porch of the house. It was a white, wood-framed house that stood at the top of a red-clay bank. My brothers and I occupied the bedroom that was next to the kitchen. The bathroom was beyond the kitchen, in an alcove toward the back door. Since the amount of heat generated from our coal-burning heater didn't warm the nook and bathroom, Mother again used the galvanized steel tub to give us our weekly baths in the kitchen during the winter. She also provided us with a chamber pot at night because the bathroom was too cold.

Life at this little house was exciting. Summer meant none of the Willis children wore shoes. We went the entire season without them, except for during church. It was a common practice among the locals. After a winter of wearing shoes, our feet were tender, and even a small rock hurt when we stepped on it. Within a few weeks, our feet were already toughened, like leather, and we could go anywhere we wanted to go without difficulty.

Behind the house was a pasture surrounded by a barbed-wire fence. A gate from our backyard served as an entrance into this field where a barn stood, farther back, full of hay. One day Johnny, Randy, and I were playing in the barn. I didn't notice an old, hidden pitchfork. As I was running, I stubbed a toe on the pitchfork. "Ouch, my toe! Ouch, my toe!" I screamed and cried in agony. Daddy came and carried me to the house. Mother examined my toe and cleaned the wound, which was very painful.

"I'll have to put some Mercurochrome on it," she stated.

"No, Mother, please—not Mercurochrome. It'll burn too much!"

"Mikey, I have to, or it'll get infected," she said as she began pouring in the stinging, bright-orange potion. I cried as the ointment made its way to the deepest part of the wound. Either Mercurochrome or Merthiolate, both antiseptics, were a child's worst nightmare, something to be avoided at all costs. Pepto-Bismol was also a tonic to be shunned. Mother gave the pink potion to me for an upset stomach. The awful taste always made me vomit. She never figured this out. I didn't find out until much later that Pepto-Bismol was meant to settle the stomach, not make you throw up. In our household, you almost had to be dead to be taken to a doctor. Only twice during my childhood did I see one. Avoiding the doctor and the dentist was a common practice among the people of the Blue Ridge Mountains. They were expensive visits.

═╬╬═

Saint John's Episcopal Church was a curiosity. We liked to play around it, although we didn't usually go near the cemetery in the back of the church. We even occasionally looked inside, since it was never locked. We knew by instinct not to disturb anything. Mother forbade us from even entering. Still, sometimes, the temptation was too much.

The church building was a tiny wood frame with natural wood siding and wooden shingles. There was a small wooden cross at the top of the entrance. Inside there was seating for perhaps sixty people. An old Crown organ with pedals provided music. All the interior décor was natural hardwood including the pews, altar, and pulpit. Sunday school classes were held next to the church in a small fellowship building. It too was made of natural wood siding and had a tin roof.

One day a member of the church told Mother that my siblings and I were invited to Bible school the next week. This news pleased Mother since it meant for a whole week, during the mornings, she would be free of us. Even though Daddy protested our going to an Episcopal church, she sent everyone but Deborah and Dawn, who were too young.

We enjoyed the Episcopal bible school. The elderly priest, Dr. Rufus Morgan, was the founder of the little church. We had never heard of or seen a priest before. I thought Father Morgan's clerical collar was fascinating. The church pews had kneeling benches, something our church didn't have. At Mount Hope, only Daddy kneeled, but only on one knee, as he prayed before the offering and before he preached. Here, though, everyone kneeled on both knees during different times of the service. We also learned about the *Book of Common Prayer.* It was news to me that prayers could be written down. I thought that was reserved only for the Bible. Furthermore, if I prayed these prayers, I wondered if God heard them since they were the prayers of someone else.

One morning during Bible school, we had a class on the porch of the fellowship building. The children had helped construct the lesson on a long scroll of paper the day before. The students painted a large cardboard box and converted it into a TV. Next, they cut slots on either side of the screen. A teacher told the Bible story while pupils feed the scroll through the slots. We had an excellent time until Margaret, one of the little helpers, fell off the stage. The next week, Mount Hope began a two-week Bible school, which meant Mother got relief from us for three full weeks. She was jubilant.

Across the road from our house lived Farmer Wood, who along with his wife, daughter, and son-in-law, James Henry, worked a farm. He had cows, chickens, guineas, and all kinds of other farm animals. He also had hay fields, where giant haystacks were mounded. But Mr. Wood had a problem. An old hound dog loved to catch his guineas. These birds traveled in a large flock and roamed all over the farm. At some point each day or so, the hound dog attacked the birds and secured his meal. One day Mr. Wood called the sheriff. A deputy came to hunt the dog. They found him in our backyard. All of us were made to go inside. We heard a loud gunshot. Afterward, my mother allowed us to return to the yard, where we saw the deputy with his shotgun. It was still smoking. In the backyard the old hound dog lay dead with a large hole in his side.

While we lived next to Saint John's, Daddy got a glove, baseball, and bat for Johnny and me to share. We were both left-handed, so, Daddy thought one glove was sufficient. I didn't want to share the glove with Johnny. I said to Daddy, "I can't use this glove. I throw with this one." I pointed to my right hand.

"I'll be dad gum. I thought you threw with your left hand." I couldn't share the right-handed glove Daddy had gotten for Randy. It was much too small. Daddy bought me a right-hander's glove of my own. From then on, I did everything with my left hand except throw a baseball, which became an easy righthanded skill.

Flat tires were a regular occurrence in the 1950s with any vehicle on the road. We often watched Daddy as he got out along the roadway to change a flat, using the spare tire. It was always great fun to watch. Daddy was a "Dodge man." He thought Dodge made the best cars, and he traded one after another, but they were all used vehicles.

One day Johnny, Randy, and I were playing around Daddy's old Dodge when six-year-old Johnny came up with the idea of driving a nail in one of the tires so Daddy would have to change it. Everybody agreed this was an excellent plan. I hammered the nail right into the side. "Daddy, Daddy!" Johnny yelled. Daddy came to the car.

"You have a flat tire," I said, pointing to the nail on the side.

"Dad gum, how in tom-thunder did I get a nail in my tire way up on the sidewall like that?"

"Yeah, and we didn't put a nail in it either," Randy said.

"I'll be; I don't know what I'm going to do with you boys. Move out of the way; I've got to get to the station before all the air goes out."

"Can we go too?" I asked.

Daddy looked at me with a long pause, "Yeah, get in, all three of you."

One afternoon Mother made popcorn for all of us. She and Daddy began arguing—Daddy was yelling at Mother, and she swore at Daddy. Suddenly, Mother picked up the bowl of popcorn and threw it at Daddy. A plethora of curse words followed the popcorn. "You goddamn son of a bitch!" she yelled. The white puffed kernels went all over Daddy. He jumped up, and just as it looked like a fight was to follow, they both began to laugh. I didn't understand this strange behavior; it was scary to me.

In the fall, Johnny started first grade. As he left the house with Elaine and Gloria to board the long yellow school bus, I was mad. "I want to go to school too," I cried.

But Mother said, "You'll get to go soon enough, next year."

"But I want to go with Johnny," I said.

"You'll have to wait. Johnny's older than you." Johnny and I had never been separated; this was the first time. We were "Irish twins"—our birthdates were only eleven months apart. Mother told everyone I had been born prematurely and that was the reason for our close birthdays. I accepted this explanation until I was grown and discovered that my birth certificate showed that I was born full-term. It seems Mother had hidden the truth to cover her embarrassment. I began calling Johnny "my equal-like brother," meaning we were of *equal* or the same age. Johnny always paid me back on his birthday, March 13, by reminding me that, indeed, he was a year older than I was after all.

At Christmas in 1957, while we lived next to Saint John's, Johnny, Randy, and I got pop guns—rifles that shot cork bullets. We were happy with what Santa Claus had brought us.

Later in the day, while Mother was cleaning up the kitchen from our Christmas meal, the three of us put our new guns to the test. Each took aim at a glass Christmas ornament, and with high accuracy, we picked them off, one by one. This competition continued until almost every ball on the tree was gone.

"What in the hell are you boys doing?" Mother asked when she saw what we had done. She whipped each of us and took our guns away. Then she began crying. "I can't have anything around here anymore. You blame young'uns destroy everything! I've had those Christmas decorations ever since I got married to your Daddy." I felt sorry for Mother, and I felt bad we had made her cry. I wished we had not shot off all those Christmas balls.

In March 1958, just after we moved to the Mount Hope parsonage, Mother gave birth to Phillip, the last child born to our family. Mother had given birth to four boys and four girls between 1946 and 1958. When Phillip was born, she wasn't yet thirty years of age. I always wondered why she seemed to just suddenly quit having babies; years later I found out that on that eighth trip to the hospital, she also had a tubal ligation. Mother and Daddy never told anyone.

CHAPTER 7

THE MOUNT HOPE PARSONAGE

The Mount Hope Baptist Church parsonage was under construction for much of 1957. Daddy took us there to inspect the work on Sundays and Wednesdays. We were excited about the new home that we were moving to. Visiting the construction site was always a great occasion. On a big pile of dirt, Johnny, Randy, and I played King of the Hill and slid down the mound over and over. We were disappointed on moving day in early 1958 to find the high hill removed, replaced by a level yard. Straw covered the ground, as it was winter and grass wasn't yet growing. Winter rye sprang up first to protect the soil from erosion until the new grass grew in the spring. Later, when the grass grew high enough in the backyard, Johnny, Randy, and I burrowed tunnels and tramped trails through it with great delight.

The members built the parsonage on a plot of ground between the church and Patton Road to the west. It faced the highway, separated from the road by a large front yard. An old hollow oak tree stood at the edge where Daddy parked the car. Later, Daddy attached a basketball goal with a plywood backboard to the tree so we could shoot baskets.

A coal-burning heater situated in the living room warmed the ranch-style, redbrick house. We opened the windows for summer cooling. The house had no front porch or even a sidewalk. Instead, long planks served this purpose so the family and visitors could negotiate their way from the car to the front door through the muddy yard. A wooden skid was placed at the doorway to serve as a landing. The kitchen door opened to an immediate six-foot drop-off; there were no stairs. The only other exit was downstairs, through the basement. During the four years we lived there, there was no sidewalk and no kitchen-door stairs.

The house had three bedrooms, a living room, a kitchen and dining room, one bathroom, and a study for Daddy. On moving into the parsonage, the girls were assigned the bedroom on the east side of the house, next to the study; Daddy and Mother had the middle bedroom, and the boys had the bedroom located to the west. A long hallway connected these bedrooms, which opened into the dining area of the kitchen and opened into the living room.

The kitchen had new appliances, including an electric stove with an oven and a refrigerator. It was the largest house in which we had ever lived. The study was truly that; it had no closet. The scale model of the home showed this study was to have an entrance, essentially giving the face of the house the look of having two front doors. This original plan was later changed, leaving a single front door opening into the living room. Mother played a significant role in getting the parsonage redesigned.

"John, two front doors will look awful. You can't put two front doors on that house!" she said.

"But Mildred, when other preachers and members of the church come to visit, I want them to be able to get right into my office."

"When they come, you need to visit with them over at the church, not in the house!" Mother won the argument.

The bathroom was much larger than any we had had before, and for the first time, we had adequate hot water to fill the bathtub. Mother no longer had to boil bathwater on the kitchen stove. We took our baths in shifts, especially during school months and on Sundays. All the younger children got one scrubbing in the tub every Saturday night. Johnny, Randy, and I took ours together. One time in the bathtub per week didn't mean we went dirty the rest of the time. Every evening, before bedtime, Mother gave us full dab baths using a wash pan, hot water, and plenty of soap. Mother had begun this practice in the past due to the lack of sufficient hot water in the homes where we had lived. Once we moved to the parsonage, she continued it out of habit.

Mother insisted on cleanliness, and particularly on clean hands. On our coming out of the bathroom, she always asked, "Did you wash your hands?" It took only a few whippings to get the point across.

The basement had a dirt floor except for a small concrete pad that contained fixtures for a washing machine. Next to the concrete pad was a pile of soft lump coal placed there for use in the upstairs coal-burning heater. Anytime we opened the door, an earthy, damp, musty smell wafted up the basement steps from the dirt floor.

When we moved to the parsonage, Mother had an old wringer washer, which was replaced by a new automatic one a few years later. She discharged water down a drain that emptied into a ditch running beside Patton Road. I loved to watch Mother wring out the wet clothing between the rollers of the wringer washer. I wanted to help, but she didn't let me. "No, Mikey, you can't help; you'll get your hand mashed off," she said. Clothes were hung to dry on a clothesline in the backyard. It was many years before we got a clothes dryer.

Every morning I watched Elaine, Gloria, and Johnny board a little yellow school bus for the short trip to Cartoogechaye

Elementary School. You could see the school from our house, less than half a mile away. Even though it was a short distance, Mother still insisted her children ride the bus. She was afraid of the traffic on the highway. Also, school officials discouraged walking. Willie Dalrymple, whose rental house we had lived in, was the bus driver. He had a cleft palate and spoke with a lisp. Mr. Dalrymple and his wife, Blanche, had an intellectually disabled son, Tommy, who drove a tractor everywhere. North Carolina would not issue him a driver's license, but he could drive farm equipment without one. When driving by, Tommy always waved. He was always happy, and I liked him. The Dalrymple family attended our church. Mrs. Dalrymple was a kind, warmhearted woman. I was always respectful of Mr. Dalrymple and Tommy since both Mother and Daddy instilled in us the duty to be kind to those with disabilities. Any hint of discourtesy brought immediate correction.

Shortly after we moved into the parsonage, the church announced that the members would give us a *pounding* after the service that evening. Afraid that we were all going to get whipped, I asked Daddy when we got home, "What's a pounding?"

"It's where they bring all kinds of food, as a gift, to the preacher and his family."

"Then why is it called a pounding?"

"Son, I don't know. It's just a term they use."

"Why can't they have it at the church rather than here, John?" Mother asked. "I don't want all of them in here looking at all this old beat-up furniture!"

"Mildred, it'll be all right; they just want to be friendly."

"I think they're just nosey," she retorted. She was right. Our furniture had taken on wear from years of use and the toll of eight children. That evening, after church, all the members stacked loads of groceries on our kitchen table and gathered in our living room for fellowship. Members held poundings at the parsonage on a regular basis. While always appreciative of the members' gener-osity, Mother did not like groups like this gathering in our home.

"A parsonage is like living in a fishbowl," she said. "The whole church acts like they have a right to come in here anytime they want; I hate living here. Someday I hope we can have our place, and then I'll decide who comes."

⥱ ⥲

In late spring, Daddy cut the high rye grass that had grown in the Mount Hope parsonage yard over the winter. He had let it go too long and had to take a sling blade to it. Mother was embarrassed by the length of the grass. "John, all the neighbors and the whole church will be talking about how awful our yard looks. Do you want them saying that?"

Johnny, Randy, and I helped Daddy. After the rye had dried, we gathered all the straw into small bundles and tied each with a stalk. "Bob Parker can use this hay to feed his dairy cows," I an-nounced. The next time Mr. Parker came by the house, Mother had him stop to pick up our donation. The many bundles looked tiny when Bob loaded them into his farm truck. I thought to my-self, *That straw won't last any time for those cows. They'll eat it all up in just a few bites.*

Mr. Parker, a member of our church, and his brother, Cecil, owned the cornfield that grew to the west of the parsonage. Corn was visible as far as the eye could see, as well as on a larger field farther away. A silo and large barn were visible in the background. Holstein cows roamed the pastures nearby. One of my great plea-sures was to watch Bob and Cecil plow the cornfields with their big tractors. Neal, Bob's son, rode along with either his father or uncle. In a few years, he was plowing these fields by himself. Neal was my age, and I was envious of him because I wanted to ride the tractors and work on a farm too.

After the corn had tasseled each year, Bob allowed Mother to pull as much field corn as she wanted. While it was meant for silage and not intended for human consumption, we found the roasted ears to be a delightful addition to the supper table.

Bob and Cecil also owned the hay field above the parsonage, on the other side of the highway. Once the hay grew high enough, it was cut, allowed to dry in the sun, and then bundled with a machine into square bales that were then loaded into a truck and taken to the barn. When we were older, Bob allowed Johnny, Randy, and me to help Neal load the hay bales on the back of the truck. We took them to the barn, where we stacked them. This job was hot and sweaty and made me quickly reconsider my desire to be a farmer and diminished my envy of Neal.

Bob also had Daddy come and get free milk. The raw, unpasteurized milk was rich in butterfat, which rose to the top of the glass gallon containers Daddy used to catch the liquid from the faucet of a large tank. This milk had to be shaken up before pouring. I loved the delicious taste. We could never predict when we would get milk from the Parkers since it was only available when the cows produced too much and the cooling tank was overflowing. The Parker Dairy Farm was a big operation. I often accompanied Daddy to the farm, where I observed Bob, Cecil, and Neal attach automatic milkers to each cow. These fed the milk directly into a tank. When given the opportunity to hand milk a cow, I declined. "Ugh, that's nasty!" I said.

"Come on, Mikey, give it a try," Daddy urged.

"No, I don't want to milk that ugly cow." I couldn't bear the thought of touching one of those long, dangly cow's teats.

⇒+ +⇐

When spring arrived, Daddy made a garden in an area beyond the backyard that the church members had cleared. He planted potatoes, corn, yellow squash, green beans, tomatoes, and many other garden vegetables. He required all of us to assist in this task, which we dreaded because the work was hot and interfered with our playtime. Daddy was a harsh taskmaster who made this miserable job worse with his angry orders and demands, which seemed impossible to obey. He dispensed numerous whippings when we worked in the garden. As the season wore on, mercifully, Daddy grew tired and abandoned it to the weeds because he had revivals to run, which meant he was gone much of the summer.

Sometimes Mother complained, "John, what do you think the members of the church are going to say about that overgrown garden? They'll say, 'Why, the preacher can't even grow a garden.' Is that what you want people to think?"

He didn't respond—he just kept on preaching his revivals.

Mother worked the garden the best she could. Thus, we reaped some benefit from our labor. Daddy's garden-making pattern was repeated every spring that we lived in the Mount Hope parsonage. Because of his disinterest, my siblings and I never learned how to make one.

Chores were minimal throughout our childhoods. For the boys, work consisted of taking the table scraps to the edge of the yard for disposal. We took turns at it but often argued over whose time it was. We also had to dispose of the trash. At first, we took it to an open pit down by Cartoogechaye Creek that the church had bulldozed just for that purpose. After complaints and state authorities had arrived for an inspection, it was ordered closed. Another bulldozer came to seal it up. Afterward, Daddy obtained a fifty-five-gallon steel drum so that we could dump the trash there. He vented it at the bottom with holes. Trash was collected here and burned. Mother always removed the aerosol cans to prevent them from blowing up. One time while she wasn't watching, though, I threw one in anyway, since I wanted to see it explode.

"Good God, what the hell are you doing, Mikey?" she yelled. "You little dipshit, you'll get us blown up. Do it again, and I'll beat the shit out of you. Do you understand me?"

"I didn't do it; you must have missed one!" I protested.

"Missed one, my ass. I know what you did, and don't let me catch you doing it again, you little hoodlum!"

My sisters had more chores than my brothers and I did. They had to wash the dishes and help Mother with cleaning the house. The boys never had to wash dishes, since Mother said it was "a woman's job." Still, when we got older, my brothers and I had to clean our bedroom. Not having to work didn't mean we lived a comfortable life, for whippings were frequent and unpredictable.

One day I decided to try to go all day without one, a difficult task to accomplish. Things went well at first. For much of the day, I was diligent in obeying all of Mother's orders and in staying out of her way. In the afternoon, without warning, Mother whipped me. I didn't even know what I had done wrong. Hugely disappointed, I never attempted the feat again, concluding that going a whole day without a whipping was impossible.

Summer came, and Johnny was finally out of school. It was the time of year when I had always shed my shoes as outdoor play began. Remembering the pitchfork from the last summer, I decided this one would be different. I said to Mother, "I'm not going barefoot anymore. I'll wear shoes from now on."

She complained, "Son, that'll cost us an extra pair of shoes each year."

"But...I don't want to go barefoot!"

"If you insist, I can't tell you no," she said. I couldn't believe Mother gave in so quickly—I had expected a big fight over the issue.

⊨⊣ ⊢⊨

Mount Hope and all the surrounding territory was our summer playground. Johnny, Randy, and I played in our new yard, inside the basement, in the churchyard, inside the church, in the woods, inside the outhouses, in the cornfields, in the hay field, and in and around Cartoogechaye Creek. Mother sent us outside after breakfast and demanded we not return until dinner at noon. After dinner, she sent us outside again and told us not to come back until supper. These were commands we happily obeyed.

⊨⊣ ⊢⊨

Bible school interrupted our summertime routine, but it was something I enjoyed. Daddy always held a two-week Bible school at any church he pastored, and Mount Hope was no different. I liked Bible school because children attended from the entire community, not just the boys and girls we saw on Sunday. In addition to Bible lessons, there were crafts to learn, followed by refreshments and then playtime.

I didn't like activity time because I couldn't make anything, regardless of how hard I tried. In my early Bible school years, if the craft was to color and glue macaroni on a piece of construction paper to resemble some object, mine was always the messiest. It didn't matter if the teacher bragged about how beautiful it looked. I knew it was perfectly awful. When I was older, if the craft at Bible school was to make a birdhouse or shoe-shine box, mine never placed in the competition. I had no skill whatsoever when it came to working with my hands, but I could run and play with the

50

best. I enjoyed this part of Bible school the most, along with the refreshments.

The 1958 Bible school was most memorable. I had a fight with Tuddy Basden, which was my first. Tuddy was a large boy, my age, and a bully. I had never encountered a bully before, but Tuddy didn't frighten me, even though he had scared all the other boys from the churchyard. I was much smaller than Tuddy. He had everyone on the run except for me. I stood my ground.

"Mikey, you'd better get out of this churchyard and go home, or I'm going to crush you," Tuddy said.

"You can't flatten me, you fat old cow," I retorted, and with these words, the fight began. I threw punches but to no avail. Tuddy was too big. The blows landed without effect on his oversized body. With one big thump, he sat down on top of me. Squashed, I couldn't breathe. Mercifully, someone arrived and pulled Tuddy off. Daddy came to see what had happened.

"Son, why were you fighting?"

"Because Tuddy is bossing everyone around, and he told me to go home," I replied.

"The two of you will not fight while on this church property anymore. Do you understand?" he said.

"Yes," we both said. I was surprised—Daddy didn't whip me that afternoon when we got home. After the fight, one of only a few I lost during my childhood, Tuddy didn't bully me anymore. From this scrap, I learned valuable lessons I employed in future fights. I learned it was necessary to be quick, to use the element of surprise, and not to get locked up with your opponent. I also learned it was important never to let your opponent sit on you.

⟞✠ ✠⟝

One day Johnny, Randy, and I were at the edge of the backyard near Patton Road, close to the ditch that separated the yard from the road. I decided to move a big rock that was there. I pushed and shoved, but I couldn't budge it. Johnny came over to help, but the two of us couldn't move it either. We recruited Randy, and the three of us were finally able to turn the boulder over.

Underneath, we found what appeared to be worms—a whole pile. We sat down among them. They looked different from others we had seen, for even though they were the size of night crawlers, they were darker and scaly. As they began to slither away quickly, I yelled, "Let's catch them!" and we went after the worms.

"They don't look like worms to me," Johnny said.

"I'll get a stick and catch one," I said. After securing a stick, I got one of the last remaining worms on it. All the others had slithered into the underbrush and were gone. This one began creeping toward my hand. As it drew closer to my fingers, I switched ends, holding the stick on the opposite end. The worm then headed back along the stick toward that hand. This pattern continued for several trips until Johnny came up with an idea.

"I'll go to the basement and get a jar to put it in," he said.

"That's an excellent idea," I replied. Once the glass jar was retrieved, I shook the worm off the stick, and Johnny screwed the lid shut to keep it from escaping.

"Mother, come and see what we have!" Johnny yelled.

She came outside. By this time, Johnny had put the jar behind his back to surprise her.

"What do you have?" she asked.

"Look," Johnny said, as he shoved the glass jar into her face.

"Ah...shit!" Mother let out the loudest scream I had ever heard in my life. Her squeal frightened Johnny so badly he dropped the jar, shattering it into tiny pieces. "It's a snake! Get away!" she bellowed as she retrieved a shovel. In a few short blows, she had killed the tiny little creature. "What the hell were you boys thinking? Why in God's name were you playing with snakes? Don't you know they can kill you? I don't know what kind of snake it is, but I'll keep it until John gets home. He'll know."

We waited the rest of the day for Daddy to come home to inspect the little dead snake. After looking at it, Daddy said, "Boys, you got yourselves into a nest of baby copperheads. If you ever find others, stay away from them. One bite from a copperhead can kill you—even one this small!" Afterward, we became very watchful for snakes regardless of their size, shape, or color.

As pastor of Mount Hope, Daddy had the weekly responsibility of keeping the grass of the parsonage and the church trimmed. The church deacons ensured the mowing job got done by purchasing a new gasoline-powered, self-propelled push mower for Daddy to use. Daddy, always wanting to look the part of a preacher, wore his suit and a tie to accomplish the task.

"John, you look plum silly out mowing in that suit and tie," Mother protested. Her objections didn't stop Daddy. Every week he was outside mowing in his suit.

"Let me mow!" I declared one day.

"You're only six—too young to mow," Daddy replied.

"At least let me try."

Under Daddy's careful supervision, I mowed a swath of grass. After that first time, Daddy let me mow larger and larger areas. By the end of the summer, he had lowered the mower's handlebars, so I didn't have to reach over my head to control it. From then on, until we left Mount Hope, I regularly mowed the parsonage and church lawns.

CHAPTER 8

CARTOOGECHAYE ELEMENTARY SCHOOL

When September 1958 arrived, it was time for me to start school. I was excited as I walked down to the bus stop that first morning with Elaine, Gloria, and Johnny to ride Mr. Dalrymple's bus to Cartoogechaye Elementary School. Elaine led me along the long hallway of the school to the first-grade classroom, where Mrs. Corbin met me at the door. In just a few days, I no longer needed Elaine or Gloria's assistance to find my class. I told them I could get there by myself.

I was eager as I entered the classroom for the first time. Ever since Johnny had started school a year ago, I had been waiting for my chance to attend. First grade was an excellent place to be. Mrs. Corbin had already assigned me a seat when I arrived that morning.

"Mickey, your seat is over here," she said.

"Mrs. Corbin my name's Mikey, not Mickey,"

"I'm sorry Mikey; I thought your mother said it was Mickey. I'll be sure to call you Mikey from now on."

The first-grade classroom soon filled with boys and girls from all over Cartoogechaye, both the upper and lower sections. Some, like me, were very anxious and excited to be at school. Others cried and were afraid. Mrs. Corbin did all she could to reassure us that school was a fun experience and that a good education was vital. Children from all socioeconomic backgrounds were in my first grade. Still, there were no African Americans at Cartoogechaye Elementary School, as the Macon County Schools had not yet fully integrated as required by the US Supreme Court decision of 1954. If there had been, it still would not have brought integration to Cartoogechaye, since no African Americans lived in the community. However, there was a Cherokee Indian girl who was assigned a seat right next to me.

Mary was a chubby little girl with jet-black hair, rosy cheeks, and a dark complexion who always seemed to be sick. When it got cold, she arrived chilled to the bone with a runny nose. To my dismay, Mary wiped snot on her sleeve, something Mother would have whipped me good for doing. To make matters worse, she picked her nose and wiped the gleaming green globs on the front of her dress. Although I felt sorry for Mary, I was greatly relieved when Mrs. Corbin announced one morning she had moved and wasn't returning to our school.

Several classmates came without shoes and wore ragged clothing. The school maintained a small clothing storeroom where staff kept used shoes and clothing for them. However, the stock was often inadequate, as some children still couldn't find appropriate attire. Billy was one such boy. He had no shoes, and none fit him from the clothes pantry. The next day I brought a pair of my boots, still in good condition, to give to Billy, but they were too small.

"Billy will take the boots to his younger brother, Sammy. He'll be able to wear them," Mrs. Corbin told me. "That was a thoughtful thing you did for Billy," Mrs. Corbin said. "Mikey, you inspired someone else to donate a pair of shoes for Billy. Now both he and Sammy have shoes—thanks to you!"

Besides socioeconomic differences, there were also noted differences in hygiene and awareness of it. Mrs. Corbin had to deal with these issues as they arose, including, most memorably, Annie's problems. Almost daily, Annie soiled herself while she sat in her seat or in the bathroom located in the back of the classroom.

"Shoo! Mrs. Corbin, Annie's messed on herself again," the class said almost in unison each time this happened. Or someone would report, "Mrs. Corbin, Annie's in the bathroom and won't come out. It smells awful!"

At these words, Mrs. Corbin's face turned ashen gray as she headed back to help Annie. Most of the time, Mrs. Corbin had to get a dress from the storeroom and change Annie's clothes.

━┼ ┼━

The first-grade classroom was fantastic. As you entered, on one wall was a large drawing of a clown holding balloons on strings that stretched up the wall to the top of the ceiling. On each balloon was written the name of its color: red, blue, green, yellow, orange. We used these balloons to associate each word with its color as we learned to read. The alphabet and numbers, on a green background with white letters, were displayed above the green chalkboard. Mrs. Corbin used these to help us to print both upper- and lowercase letters and numbers.

At home, Mother and Daddy took the education of their children casually. I was left on my own to do my homework or not and to make good grades or not. Fortunately, for me, I liked school and sought to do my best. I was a good student, making As and Bs. Still, recess and mealtime were my favorite activities.

Within the first few days of school, I had my first girlfriend, Martha. She was a cute, blond-haired girl and irresistible.

At mealtime, we walked single file into the cafeteria, with one student leading the way. At home, we called this meal *dinner*, but here it was called *lunch*. Students got meat, vegetables, rolls, dessert, and milk. Sometimes you didn't know what you were getting. The children called one substance "pig brains," and I believed that's what it was for a long time. It didn't matter to me; I thought the meal was very delicious. Lunch was twenty-five cents a day; extra milk was three cents; and ice cream, a special treat, was ten cents. Mother always sent three cents a day for extra milk. Sometimes, she gave us a dime for ice cream. I always bought ice cream if I got a dime. If I didn't buy the extra milk, Mother let me keep the money. At the age of six, I began saving. I used these funds at Christmastime to buy gifts for Mother and Daddy.

After lunch, Mrs. Corbin had all of us take naps. She gave us gray wool blankets that we spread out on the floor and laid down. They were itchy and uncomfortable. I could never go to sleep, as I had never taken a nap in the middle of the day. Mother never made me do this at home. Mrs. Corbin awarded every child who went to sleep a gold star. Most of the children had many, but I had none. I couldn't go to sleep, and the harder I tried, the worse it got. She asked me one day, "Mikey, why don't you go to sleep during nap time?"

"I don't know, Mrs. Corbin. As hard as I try, I just can't sleep."

"Keep trying," she replied. I finally faked it and had three stars by my name, but I felt guilty because I thought I had cheated.

"Mrs. Corbin, I didn't earn those stars; I only pretended to go to sleep," I finally told her.

"Mikey, I know you went to sleep. You can't fool me," she replied.

During nap time, I watched Mrs. Corbin work at her desk. I was particularly intrigued by a calendar she used to teach us about the days and months of the year. It worked somewhat like a puzzle. Each month letters and numbers were removed and rearranged and blanks were inserted to even things up once all the other pieces were in place. I noticed on the calendar the number 1958 never changed. I always wanted to ask why but was embarrassed to ask, since I thought it was something I should already know. After Christmas break, I found out. The first thing Mrs. Corbin did was change December *1958* to January *1959.*

Upon our return from Christmas, I said, "Mrs. Corbin, guess what I got for Christmas!"

"What did you get?"

"I got a BB gun!"

"No, Mikey, surely you didn't. You're only six!"

"I did, and so did Johnny and Randy."

"I see. So, Johnny is seven, you're six, and how old is Randy?"

"Randy's five."

"My, my, you boys had better be careful with those BB guns. I can't believe your parents got them for you. You could shoot each other," she said.

After Christmas, Mrs. Corbin announced, "Students, you will no longer be taking naps after lunch each day. All of you have adjusted well to school, and napping will no longer be required." Unlike many of my classmates, I received this news with great enthusiasm because it meant no itchy wool blankets, no more pretending to sleep, and no more competing for gold stars.

Mrs. Corbin used the changing of the calendar from 1958 to 1959 to tell us about Alaska. It had been added to the United States to become the forty-ninth state. Later, she also told us that yet another state, Hawaii, was soon to be added, bringing the total number of states to fifty.

By the end of first grade, I had zero absences from school. Almost all my classmates had been out at least a few days each. Absences from school were a rarity for me throughout my years in school. I always enjoyed good health and somehow avoided most of the communicable diseases that came around.

⟫ ⟪

In 1959, I was in Mrs. Cabe's second-grade class. On my first day in second grade, while I was standing in the lunch line next to Joe Mashburn, Mrs. Corbin said, "Joe, you've grown since last year. Why you must be a foot taller." I straightened up next to Joe and stood as tall as I could to measure just how much taller he was than me. "Mikey, you've grown too," Mrs. Corbin said after realizing I had overheard. She had always been very kind to me.

Things were different with Mrs. Cabe. While Mrs. Corbin was young and cute, Mrs. Cabe was old and gray haired. But, more importantly, I soon learned Mrs. Cabe also had a mean streak.

I knew many of the second graders from first grade, but there were new faces too. One was Wally, a big boy who had a bigger desk than the rest of us and was assigned a spot in the very back of the room. He had failed a few grades and was old enough to be in the fifth grade. Wally was intent on intimidating all the boys. One day while Mrs. Cabe was busy with other matters, Wally made the mistake of taking me on, right in the classroom. "Mikey, you're a big baby, just a big baby!" he taunted.

His barb raised my fiery temper. "Wally's a baby; Wally's a baby!" I told him right to his face.

To my surprise, Wally began to cry. "Miss Cabe, Mikey called me a baby," he wept.

"Mikey, did you call Wally a baby?" she asked.

"Yes, Miss Cabe, I did, but he called me one first."

"Come to the front of the room," Mrs. Cabe demanded. I complied as she was writing something on a sheet of construction paper. When Mrs. Cabe finished, the sign read, "Mikey is a baby."

"Turn around," she demanded. I followed her instruction. She then pinned the sign to my back. "Now you wear that sign the rest of the day," Mrs. Cabe told me. "You may return to your seat now." I heard laughter from my classmates as I sat down. Mrs. Cabe returned to her work, while I sat stewing. *I will not have this sign on my back all day*, I told myself. *In fact, I'll not wear it another second.* I reached behind me, ripped off the sign, and wadded it up.

"Miss Cabe, Mikey's taken off his sign," I heard someone say. She looked at me with fire in her eyes for one of the longest moments of my life. I defiantly stared right back, having decided she couldn't whip me any harder than what I got at home, and I was ready to take it rather than wear the sign again.

"That will be all right," she said to the unknown informant and returned to her work. When we got in line for lunch, I threw the wad of paper into the trash can. By the end of the week, Wally and his big desk had been moved out of our classroom and down the hall to the fifth grade.

Across the aisle to my left sat Tony, a small boy who seemed unsure of himself and was very fidgety. He was a poor student who didn't do well on his exams. Since I was left-handed, during exams, it was easy for him to see my paper. I noticed during one test he was copying my answers, word for word. His actions startled me because I was afraid Mrs. Cabe would think I was cheating too. It also angered me, as I didn't like Tony copying my answers. I deliberately began putting the wrong answers on my test. I waited for Tony to finish his cheating, and just before the exams were taken up, I erased and corrected my answers. Tony made an F. I didn't have to worry anymore about him copying from me.

Second grade was a time when the bullies in the classroom tried to exert themselves. On the playground, I met these boys head on. I wasn't afraid of them, but more importantly, I decided no one would bully me. It took several fights to establish this fact, but they soon left me alone. The teachers were either nonobservant of these fights or simply let them run their course. Whatever the case, fights usually ended without teacher intervention.

Fighting was a way of life among these Cartoogechaye boys. Because we had moved into the community and were not natives, my siblings and I were outsiders and targeted. Students taunted Elaine and Gloria relentlessly. Johnny was like me, a fighter. While Johnny and I were not bullies, we did defend ourselves. Some of the ridicule came because we lived in "that big new house" everyone saw from the school. They were jealous of a family they viewed as having more, "down in the valley," while they lived modest lives in the mountains of Cartoogechaye. They didn't realize that we were poor as well.

At home, we had conflicting advice about fighting at school. Daddy always said, "Boys, if I find out you're fighting, I'll whip you when you get home. Remember, the Bible teaches us to turn the other cheek."

Mother followed up on Daddy's advice when he wasn't around. "Boys, if you're picked on and don't fight back, *I'll* whip you when you get home." Johnny and I followed her advice rather than Daddy's. But he didn't mean what he said since he never carried out his threat to whip us for fighting.

Mrs. Cabe read a book to the class because she said it reminded her of the time she had taught in a two-room schoolhouse located nearby. The book was titled *The Thread That Runs So True* and was by Jesse Stuart. It depicted Jesse's struggles as an eighteen-year-old first-year schoolteacher in a one-room schoolhouse in the hills of eastern Kentucky. I became engrossed in this tale from an earlier era of the twentieth century and in the intrigues Jesse endured among people who viewed him as an outsider. He had to fight for respect, just like me. I identified with Jesse's struggles and how he coped with getting along. Mrs. Cabe read a portion of the book to us each day. After Mrs. Cabe had finished the book, I said to my-self, *Someday I'll write a book about my struggles here in Cartoogechaye.*

⊶ ⊷

In 1960 I was in Mrs. Wilson's third-grade class. Fighting would have been behind me if it had not been for Randy, who was in second grade. For some reason, the bullies kept getting the best of him. Randy's answer to this dilemma was to call upon me for as-sistance, which I provided. I took up for him, and over the course of the year, I whipped many of the second graders in defense of Randy. On one such occasion, Randy came running. "Mikey, they took off their belts; they're going to whip me!" he said.

I looked down the hallway, and sure enough, several boys had their belts off and were waving them in the air. I took mine off and went screaming toward them. "I'll whip you all! I'll whip you all!" I shouted as I slung my belt wildly over my head. Randy took his off and was right behind me, swinging away too. All the boys bolted for the exit door as fast as they could.

Mrs. Wilson was a nice teacher who was easygoing for the most part. Whenever conflict erupted in her classroom, she usually resolved it by having the two offending parties apologize to one another in front of the entire class. One day on the playground, Jerry and I got into a fight. Mrs. Wilson intervened and stopped the fight, which was unusual. Once we returned to the classroom, she said, "Mikey and Jerry, come to the front of the room, please." We complied. "Now, each of you apologize to one another," she demanded.

"I'm sorry," Jerry said. I just stood there; I was still mad.

"Mikey, go ahead; you're next," Mrs. Wilson said.

"I can't apologize, Miss Wilson. I'm not sorry!" I said.

Startled, Mrs. Wilson paused to regain her composure. "Go sit down Mikey. This class has too much to do for you to stand there all day," she scolded.

In third grade, art was a weakness. I made As and Bs in everything else, but art was my Achilles heel. During class one day I came up with the idea of tracing my art piece for submission. It was the best artwork I had ever done. "What an excellent piece, Mikey," Mrs. Wilson said, admiring my work as she attached it to the corkboard.

"Mikey traced it," someone called out from behind me.

Others said, "Yes, he did!"

I slumped in my seat, knowing they had caught me. To my surprise, Mrs. Wilson ignored them. The A she gave me stood, but I had learned my lesson. There were no more art tracings from me.

In social studies, we learned about the upcoming presidential election. I was surprised to hear that anyone other than Dwight D. Eisenhower could be president. After all, he was the only one I had ever known. The contest was between John F. Kennedy and Richard M. Nixon. Both in class and at home, I became completely fascinated by this election. Daddy, a lifelong Democrat, was for Nixon, the Republican.

"Kennedy's a Catholic, and he'll have to take orders from the pope in Rome if he's elected," Daddy argued. "The whole country will be ruined if Kennedy becomes president." Because of Daddy, I became a Nixon supporter. Mother remained silent about her opinion. On the night of the election, November 8, 1960, I had to go to bed before the election results were known.

The next morning I asked Mother, "Who won the election?"

She said, "Kennedy won. He'll be our next president."

School was out on Friday, January 20, 1961. That day, on television, I watched as John F. Kennedy became the thirty-fifth president of the United States. By then, most of the talk about how the pope would be running our country had ended. Instead, there was genuine excitement about this new, young president. My awareness of the presidential election carried over into a wider interest in current events in general. I began to watch the news on television at home and paid closer attention to the discussions at school.

The Peace Corps was one of the topics. President Kennedy announced the creation of this new volunteer program on March 1, 1961, just after his inauguration. The mission of the Peace Corps was to aid nations around the world, to help them understand the United States, and to help the United States understand them. Everyone was excited about this new program. Many young people signed up to participate.

The Space Race also got my attention. It heated up on April 12, 1961, when Yuri Gagarin, a cosmonaut from the Soviet Union, became the first human in outer space. The United States had competed to get to outer space first, but delays in the American launch schedule resulted in Astronaut Alan Shepard arriving there more than three weeks later, on May 5, 1961.

The idea of space travel was almost more than a boy could ponder. Interest in the Space Race was tempered, though, by the frightening Bay of Pigs Invasion of Cuba in April 1961. Tension filled the nation and our schoolroom as we discussed what was going to happen. Many people believed Cuban president Fidel Castro was a menace and it was important to stop him. Others were wary of the war's consequences.

The crisis followed the U-2 Incident of May 1, 1960, in which an American U-2 spy plane was shot down over the Soviet Union. Our government at first denied the plane's purpose and mission but then was forced to admit its role in covert surveillance when the Soviets produced the aircraft's remains and surviving pilot, Francis Gary Powers, as well as photos he had taken of Russian military bases. The incident was a great embarrassment to the United States and prompted a marked deterioration in its relations with the Soviet Union. Talk of World War III soon subsided, however, as the Cuban invasion proved to be a failure. Afterward, Castro sought closer ties with the Soviet Union, which had terrible results over the next year and a half.

Attention once again returned to the Space Race when Kennedy presented a plan to send a man to the moon and back by the end of the decade. Going to the moon was almost incomprehensible, a notion that seemed more like fantasy than reality.

In the third-grade, I gained enough confidence to enter the marble games on the playground. Still, I was smart enough not to get into a game with the older boys, who were much better. But in my age group, I could compete with the best. The prize was to take the most and best marbles from the big ring we drew on the ground for competition. We had a great time playing marbles.

I also became more mischievous. On the playground one day, I wrote a note and hid it. I then gathered a group of boys for the stated purpose of playing tag, but before we could start, I found the note. "Hey, this says, 'A ghost was here,'" I told the boys. They all looked at the paper with alarm.

"Let's show it to Mrs. Wilson," Jackie said. Off they went.

Mrs. Wilson came. "All the boys are scared. They say you found this note. Is that right, Mikey?" she asked, showing it to me.

"Yes, Miss Wilson, I found it."

"Then tell the ghost to learn to spell. It's *ghost*, not *gost!*" Miss Wilson said with a laugh.

In 1961, I had Mrs. Wilson a second time, for fourth grade. The third and fourth grades had grown too large. The solution was to take some of the students from the third and others from the fourth and create a split classroom that Mrs. Wilson taught. I didn't like this arrangement since it meant I was no longer with many classmates with whom I was friends from first grade. This split classroom created trouble on the playground, as some of my former classmates now teased me for being in a class with third graders. My reaction was to fight, which resulted in blows between Bobby Crawford and me. I had always considered Bobby to be one of my best friends. He attended Mount Hope, and I had been to his house to play on many occasions. Bobby was a little bigger than I was, and his punches hurt. I fought back, landing the hardest blows I could. As the fight progressed, I felt myself sinking. About the time I thought I'd lost, Bobby, suddenly and without warning, broke from the battle, began crying, and ran from the playground. He ran all the way home, east along the highway to Patton Road and south, past the parsonage, to his house, another quarter mile. I was stunned, and so was Mrs. Wilson and Mrs. Wallace, Bobby's teacher. The next day, Mrs. Wilson called me out into the hallway to meet with Bobby and Mrs. Wallace. This time, I needed no prompting from Mrs. Wilson.

"I'm sorry for fighting," I confessed to Bobby.

"I'm sorry too," Bobby said. These formal apologies ended the matter, but I was genuinely regretful for having fought a good friend. We had a strained friendship after that, but I finally established myself as a fighter. I didn't have to brawl anymore at Cartoogechaye Elementary School.

That previous summer, upon returning from one of his revivals, Daddy had bought Johnny, Randy, and me corncob pipes. He often brought us toys after he had completed a revival tour. We came to expect and look forward to his gifts. In the fall, I took my corncob pipe to school to show the other boys. I was very proud of it.

"You haven't smoked it yet," said Wayne.

"I don't have any tobacco," I said.

"You don't need it. We can go over into the cornfield and smoke corn silk," Wayne said.

"You mean you can smoke corn silk?"

"Why, yes, I do it all the time at home," Wayne said.

Fred, who was standing beside Wayne, agreed. "I've smoked corn silk too and rabbit tobacco," he said.

With some apprehension, I darted into the woods at the edge of the playground with Wayne and Fred and crossed the fence into the Parkers' cornfield. Dried corn tassels were hanging from mature ears of corn. They were awaiting their harvest as silage. Wayne filled my pipe with corn silk and lit a match he just happened to have with him.

Wayne took a puff and passed the pipe to Fred. After Fred had a drag, he gave it to me. I sucked in the hot, burning corn silk. Not being used to smoke filling my lungs, I immediately coughed, nearly choking. "That's good!" I said although I didn't take another puff. Wayne and Fred finished it off. I cleaned out my pipe before the three of us returned, unnoticed, to the playground, but I had ruined my corncob pipe. I couldn't take it home because Mother and Daddy would know what I had done. I quietly "lost" the pipe in the woods by the end of recess.

The Cold War returned as a topic of discussion in the fourth grade because of the Berlin crisis, which had begun the previous June but had accelerated. I had watched throughout the summer on television as the events of the crisis unfolded. Then, on August 13, 1961, East Germany closed the border to West Berlin. After sealing it off, the Communists erected the Berlin Wall. Many parents believed World War III was imminent. It was a scary time that finally ended in a standoff. Still, the wall remained.

The Space Race, in contrast, produced feelings of glee when John Glenn became the first American to orbit Earth on February 20, 1962. After his space flight, I wanted to be an astronaut.

As the end of school neared, in the spring of 1962, I didn't yet know fourth grade was to be my last year at Cartoogechaye Elementary School.

CHAPTER 9
SEMINARY

In 1958, just after we moved into the Mount Hope parsonage and the same year I started school, Daddy went back to seminary. He enrolled in Southeastern Baptist Theological Seminary in Wake Forest, North Carolina, where he graduated with a bachelor of divinity degree on May 19, 1961. During the time that Daddy was attending school, he left home the first of each week and did not return until Friday evening. On Saturdays, we had to be very careful not to wake him, since he slept late after a long, hard week at the school.

Mother and Daddy had always been harsh disciplinarians, even though their punishment was inconsistent and unfair, driven mainly by anger. Mother's whippings hurt, but she didn't have the strength to injure. Daddy's punishments could harm and often did, especially when his temper rose high enough. His extended periods of absence created tension at home and became the source of great resentment and depression for Mother since she was left with eight children in her care while he was away.

While Daddy was at the seminary, Mother was trapped at the parsonage, as she didn't drive. In fact, Mother never drove a car her entire life. If she needed something, she waited until Daddy was home on weekends because she was reluctant to seek anyone's assistance. This attitude only reinforced her feelings of isolation. Added to Mother's distress was the fact Daddy ran revivals between seminary sessions, meaning he was gone virtually all the time. We didn't see him very much, and when we did, he was often tired and irritated. As Mother's despondency grew, she became increasingly troubled, and her whippings intensified. Her swearing became much more pronounced, and when Daddy was home, she agitated him with stories of our disobedience, which provoked him to punish us. I often dreaded Daddy's arrival, for, depending on his mood, it could result in a beating.

It was an odd situation. On the one hand, while Daddy was gone, I missed him and was afraid at night, for no one was home to protect us. His absences seemed to last forever, which created a sense of loss and confusion. The dread of his arrival was also acute, for danger then lurked. A watchful eye was necessary to avoid his anger, if that was possible. Many cruel incidents occurred during these years. One happened at the supper table because I got mad and smacked the chair with my hand. "Son, get down there and kiss the seat. You shouldn't be getting mad like that," Daddy said.

"I'll not do it," I said.

Daddy grabbed hold of me and began shoving my face toward the chair seat. "Son, I'll not tolerate your disobedience; so, kiss it, now!" he shouted, becoming angrier.

"No, I won't!"

He began hitting and punching me and shoved my head toward the seat. Now, almost hysterical, he said, "Son, you kiss that chair, or I'll kill you!"

By now I was afraid for my life and cried profusely. Fearing Daddy's rage, I kissed the seat. However, I said to myself, *Daddy, you'll see me kiss this chair seat, but inside of me I'm not kissing it*! My outward submission satisfied Daddy, ending the beating and maybe saving my life.

My father sometimes came home and lined all eight of us up, from the oldest to the youngest, and whipped us all with a belt for what he called "general principle," meaning he suspected we had been disobedient in some way during his absence—even though neither he nor Mother had any proof of it. A whipping was then necessary to correct us for these unknown misdeeds. Daddy seemed to take great delight in these whippings, while Mother stood by approvingly. Mother and Daddy also encouraged us to tattle on one another if some misdeed was committed.

"I'll whip any of you young'uns who knows something but doesn't tell it," Daddy stated. Every time he beat us, he asked, "Did anyone else know about this?" The child punished was required to name the conspirators, if they existed, and then they too were whipped. It didn't take long for alliances to vanish among the brothers and sisters. None developed close bonds since all feared the consequences of keeping silent. We were afraid not to tattle.

When Johnny, Randy, and I got BB guns for Christmas in 1958, Daddy warned us he would shoot the first one of us with the air rifle who injured the other. This circumstance didn't take long to occur, given Johnny was seven, Randy was five, and I was six. It happened while we were shooting metal cans just after Christmas. Randy had stacked them up, but as he was moving away from the targets and while I was aiming, the top can fell off. As I pulled the trigger, Randy rushed back toward them, and I inadvertently shot him on the wrist. Randy screamed in pain. "Mikey shot me; Mikey shot me!"

Daddy came rushing out of the house. Randy's injury was minor, but it didn't matter to Daddy. "Son, didn't I tell you I'd shoot you if you shot someone?"

"Yes," I said as I began to cry. "I didn't mean to—it was an accident," I pleaded.

He was unmoved. "Come around to the back of the house and give me your gun," he said.

"Please don't shoot me," I cried. "Please, don't."

"Line up against the back of the house," Daddy demanded. I complied. "Turn around with your face to the brick, and cover your eyes with your hands." He shot me in the back of my right leg. I screamed in pain as Daddy said, "Now let that be a lesson to you!"

During these years Mother's despair descended into manipulative and suicidal behavior. Sometimes she would threaten to take her life by going to the church, turning on a propane heater, and killing herself by carbon monoxide poisoning.

"No, Mother, please don't do it," we would cry and scream as she got up from her chair.

"Yes, I'm going to do it now," she would reply as she headed to the door.

"Please don't go," we would plead as she turned the doorknob.

"If I stay, will you be good?" she would ask as she opened the door.

"Yes, we won't give you any more trouble," we would say.

"Fine, then I'll not go." She would close the door and return to her chair.

This drama was repeated over and over during these years. Other times Mother threatened to run away and never return. "I'm leaving this house, and you'll never see me again," she would say.

This threat always evoked panic, followed by our pleading with her not to leave. "Please don't go, Mother," we would cry and scream.

"Yes, I'm leaving now," she would say as she headed toward the door.

"Please stay, and we'll be good."

"Okay, if you'll quit your fighting and arguing, then I'll stay."

She often said she wanted to die. "I can't stand it anymore. I don't want to live; I wish I were dead," was her constant refrain. Mother was the unhappiest person I knew. For me, this turmoil created fear of the dark and fear of death—my death or that of my brothers and sisters or Mother and Daddy. I dreaded the night because at bedtime my fear was greatest. To calm my nighttime anxiety, Mother and Daddy put a Roy Rogers night-light in the bedroom where I slept with Johnny and Randy. It was in the shape of Roy's gun. While it did provide some comfort, the uneasiness and fear remained.

To keep death away, I began a ritualistic incantation to ensure my family's safety. Of death, I said for each of my siblings and Mother and Daddy, "I just know it will happen; I know it will." Stating death was sure to happen, I reasoned, guaranteed it would not. The proof of the effectiveness of my prayer came each morning when everyone was still alive. This one-sentence charm was expanded over time as the thought of death continued to torment me. No longer was it good enough to pray a one-sentence incantation for the whole family; I had to pray it for everyone, a total of ten times. As fear continued to trouble me, I expanded the spell again, repeating it ten times each for everyone, for a total of one hundred times.

These nighttime supplications became exhausting, yet I kept them going for years. After all, I reasoned, a missed recitation meant certain death for someone in the family. I began this practice when I was six. It ended at the age of ten, when one night I was so exhausted I went to sleep before completing the ritual. The next morning, realizing what I had done, I hurried to see if anyone was dead. When I found everyone alive, I was relieved.

That night, I decided to try it again. I went to sleep without invoking the petitions. Again, the next morning, everyone was alive. After that, I concluded I didn't have to say the prayers anymore. This emotional, chaotic, and troubling lifestyle was our homelife— the dark backdrop of the Willises' existence. For me, somehow, it was normal. I had nothing else with which to compare it.

CHAPTER 10

CARTOOGECHAYE CREEK AND THE WOODS

I loved Cartoogechaye Creek. It was my refuge. I could go there and not worry about anything. The creek was a quiet place where I enjoyed the magnificence of the outdoors. I loved the smell. The air was fresh, and I felt at peace. It had all life could offer. I knew every inch of the creek within a mile, east or west, of the Mount Hope parsonage. From the first time in 1957 that I peered over the Patton Road Bridge and into the water below, I was in love with this creek. From the top of the bridge, I could see a large rock jutting out from the middle of the stream that I loved. Occasionally, I waded out in the swiftly moving water just to sit on this exposed bedrock. Sometimes I tried to fish there, but the spot wasn't very good for fishing. Mainly, I contented myself with sitting and enjoying the sound of the water as it rushed along.

We began fishing this creek almost immediately after moving into the parsonage. At first, Daddy fashioned fishing poles made of a cane for Johnny, Randy, and me, adding a line, hook, and sinker to the end. These poles were awkward and difficult to use. Maneuvering them to avoid the trees and the brush along the bank was almost impossible. I often got the line hung up. I could never catch a fish with my cane pole, but Johnny could. He was always a better fisherman than I was.

Daddy, observing our problems with the cane poles, bought us fishing rods with casting reels from the downtown Franklin Western Auto. With these we became successful fishermen, bringing our catch home for Mother to clean. During the summer months, from the time I was six years old, I rose early. Getting up at dawn, I headed down to Cartoogechaye Creek, where I fished until I heard Mother's call for breakfast. Johnny and Randy often joined me. Mother's call was a high-pitched whistle that, in the morning air, could be heard very clearly from anywhere along the creek bank. Mother sounded this call by placing her thumb and index finger on her lower lip while forcing air through her front teeth and out her mouth. It was an impressive whistle—one I could never replicate as hard as I tried. After breakfast, we returned to our fishing or played in the woods and fields until we again heard Mother's whistle to come to dinner.

There were many good fishing spots. One was at the edge of a cornfield where a branch converged with Cartoogechaye Creek. I caught some of my largest trout in this fishing hole—rainbow and brown trout. We considered anything else inferior. When we became older, Johnny, Randy, and I also cleaned our catches. Mother wrapped the trout up and froze them until we had a "mess." She then served them up for the entire family in a fish fry. I loved these special suppers. The smell of the trout cooking on the stove in an iron skillet was what kept me going back to the creek bank. I also loved the savory taste. We usually had several fish fries each summer, depending on the success of our fishing. Daddy laid down only one rule. Under no circumstances were we to fish on Sunday, for that was the Lord's Day—a day of rest not to be violated. After all, Daddy reasoned, fishing was work.

"No fishing will be done on Sunday. It is toiling, and you can't do it," he warned. We obeyed this rule for fear of a whipping. I violated Daddy's rule only once. One Sunday, just after trout season had started and Daddy had left to preach an afternoon church service, I was anxious. I couldn't tolerate the idea of letting a perfectly good, sunny afternoon go to waste while there were trout to be caught. I sneaked down to Cartoogechaye Creek and put in a line. The fish were biting well that day, and it didn't take long for me to land one of the biggest trout I had ever caught. My dilemma became immediately evident. I couldn't take the fish home, as my transgression would then be exposed. Mother would certainly tell Daddy. Repressing a burning desire to show off my excellent catch, I carefully removed the hook from the jaw of that great trout and released it back into the water. I watched regretfully as it swiftly darted away.

Earthworms were the bait of choice. They were easily found in the moist clay next to the parsonage or near the creek. Sometimes I used grub worms, crickets, grasshoppers, and other giant insects—whatever was abundant and typical for trout to eat. One summer the trees were filled with an infestation of big green caterpillar-type worms. When a strong wind blew, they fell from the leaves they were consuming, caught themselves on a web-like tether, and reeled themselves back up. Sometimes these strange caterpillars dropped into the water from the trees overhanging the creek. Seeing them fall, I realized the fish ate them. I began using the worms as a source of bait.

Daddy bought spinners, which became the bait of choice where there was enough room to cast out and reel them back. Sometimes the water was so clear I could see the trout chasing the spinner just before it hit. The excitement from spinner fishing kept me repeatedly casting for hours. I used a three-hook spinner until they were declared illegal by wildlife officials. From that time forward, only one hook was acceptable. To comply with the law, I cut two of the three hooks off my favorite spinner to avoid its loss, if caught by a warden. It didn't matter, for in all the years I fished Cartoogechaye Creek, an officer never stopped me. And, although I had them, there would not have been any consequence if I had not had a fishing license or trout stamp. If spotted, I was prepared to rush home and retrieve these documents, since I never carried them with me.

The Patton Road Bridge was a trout-stocking location for wildlife management. We were always on the lookout for their arrival because it meant a fantastic day of fishing. My brothers and I spied on the officers until they left. By that time, Mother had opened a can of whole kernel corn, which we used for bait. We knew these newly stocked fish were fed similar-looking food in the stock ponds and would eat the corn readily. We never told any of our neighbors when the officers supplied the stream since we wanted to catch as many trout as possible for ourselves.

I felt guilty using the corn to catch the unsuspecting prey so quickly. I didn't feel I was giving them a sporting chance. But the guilt wasn't enough to keep me from doing it. The tug of a trout on the end of a fishing line was too tempting, even if the fish had been newly stocked. The fishing frenzy didn't last long. Within a few days, the trout dispersed and became accustomed to eating natural food. We then put the corn away until the next restocking. It was easy to tell stocked trout from native trout. The fishery clipped one of the small front fins of the stock trout, while a native had two full front fins. There were not many native trout in Cartoogechaye Creek. In fact, I never caught one in all the years I fished there.

⇥ ⇤

When not fishing, I liked to roam the cornfields and the woods along Cartoogechaye Creek. The magnificent Blue Ridge Mountains were visible from all directions. Many times, I explored these cornfields alone, but at other times I went with Johnny and Randy. It was easy to get lost in one, especially when the stalks grew high over one's head. I sometimes panicked until I got my bearings. Getting lost in a cornfield was an embarrassment, something to which I never admitted.

One of the grandest sights was the white-tailed deer that regularly ventured out of the woods to feast on the golden grains these fields offered. Near Mount Hope Baptist Church, we frequently observed deer as they came out of the woods in the early evening and into the hay field above the parsonage, across the highway. We watched quietly so as not to scare them, for they spooked very easily. One evening as we watched the group, a car pulled off the road in front of the parsonage. We thought the occupants wanted to enjoy the scene, just like we were doing. Shortly after that, we heard a loud shot. The smoke from the end of a rifle puffed up from the driver's-side window. The car sped off, squealing its tires. At the crack of the gunshot, all but one of the deer fled for the safety of the woods. The remaining doe was down. It wasn't a clean shot. The doe flailed on the ground, struggling to run but couldn't— the wound had broken her back. We called the wildlife officers. They arrived, put down the doe, and completed a report.

"Who would want to shoot that deer?" I asked Daddy.

"Son, there are mean people in this world who'll do just about anything," he said.

"I hope they fry that asshole! He could have shot one of the young'uns," Mother interjected. They never found the shooter, and it was a long time before the deer returned to the hay field.

⊷ ⊶

The woods were the site of many adventures, full of old logging roads, the significance of which I didn't understand at the time. The woods were a place of solitude and exploration year-round. I felt at peace in the woods, close to nature and the beauty of the world. Time seemed to stop when I was there. The sun peeking through the leaves, the breeze in the air, and the rustle of the trees allowed me to drift off to another place. I spent hours in that creation, free of the problems in this one. The woods were a place of refuge. I went there when times were tough, when Mother and Daddy were harsh, or when life just seemed full of trouble. I took solace and found security there. In the woods, I also imagined the future. *What will it be like in the year 2000?* I wondered. *How will the world be different, and how will life be changed?* "I'll turn forty-eight in the year 2000!" I said. "That's older than I can imagine!" *I hope I'll be successful.* It was these things, and much more, that I pondered while walking through in the woods.

Whatever the future held, I had already decided one thing: *I will make something out of my life. I'll not be a ditch digger!* This idea came from Mother, who often said, "Mikey, you're good for nothing! When you grow up, all you'll be good for is digging ditches. You'll never have enough gumption to do anything else." Mother's statement made me believe ditch digging was the worst job anyone could have, and I was determined not to be a ditch digger.

The old logging trails I followed in the woods came from an earlier era of the Appalachians when clear-cutting of the forests was a common practice. Beginning in the nineteenth century and continuing into the early twentieth, all healthy trees were cut and sold to sawmills, most of the tall old-growth timber. Thousands upon thousands of forest acres were exploited by use of these logging roads, along with the use of creeks as skid trails and the building of flumes. Clear-cutting left the region's forest resources in a state of ruin, which led to the development of the profession of forestry. Consequently, what I observed were new-growth trees that were relatively small. There were very few large trees left in the woods. I didn't know this history, which made it easy to enjoy the beauty of these reemerging forests.

The woods immediately surrounding the parsonage were full of rabbits, squirrels, various species of songbirds, and white-tailed deer. In the fields and underbrush, one could flush out pheasant, quail, and dove. Near Cartoogechaye Creek, field mice and other small animals were abundant, and occasionally a ground-hog could be seen. Opossums were nasty creatures that roamed at night and got into our garbage. Skunks were a menace as well. One night our dog got into a fight with a skunk in our basement and was sprayed, sending the foul odor throughout the house. It was winter, and we didn't get rid of the stink until spring. The scent clung to our clothes and was an embarrassment when visitors came to the parsonage. When springtime arrived, we opened all the doors and windows to allow the winds to sweep the smell away. Our dog's confrontation with the skunk had made for a very long, smelly winter.

Mount Hope was also a haven for stray dogs and cats. These animals were set out by their owners. They roamed the woods immediately to the back of the church and parsonage. Some of the dogs became our pets; others we chased away. Sometimes hunting parties were organized to kill off the vagrant dogs. The cats were a different matter. These strays became feral and lived in the woods surrounding the church. We called them "wild cats," because the feral cats terrorized us as they scampered away, especially if we stumbled upon them while playing in the woods.

Deeper in the mountains, far away from human habitation, black bears, wild turkeys, and wild boars roamed. Some said the elusive mountain lion also lived there. The wild pigs were not native to the Appalachians. Rather, they had been imported from Europe in the early twentieth century and placed on game reserves for hunting. Some of these European hogs eventually escaped and came to populate many areas of western North Carolina, including the Great Smoky Mountains National Park located thirty miles from our house.

One day as we played in the yard, a wild boar came running into our yard.

"It's a devil; it's a devil!" my sisters screamed hysterically as all of us ran panic-stricken into the house.

"My God, if I knew how to shoot, I'd kill that bastard!" Mother screamed. From then on, we were very watchful for these ugly beasts with their long tusks and menacing faces.

Snakes were commonplace too. Copperheads and rattlesnakes were the main enemies that we were on the lookout for. There were also many nonpoisonous snakes. I didn't fear snakes, but I did have a healthy respect for the dangerous ones, for I knew they could kill. I also knew a black snake's bite wasn't very pleasant. I avoided them as well. Other reptiles and amphibians included turtles, frogs, lizards, and salamanders. It was an unfortunate event for these creatures if we caught them, as we always tried to keep them as pets. Mother soon demanded their release, concluding they would die of hunger if we didn't let them go.

⊫⊣ ⊢⊨

The woods were full of hickory, maple, oak, poplar, sassafras, dogwood, willow, birch, elm, walnut, and various types of evergreen. One tree missing was the American chestnut. These trees had been devastated by the chestnut blight, a fungal disease, in the early twentieth century. I had never seen one, but I heard about these majestic trees and their roasting nuts from Granddaddy Willis, who told us about them during one of his rare talkative moments. On the farm, in the Willis Cove, they released the hogs into the woods to fatten them up on chestnuts in the fall once they had dropped from the trees. Granddaddy also told us the story of how he lost his right eye as a young boy when a roasting chestnut popped out of the fireplace at home and blinded him.

Old chestnut boards, usually collected from dilapidated barns, were prized possessions that were used to fashion furniture, paneling, and other items. Finding wormy chestnut was even rarer. This wood came from defective trees with insect damage—long-dead blight-killed trees. The wormy wood became fashionable for its rustic character. Sellers of chestnut or wormy chestnut boards commanded a hefty price. The American chestnut tree was mythical, only talked about in the past tense.

⋙⋘

In the Blue Ridge Mountains, each season had its characteristics, all delightfully different. The budding of the trees in the woods signaled spring was approaching, a fantastic time of year. As spring advanced and the temperatures rose, the dogwoods bloomed, and various kinds of wildflowers began growing on the forest floor. It didn't take long for the woods to be green and alive with all the colors of spring. Numerous varieties of mushrooms, mosses, and fungi also emerged in the spring. My mother always told us, "Boys, make sure you don't eat any of those mushrooms. Some are good, but others are poisonous, and you can't tell them apart. So, don't eat the mushrooms!"

In the summer, the leaf cover of the trees provided shelter as we played in the woods or fished along the banks of Cartoogechaye Creek. We were watchful for poison ivy, which grew among the trees and near the banks of the creek. Contact with its leaves resulted in an itchy irritation, at least for my brothers and sisters. Fortunately for me, I didn't get these rashes. In fact, I could roll in poison ivy without effect, but I didn't, preferring instead to maintain a healthy respect for the plant despite my seeming immunity. I had seen too much suffering from my siblings and remained cautious.

In the fall, my favorite season, the color of the woods turned to orange, red, yellow, and purple. I loved the fresh, crisp air and the smell of the turning leaves. Once they had fallen and the cold had arrived, I loved to stomp through the dried-out leaves. Each Christmas Mother sent us to look for the perfect cedar tree for a Christmas tree. Bob Parker gave Daddy permission to cut these cedars from his property.

In the winter months, the scene of snow piled deep among the barren trees was a fantastic sight. Daddy loved the snow too. Many times, after it started to fall, he loaded us up and headed east toward Franklin. It was a challenge to see if we could get to the grocery store and back without ending up in a ditch. Daddy never canceled church services for snow either. Because of our large family, he always had at least ten in attendance. He bragged to his preacher friends that on the worst snow day of the winter, he always had at least a dozen of his members in attendance. Daddy's statement was true since it was certain a few others would show up along with us. We usually had several big snowstorms each winter, which we enjoyed immensely.

By winter's end, I was always ready for spring. Spring fever usually began in mid-February. Sometimes I put on my coat, went outside, lay on the ground, looked up at the bright heavens, and pretended it was spring. The sunshine in my face and blue sky allowed me to imagine spring was already there. One day Mother saw me lying on the ground, came to the door, and said, "Shit fire, Mikey, get up off the ground before you freeze your ass off! What the hell are you doing lying on the ground like that in the dead of winter? Don't you have any sense at all?" I got up but didn't reply. Mother would not have understood.

$$\Longleftarrow\!\!+\ +\!\!\Longrightarrow$$

My love for the Blue Ridge Mountains was immeasurable, and the rest of the family enjoyed them equally. We were just as awestruck by the beauty of the mountains as were the tourists who made special trips to see them. Day-trips were regular affairs when Daddy was home, usually on Saturday or Sunday afternoons, if he didn't have to preach. Spring, summer, and fall were perfect times for sight-seeing. We especially liked to take trips in the fall, when all the colors of the Blue Ridge Mountains were on display. Sight-seeing was wondrous considering that the Nantahala National Forest, the Pisgah National Forest, and the Great Smoky Mountains National Park were nearby.

In Macon County, we traveled east from Franklin to Highlands and stopped at all the falls along the way. We visited Wayah Bald and Standing Indian and toured along the Nantahala River Gorge. If our trip was going to be long, Mother packed a picnic lunch. We drove to Cherokee, through the Oconaluftee, and into the Great Smoky Mountains National Park. It wasn't uncommon to see black bears come out of the forest for the chance at a meal from a picture-taking tourist or a garbage can. We stopped at Newfound Gap, where we observed some of the most spectacular scenes in the entire park. Sometimes we visited Aunt Dorcas and our cousins in Sylva, before proceeding toward Waynesville and Canton over the Balsam Mountains. Through the years, we never got tired of these day-trips. They were rare times of family fun and enjoyment.

CHAPTER 11

SOUTHERN BAPTISTS

Mount Hope Baptist Church belonged to the Southern Baptist Convention. Daddy was a Southern Baptist from his youth, from the time Grandmother Willis had first taken him to Calvary Baptist Church in Canton. He believed the Southern Baptists were the closest thing on earth to the church Jesus originally founded and that the doctrines and practices of the denomination were exactly like those Jesus taught. Daddy said there were other churches with Christians, but it was Southern Baptists who most closely followed Christ. He pointed to the Methodists and the Presbyterians as examples of denominations that had Christian members. Daddy was respectful of the Methodists because it was the church where his parents were members. He was also first baptized there. My father believed in baptism by immersion, as did all Southern Baptists. The ordinance was intended for both adults and youths who had been "saved" or "born again." After salvation, an individual was immersed in water and allowed to join the church.

He also believed it was sinful for Christians to drink alcohol, a practice condoned by many Methodists and Presbyterians. While the Pentecostals believed many of the same doctrines held by

Southern Baptists, Daddy was wary of them because they spoke in tongues, conducted healing services, and were very expressive in their worship. He called them "holy rollers" because he said they sometimes rolled in the church aisles during their services, which to me was a scary notion.

Grady Reece, the pastor of a nearby Pentecostal church, at times stopped to visit with Daddy. He always drove an old battered pickup truck. Reverend Reece was a pleasant man who was always friendly. At first, I was afraid of him because of the stories I had heard about Pentecostals, but over time, as he continued to stop by, I began to wonder why Daddy had such a low opinion of them. Grady Reece seemed very rational to me. Regarding the issue of Pentecostalism, Daddy gave us a mixed message. At home, he didn't let us play Holy Roller, and when Oral Roberts's television program was on, he didn't let us make fun of his healing services. Oral Roberts, a Pentecostal preacher, along with Evangelist Billy Graham, pioneered televangelism in the 1950s. We watched Oral Roberts's program weekly. Regarding these televised healing services, Daddy said, "If it is his will, God can heal anyone."

As for Catholics, Daddy objected, just as he did with the Methodists and Presbyterians, to their practice of infant baptism and their drinking of alcohol. He questioned whether they were even Christians because of their many traditions and beliefs that he thought strayed from the teachings of Jesus. He was also suspicious of the pope. Daddy was also critical of the Episcopal Church because of its many formalities and the practice of reading prayers from the *Book of Common Prayer*. He maintained this position even though the Reverend Rufus Morgan, who headed the local Episcopal church, was hugely respected, not only in the Cartoogechaye community but also throughout Macon County. "Catholics and Episcopalians call their preachers 'Father,' but the Bible teaches that no man should be called father," Daddy said. He was kinder to the Jews, believing they were God's chosen people, making it necessary for Christians to be respectful of them even though they didn't believe Jesus was the Messiah. According to Daddy, all other religions were false and a danger to all Americans and the world.

I had no reason to doubt Daddy's teachings and beliefs. After all, except for Saint John's Episcopal Bible School, I had never attended a church that wasn't Southern Baptist, nor had I been exposed to any other religion but Christianity.

Mount Hope Baptist Church was full of activity. As pastor of the church, Daddy was at the center. He, along with the deacons, controlled everything that happened. There was an annual business meeting at which the members of the congregation elected the deacon board and many other positions. After the annual meeting, it was left up to Daddy and the deacons to get things done. Very rarely did the entire congregation assemble for a called business meeting. Babs Neely served as secretary. Many of the visitors thought Babs was the preacher's wife since she was very attentive to Daddy's needs before and after each service.

At Mount Hope, church services were held on Sunday morning, Sunday night, and Wednesday night. Sunday morning services consisted of Sunday school, followed by a worship service. Sunday school, which began at ten o'clock and continued until ten forty-five, was held to teach the Bible to all age groups. Age levels included preschool, primary, junior boys and girls, senior boys and girls, and men's and women's adult classes. Sunday school attendance at Mount Hope averaged around sixty. The Sunday morning worship service, which started at eleven o'clock, averaged around one hundred and always followed the same order. It began with the singing of hymns led by Kenneth Crawford, the song leader. Mavis Dowdle, the piano player, accompanied Kenneth on the upright piano. A choir, positioned on the podium behind Daddy and Kenneth, assisted.

The congregation usually stood for the singing of the first song and then sat for the next two. If a hymn was long, it was customary for Kenneth to announce we were to sing the first, second, and last stanza. It irritated me if a verse, usually the third, was left out. "If the songwriter took the time to write that verse, then we should take the time to sing it," I reasoned. I voiced my displeasure to Daddy, but it didn't matter. Kenneth Crawford continued to leave out the third verse of most four-stanza hymns.

Mavis's piano playing had a double clomping sound to it since she hit the piano keys with her right hand first, followed by her left hand. Mavis couldn't play the piano by pressing both hands to the keys at the same time. We sang from the *Broadman Hymnal*, a songbook used by many Southern Baptist churches. There were many favorite hymns, including "Amazing Grace," "At the Cross," and "Higher Ground." Following the song service, Daddy welcomed members and guests, made church announcements, and took up the offering. He always prayed before the offering was taken up by getting down behind the pulpit on his right knee with his left knee up, a half-kneeling position. This style was somewhat unique to Daddy, although I did see other preachers use it. Usually, the minister only stood and prayed.

During the offering, Kenneth Crawford either led the congregation in another hymn, or special music was presented by a member or by an invited guest. After this song, Daddy read a text from the Bible, introducing his message. Before preaching, he once again kneeled behind the pulpit and prayed, after which he began his sermon. He almost always started his message with humor, and for the most part, his words were temperate. Still, they had enough fire to them to occasionally evoke an "amen" from the audience. At other times, he became emotional and broke into weeping at just the right moment. Daddy's sermons had charm, were filled with affection for his members, and displayed a passion for the Bible while still staunchly adhering to the doctrines of the Southern Baptist Church. These attributes were what made him admired by his members and successful at his profession.

The Mount Hope church services were also very moderate. It was very unusual for anyone to shout, although sometimes one of the older members or a guest did. I was always embarrassed by these outbursts. Daddy sometimes began crying in the middle of his sermon if he broke into an old hymn, a cappella style. "The Wayfaring Stranger" was one of his favorites.

I am a poor wayfaring stranger,
While traveling through this world below;
There is no sickness, toil, nor danger
In that bright world to which I go.

The Willis children sat on the same pew with Mother. We were required to stay very still and quiet. If anyone strayed from this obligation, he or she was likely to feel a sharp pain on the side of his or her leg or buttocks. Mother's pinch was the worst. She also whispered so only you could hear, "I'm going to beat the shit out of you when I get you home!" While sitting in the pew, I tried to stay as far away from her as possible.

The church service always ended with an altar call and a plea for the lost to come to the altar for salvation. A final hymn such as "I Surrender All," "Just as I Am," or "Softly and Tenderly" was played. Very rarely did anyone take Daddy up on this invitation since almost everyone in attendance was already saved.

The only modification to this order occurred in the months that had a fifth Sunday, when we observed the ordinance of Communion. It happened before Daddy's sermon. Small un-leavened wafers were passed out to all the members by the dea-cons, along with tiny cups of grape juice. Daddy read appropriate scriptures, and then everyone took the elements. The ordinance ended with a song such as "There Is a Fountain" or "Nothing but the Blood."

The entire worship service was over by noon. Afterward, Daddy went to the back door and shook hands with all the members and guests as they left. Mother was too busy with the younger children to accompany him to the back. It didn't matter. Guests rarely recognized Mother as the preacher's wife since she never looked, dressed, or acted the part. Of course, the members knew Mother, but they didn't know she cursed. While she regularly swore at home, she never uttered a profanity loud enough for a church member or guest to hear. I was surprised at how well Mother could control her cursing at church, given the frequency of her swearing at home.

Sunday night service was a repeat of the Sunday morning arrangement, just a shorter version. Instead of Sunday school, we had Training Union. As the name implied, the purpose of Training Union was to teach church members the basic Bible beliefs of Baptists and the church's doctrine. There were also instructions given regarding church membership, discipline, policy, and procedures. The age divisions were the same as those of Sunday school. Sunday evening services began at seven o'clock with Training Union, followed by the worship service. In the warmer months, when the windows were open, moths came into the sanctuary, attracted by the light. I passed these evenings watching both big and small moths and other flying insects circle the lights and soar from one end of the auditorium to the other. Studying these insects relieved my boredom.

Sometimes Wednesday's service was designated as testimony night, when members could "bear witness." I disliked the testimony meetings, for there were those who continued to speak on and on about when their souls got saved, how long ago, and how it had helped them through all their miserable lives. They then proceeded to tell of every trouble they had ever experienced. On and on these testaments went, which meant the service continued well past the usual time for departure.

Revivals occurred in the spring and fall, to renew the faithful and to preach the gospel to the unsaved. If there was to be any emotion displayed at Mount Hope Baptist Church, it was at a revival and almost always from a visitor or a group of guests, for they made up much of the attendance. At one of these revivals, I was standing during a lively hymn. The crowd became excited; shouts and "amen" went up. One old man became energized as the music and singing intensified, began wildly swinging his arms, and shouted, "Hallelujah." I was in the pew behind him. Before I could duck, he had coldcocked me. I was knocked into the bench, wincing in pain. No one seemed to notice—everyone was too taken with the moment. Even the old man just shook his hand and kept on shouting. After the service, Daddy asked me how I managed to get a bloody lip.

Bible school was held in the summer, just after school adjourned. At Bible school, I studied many scriptures—some so early in life I do not even remember learning them. I memorized the Lord's Prayer (Matthew 6:9–13) and Psalm 23. These verses and many others like them were instructive and brought comfort and assurance to me during the darker moments of my childhood.

The Royal Ambassadors, or RAs, was a missions-learning club for boys, held year-round. Girls in Action, or GAs, provided the same focus for girls. While Daddy encouraged these groups, they tended to be inconsistent, having periods when they didn't meet since there was no teacher available. Through the RAs, I learned that much of the world lived far differently than we did in America.

The women of the church held meetings of the WMU, a missions organization. WMU stood for Woman's Missionary Union, which was an auxiliary organization to the Southern Baptist Convention. Mother dreaded these meetings. "Attending that WMU meeting is a waste of my time. I've got better things to do than to go over to the church to hear all that stuff," she frequently said.

"You've got to go; you're the preacher's wife!" Daddy replied.

"I don't give a damn about that!" She got her clothes together and left for the meeting.

M Night was always a big event, especially if it was held at Mount Hope. It was an annual meeting, a type of rally that rotated from church to church. The *M* in M Night stood for "mobilization." It was a competition held among the churches of the Macon County Association of Southern Baptist Churches designed to rally support for Training Union. M Night was an evening service. The church with the most members in attendance took home the M Night banner, which the winning church then displayed on a wall until the next competition. While these meetings were great fun, I was always disappointed since Mount Hope never won the award.

Fellowship dinners also played a significant role at Mount Hope. These gatherings were scheduled on occasions throughout the year, usually after church on Sunday afternoons. Unlike many Southern Baptist churches, Mount Hope didn't have a homecoming dinner. These annual reunions were held to encourage past members and former pastors to attend. Since Mount Hope didn't have a homecoming, these periodic fellowship meals served a similar purpose. All the women prepared their most delicious covered dishes and desserts. Each family brought extras, and thus, we never ran low on food. The church always served sweet tea and coffee at every get-together. After the meal, the women gathered and talked as they cleaned up. The men grouped outdoors to smoke and talk politics, farming, or the weather. The children played, boys with boys and girls with girls. Through these fellowship meals, Mount Hope provided social interaction in addition to Christian fellowship.

CHAPTER 12

JAMES CHAPEL

During the period Daddy pastored Mount Hope Baptist Church, he also pastored James Chapel in Haywood County, a little church located north of Lake Junaluska and northeast of Maggie Valley. It was a two-hour drive each way between Franklin and James Chapel. Every other Sunday, Daddy left immediately after Sunday morning service at Mount Hope, conducted the service at James Chapel, and returned to Mount Hope in time for the evening worship service. Very often, I accompanied Daddy on these trips. Sometimes Johnny and Randy also went. My motive for attending James Chapel was simple: Daddy usually stopped at a small roadside café near Clyde, North Carolina, and bought me a hot dog and soft drink after the service. For me, this treat was worth sacrificing an entire Sunday afternoon.

To reach James Chapel on time, we had to eat hurriedly at home or take a sandwich. Stopping at the small restaurant afterward was almost a necessity because, by the time we got home, evening service at Mount Hope was getting underway. Daddy always qualified his position on stopping at the restaurant before we began the trip. "We'll stop depending on my offering total and the amount of time we have left to get back to Franklin," he said. Still, it was rare that we didn't stop. James Chapel was in the backcountry of Haywood County. The trip was a winding one through the rough mountains that seemed never to end.

The services were in a rural, wood-framed church that had slatted benches on a pinewood floor. I had to be careful while sitting on these pews to avoid having my buttocks pinched by the movement of someone else sitting farther down the row. One wiggle from anyone could produce a painful result for the other person sitting there. The church baptized in a nearby creek. Since the stream was small, members created a damn by placing reinforced wooden structures into the creek bed, abutted by a homemade bridge that was used by vehicles to pass over the body of water. As the service progressed, the temporary dam stopped the flow of the stream, backing up the water, and causing a pool to form. On the Sunday of the baptism, members of the church placed and anchored these wooden barriers just as we arrived. The dam was removed immediately afterward to allow the flow of the stream to resume.

The James Chapel worship services were much livelier than those of Mount Hope. Daddy's preaching intensified to accommodate this charged atmosphere. The congregation sang from the *Church Hymnal*, which was more commonly referred to as the red-back hymnal because of its maroon color. This songbook had many hymns full of life and energy that were not found in the *Broadman Hymnal*. They included "I'll Fly Away," "I'll Have a New Life," "There Is Power in the Blood," and "I've Got That Old-Time Religion." Daddy shouted and cried along with the entire congregation during the song services. Afterward, he delivered some of the fiercest sermons I ever heard him preach. Just as he did at Mount Hope, Daddy sometimes sang "I Will Arise and Go to Jesus" a cappella style.

After the service, on the way home to Franklin, I usually got the cherished hot dog topped with mustard, chili, and onions, along with an Orange Crush. On rare occasions, the entire family attended James Chapel, especially at Christmas. All the children in attendance got special presents such as dolls or toy trucks, just for them, placed under a Christmas tree near the front of the small church. I was surprised when the song leader, who handed the gifts out, called my name. I didn't think I would get one since I was a visitor. Not only was there one for me but also for all my brothers and sisters.

By 1957, my oldest sister, Elaine, who turned eleven that year, had taken control of the radio when we traveled. It was easy for her to do since she sat in the middle of the front seat between Mother and Daddy. With Elaine in charge, the music changed from southern gospel or country to rock and roll. When the entire family went to James Chapel, on the way home, I slept on the floorboard of Daddy's old Dodge. The sound of the engine and the warmth of the floorboard heated by the motor were perfect for relaxing. It was so wide I could lie there without being kicked by my siblings, who usually had their feet up, sleeping on the car seat. Anytime all the family was in the car, I sat in the back seat, right behind Daddy. If I wanted to ask him a question, I popped up behind him, grabbed his chin, and turned his face to the right, toward me.

"Son, don't do that. You'll cause me to wreck. I don't have to see you to hear you!" Daddy admonished.

On one of these James Chapel return trips, I asked Daddy a question. His answer haunted me until I was nine years old. "Daddy, what is the age of accountability?" I asked.

"It's the age when a child begins to know right from wrong. This period differs with each child, but by the age of twelve, most every child will have reached it. Once a child reaches the age of accountability and doesn't repent of his or her sins, upon death, the child will go to hell just like any other sinner!"

Even though I was only six, this news alarmed me for I believed I had already reached that age. "I know right from wrong!" I said. The image of God that Daddy created conflicted with what my Sunday school teachers at Mount Hope had taught me, a picture I preferred. First, in preschool and then in primary class, I was taught God was kind and loving and we were all precious in His eyes. We sang songs such as "Jesus Loves Me" and "Jesus Loves the Little Children," which reinforced this message. Also, at Bible school, I was trained to believe in the goodness and love of God. Here we sang happy songs such as "This Little Light of Mine" and "Praise Him, All Ye Little Children."

For me, the "age of accountability" was a complicated issue and challenging matter to ponder. "I don't want to go to hell," I told myself on many Sundays after that. But I couldn't find the courage to kneel at the church altar and confess my sins and be saved, as was required to avoid this fate. I did try. During an altar call, shortly after learning about the age of accountability, I sneaked my way toward the front on a Sunday morning. I inched up two or three rows of pews but couldn't gather the courage to go the rest of the way.

That Sunday night, while Mother was giving me a bath, she said, "Mikey, do you want to get saved someday?" I nodded my head affirmatively.

"You're only six, so you have plenty of time. I'm sure you'll go to the altar at the right time," Mother said. It was the only spiritual conversation I ever had with her. Unlike Daddy, who always gave us biblical instruction, she didn't. The only religious thing Mother ever did was to say the blessing over our meals when Daddy was gone. Still, Mother's words reassured me.

Finally, at the age of nine during the Mount Hope spring revival of 1961, I got the courage to go to the front of the church at the invitation. I bowed in the altar just as Daddy did when he prayed, on my left knee with my right knee up, a half-kneeling position. My father led me in a prayer to be born again. From then on, I didn't worry anymore about going to hell. According to the Southern Baptist doctrine of eternal security, that was now impossible. More commonly referred to as "once saved, always saved," it meant there wasn't anything I could do to lose my salvation, not even if I continued to sin. Daddy defended this doctrine.

"Some people say they can continue to sin after salvation, but if they do, it's my opinion they never had redemption."

"But what about an individual who was saved and later backslid? Are they still saved?" I asked.

"If a person has salvation, then that settles it—they still have it regardless of what they do."

The next Sunday, after the revival ended, Daddy held a water baptism at the Cartoogechaye Creek baptizing hole. The church members gathered on both sides of the creek on that bright, sunshiny day. An occasional white cloud drifted across the sky. The Blue Ridge Mountains loomed watchfully over all of us. It was a familiar spot—I fished there often. Daddy baptized many children and a few adults that day. He started the proceedings by leading the gathered congregation in the hymn "Shall We Gather at the River?"

Yes, we'll gather at the river,
The beautiful, the beautiful river;
Gather with the saints at the river
That flows by the throne of God

I thought, *That hymn sounds more like a song for a funeral than a baptizing!* I also remembered the story Daddy told about Old Lady Snider's baptizing and how on that day, the river swept her all the way to glory. As Daddy lowered me under the waters of Cartoogechaye

Creek that afternoon, all I could concentrate on was coming out of the water alive. As I waded back to shore, I was shivering. It was still spring, and the creek was frigid.

⇌ ⇌

Daddy also conducted weddings, funerals, and Easter sunrise services. I accompanied Daddy to funerals and these early morning services, but very rarely did I attend weddings because Mother would not let me go. "No, Mikey, you can't go with your Daddy to the wedding. If you go, I'll have to dress you up, and I just don't have the energy to do it." For Mother, "dressing up" meant putting on our best attire, as opposed to regular church clothing. She couldn't fathom the idea of us going to a wedding in anything less than our finest.

Besides being restricted from weddings, I also didn't attend Daddy's revivals since they were too far away, and he usually left for an entire week when he conducted one. Funerals and Easter sunrise services were a different matter. On most Easter mornings, I got up before daylight, dressed, and accompanied Daddy to an early morning service. Daddy could preach at these sunrise services since Mount Hope didn't have one. They couldn't be located more than a few hours away since Daddy had to be back at Mount Hope before 11:00 a.m. I also had to change into my Easter outfit. Sometimes Johnny and Randy went on these journeys too, but many times it was just Daddy and me.

All the Willis children got a new outfit for Easter. Johnny, Randy, and I usually were dressed alike. Daddy's somber Easter sermon began as he first talked about how Christ was crucified and buried. His mood improved as he continued preaching about how Christ arose from the grave on the third day. By the close of the sermon, Daddy was in joyous tears.

We sang hymns such as "Christ the Lord Is Risen Today." Mother always prepared a delicious Easter dinner of ham and mashed potatoes and many other vegetables and desserts. Afterward, Daddy hid Easter eggs, which we hunted with vigor. Sometimes he had to hide them more than once. If it rained, Mother dreaded Easter because we hid eggs in the house. When we had indoor Easter egg hunts, Mother took an exact count of the eggs to account for all of them. This tally was kept to avoid finding rotten Easter eggs several months later hidden in drawers and closets. Still, this circumstance sometimes occurred regardless of Mother's best Easter egg computation.

I also attended funerals Daddy conducted. The first one was that of Farmer Wood's son-in-law, James Henry, who shot himself in the temple just after he shot and killed Farmer and Mrs. Wood. The news of this tragedy made its way all over Cartoogechaye and throughout Macon County. The Woods were the first people I had ever personally known who had died. They were our neighbors when we lived near Saint John's Episcopal Church. Mr. Wood's haystacks were visible in the fields across the road from our house, and it was his guineas the hound dog had attacked, resulting in the sheriff's deputy hunting down and shooting the old dog. Mr. Henry's family knew Daddy and asked him to conduct the funeral, and he agreed.

"I want to go to the funeral," I told Daddy.

Johnny and Randy said simultaneously, "I want to go, too."

"No, you boys are too young to go," he replied.

"Please," we all implored in unison until he finally agreed.

"I'm going to let you go to this funeral, but if you have bad dreams, don't say I didn't warn you," he admonished. We went to the funeral home for the service, getting there early so Daddy could comfort the family members before the funeral began. Johnny, Randy, and I went up to the casket and looked inside. It was the first dead person we had ever seen. We wanted to find the spot on the man's head where the bullet entered, and we were not disappointed. You could clearly see the red mark on his right temple.

"Wow, did you see that bullet hole?" Johnny asked.

"Yes, I saw it," I replied.

"Me too," said Randy. The funeral began shortly after that. In his sermon, Daddy consoled the family but then managed to preach the rest of the funeral without saying anything good or bad about the deceased and without once mentioning either heaven or hell.

"Daddy, did Farmer Wood's son-in-law go to hell?" I asked.

"Son, we'll have to leave that up to God. Only he knows if the man was in his right mind or not," Daddy said.

That night, just as Daddy had predicted, I had nightmares. They recurred for several nights after that.

My brothers and I also attended the funeral of a baby. The little girl was lying in a tiny white casket. When the funeral was over, we drove in the rain to the family cemetery, a new one just cleared in the woods for this occasion. She was the first family member buried there. The rain was coming down so hard the dirt trail to the top of the hill turned to mud, and the hearse got stuck. The grandfather took the little casket from the hearse and, in the pouring rain, carried it by himself to the gravesite.

We went to the funeral of an adult woman. Daddy allowed Johnny, Randy, and me to view the body just before the funeral service. My brothers and I marched down the church aisle to where the casket was located and peered inside. Her teeth stared back at us. We hurried back down the aisle and exited the church.

"What was in her mouth?" I asked Johnny.

"It was her buckteeth," he replied.

"I'm not coming to any more funerals!" Randy said. For three small boys, Daddy's funerals proved educational, curious, and dreadful. We went almost every time we got the chance.

⟛ ⟛

For us as the family of a Baptist preacher, church and all the activity that surrounded church was all encompassing. It was both a ministry and a profession for Daddy, and it was also his sole means of support for a family of eight children. A salary of sixty dollars per week from Mount Hope wasn't enough to feed such a large brood, even with free housing from the parsonage. While Daddy's reason for preaching was because he believed he had a call from God, there was also a strong economic incentive. It was also customary to receive pay for many of these extra activities. It was Daddy's way of supporting the family.

CHAPTER 13
PREACHERS

It seemed as though an endless parade of pastors came to visit the Mount Hope parsonage. Some even came home with Daddy on weekends from the seminary. We never knew what to expect. One Saturday morning, I woke up early having been aroused by the noise of someone snoring. To my dismay, a stranger was sleeping in our bedroom! Johnny, Randy, and I shared a set of bunk beds. Johnny and Randy slept in the lower bunk, while I slept in the upper. There was a twin bed located in the room, but for the most part, it was unused. I was petrified, frozen in fear, as I peered out from under my covers at this stranger. All I could see were two large buckteeth protruding from his open mouth. They reminded me of those of the dead woman in the casket. Fear gripped me so completely that besides being unable to move, I couldn't scream, even though I tried. *Surely that's the devil lying under those covers waiting for me to get up so that he can snatch me away*, I reasoned. *What am I going to do? How can I get out of here?*

An eternity seemed to pass before Daddy came to the door and said, "K. B., are you ready to get up? Mildred almost has breakfast ready."

Snorting as he awoke, K. B. replied, "Yeah, John, I'm awake now! I'd like some breakfast—especially coffee."

"Got some brewing. You boys get up and meet K. B. Forbes," Daddy said. "K. B.'s a preacher friend of mine, here to spend the weekend. He'll be preaching on Sunday." Johnny, Randy, and I got up and very quickly headed for the breakfast table. Only after breakfast did I learn Johnny and Randy had experienced the same thing I had. Both had cowered under the covers in fear just as I had. K. B. proved to be fun. He was very friendly and asked us a lot of questions about our lives at Mount Hope. By the end of the weekend, we were sorry to see him leave.

We didn't have to endure another surprise like K. B.'s again. Shortly after his visit, Daddy put a bed in the study for visiting preachers.

Revivals sometimes brought pastors to stay at the parsonage. One of Daddy's best friends, Harold Townsend, preached several revivals at Mount Hope. He used the spare bed at our house many times. After one of the services, to help Mother out, Harold carried Dawn, a toddler, to the house. She had fallen asleep during the church service. Rinty, our German shepherd, had been watching over the house while we were at church. As Harold approached the front door, Rinty rose, placed both paws on the doorknob, and growled very deeply. Harold slowly backed up and returned to the church with Dawn still fast asleep in his arms.

"Your dog won't let me in the parsonage!" Harold said as he related the story.

"Come on. I won't let him hurt you," I said. We returned to the house, and Rinty came running, licking me in the face and wagging his tail. He was jubilant to see me.

"I'll be! I've never seen anything like it in my life. That dog was ready to attack me just a few minutes ago, yet you can walk right up to him, and he's gentle as a lamb!" Harold said.

"That's right. Rinty's that way with any of us young'uns, but let a stranger come into the yard, and he'll attack in an instant if we give the command," I explained. "When Daddy's away at the seminary, he sleeps right here on the front doorstep. We don't have to worry about anybody coming inside unless we invite them. Rinty's our watchdog."

We had found Rinty roaming around the Mount Hope church and adopted him. Mother was glad to have the dog because of his defensive temperament. Rinty got his name from the television series *The Adventures of Rin Tin Tin*. He was a beautiful dog. We played with him every day, especially after school. Rinty had one vice that proved his undoing—he liked to chase automobiles. As hard as we tried, we couldn't break Rinty of this habit. One morning as we left to board the school bus, we spotted Rinty, dead on the highway. Because of our anguish, we asked Mother for permission to stay home from school, but she didn't let us. All day at school I couldn't concentrate on my schoolwork. My thoughts returned again and again to Rinty and how wonderful life had been with him at our house. It was all I could do to keep from crying. When we finally returned home that afternoon, Mother had already had someone come and bury Rinty. We all cried when we got home, and so did Mother.

Chaco Maunie was another friend Daddy regularly brought to visit. He attended Southeastern Baptist Theological Seminary along with Daddy. Chaco was from India. His skin was dark, and his hair was black and curly. Many people mistook him to be African American and would not seat him in their segregated restaurants. After Daddy had explained he was Indian, the restaurant employees usually served Chaco. To permanently remedy this recurring problem, Daddy suggested Chaco wear a turban, a headdress worn in India. Chaco gave it a try with good results. Almost anywhere he went while wearing the hat, Chaco had no problems. Chaco didn't wear the traditional Indian pagri, which needed to be manually tied. Instead, his maroon turban was permanently formed and sewn to a foundation. Chaco chose ease and comfort over the customary Indian practice.

At first, it seemed unusual to have someone of a different race in our house. We had rarely been around anyone who wasn't white. Mother was uncertain too since she explicitly expressed racial prejudice. Daddy reassured us. "All God's children are the same in his eyes. God doesn't see the color of a person's skin but only what's in the heart." It didn't take long for us to warm up to Chaco. He was very friendly and gentle and genuinely seemed to care for all of us.

Mother liked him too. I had never known such a caring individual. During one of Chaco's visits, he decided to prepare a traditional Indian meal for all of us. We were all abuzz about how this food might taste and whether we would like it. Hearing our talk, Mother said, "All you young'uns come here! Now you'll eat whatever Chaco serves, and if you don't like it, you'll eat it anyway, or I'll beat the hell out of you once he's gone. Do you understand me?"

"Yes," we all replied. The threat proved unnecessary because the meal Chaco prepared was wonderful. We all wanted seconds.

⇒+ +⇒

Racial tolerance was a fundamental principle with Daddy, and he put this belief into practice. On this issue, he was somewhat ahead of his time, as many of his preacher friends disagreed with him. This criticism didn't bother Daddy. When Daddy pastored Olivet Baptist Church, Wesley Grant, an African American pastor and good friend, had run a revival at our church. At Mount Hope, Reverend Hornbuckle, a Cherokee Indian who lived within the Qualla Boundary in Cherokee, North Carolina, preached a revival for Daddy, and Daddy had preached for him. Sometimes we went to visit with Preacher Hornbuckle and his family at their home in Cherokee.

Daddy also filled in at an African American church in Franklin until a new pastor arrived. But his racial tolerance was severely tested around my eighth birthday in February 1960. That is when the sit-ins at Woolworth's in Greensboro, North Carolina, began. These sit-ins were started by African American college students to protest racial segregation. The student movement quickly spread to other North Carolina cities and towns throughout the south. Mother, an unabashed racist, was furious. "Those niggers in Greensboro have brought all that desegregation shit to North Carolina. They need to take them all out and hang them from the highest tree they can find."

"Civil disobedience is wrong!" Daddy countered. "It creates unrest and undermines the law. Nowhere in the Bible did Jesus stir up riots and civil unrest. I believe all men are equal before God, but what the colored people are doing in Greensboro is dangerous, not only for North Carolina but also for the whole country." These views intensified over the spring and summer of 1961 as the Freedom Riders went into action. These student volunteers were sent throughout the South to test new laws prohibiting segregation in interstate bus facilities and railway stations. Angry mobs attacked them along the way.

Mother's open-mindedness stopped with Chaco and Reverend Hornbuckle. Her racial tolerance certainly didn't include African Americans. "The niggers are trying to take over. Somebody's got to do something to stop them before it's too late," she said. "That Martin Luther King Jr. fellow is dangerous. You young'uns stay away from any niggers you see. They're all just nasty, dirty jigaboos!"

Daddy, while displaying tolerance and acceptance of racial differences, was wary of the civil rights movement. "Martin Luther King Jr. is stirring up too much strife. That's no way to bring about change," he said. These conflicting views on racism and the civil rights movement continued to be voiced in the Willis family throughout the 1960s.

CHAPTER 14
MEALS AT THE WILLIS HOME

Meals at our home were traditional southern fare, nothing fancy. Mother was an excellent cook, skilled in the making of all kinds of food. For breakfast, we usually had eggs, sausage or bacon, grits, homemade biscuits, and gravy. Various homemade jellies or apple butter were served on the side and added to a buttered biscuit. Mother made gravy from the grease, or drippings, of the sausage or bacon. We drank milk, and sometimes we added Hershey's Chocolate Milk Mix. When Tang became popular, Mother mixed this orange-flavored drink for breakfast too. My parents usually drank coffee for breakfast. Sometimes Daddy drank Postum or chicory, which were coffee substitutes he had become accustomed to drinking during World War II when coffee was scarce.

Grits were eaten with sugar and butter or with salt, pepper, and butter. When I was young, I liked mine with sugar and butter, but as an older child, I began eating them with salt, pepper, and butter. A special treat was biscuit crumbled into a cup of half milk and half coffee, sweetened to taste. We didn't get this concoction very often because Mother didn't think coffee was good for children.

Daddy at times tried to substitute Postum for coffee when creating this mixture, but we didn't like it.

For the noon meal, Mother served leftovers. She took biscuits from breakfast, opened them into halves, and topped them with butter. She then broiled them in the oven, melting the butter and toasting the bread to a crisp. Putting jelly or apple butter on the biscuits made a delightful dessert. For the noon dinner meal, drinks included various flavors of Kool-Aid. On occasion, Mother served fresh-squeezed lemonade.

Supper was our biggest meal. In the summer, we ate fresh fruits and vegetables. A few of them we grew, but most were gifts from our neighbors or church members. What we didn't eat, Mother canned. During the summer months, this was an ongoing activity. Vegetables included green beans, peas, corn, okra, potatoes, sweet potatoes, tomatoes, cabbage, yellow squash, radishes, sweet onions, cucumbers, lettuce, and many others. Fruits included strawberries, apples, peaches, grapes, and pears.

Mother canned enough fruits and vegetables to last all winter. She used the cucumbers to make sweet pickles. The vegetables, whether fresh or canned, were fried, prepared in butter or lard, or seasoned with fatback by the time they reached the supper table. She also served pork chops and country-style steak and gravy, but her fried chicken was the best. She applied egg batter, floured each piece, and fried the chicken in hot grease in an open iron skillet. The smell of frying chicken was wonderful, and the gravy made from the drippings was superb.

Mother used dried beans from which she removed small stones and bad beans before washing the beans repeatedly. Afterward, she soaked them for a period. When she began cooking the beans, she added salt and a big slab of fatback. Mother served soup beans with homemade cornbread baked in an iron skillet. She also liked to eat fresh baked cornbread crumbled into buttermilk. I didn't particularly like this mixture. Most nights we had either mashed or fried potatoes. Sometimes we had new potatoes. We almost never had store-bought frozen french fries, since they were costly. For supper, we drank sweetened iced tea or whole milk. We never had soft drinks for either dinner or supper.

Nothing went to waste, not even mashed potatoes. Mother used the leftovers to fry potato cakes the next day. For Sunday dinner, Mother served the biggest meal of the week. Pot roast, pork roast, homemade chicken and dumplings, and ham were often on the menu. Occasionally, we had steaks. Mother never bought steaks at the store—they were too expensive. Someone always gave them to us.

Desserts included blackberry, strawberry, peach, or apple cobblers. I especially loved blackberry cobbler served hot with butter placed in the middle. When wild strawberries were in season, my siblings and I crossed the highway and went up the side of a bank where they grew. These berries were tiny, and it took a lot of work to pick enough for Mother to make a cobbler. It was worth the labor since wild strawberry cobbler was the best. She also baked homemade cakes. Our favorite was yellow cake with chocolate icing. Mother's best pies were coconut, chess, and chocolate. Fried pies were a special delight that Mother filled with peaches, strawberries, or apples.

On Sunday night, after church, we were treated to ice milk, which was a cheap substitute for ice cream. Still, sometimes we did get ice cream. Mother removed this luxury from its package, cut eight slices, and served one to each child. It didn't matter to me whether we had ice milk or ice cream since I buried mine in Hershey's chocolate syrup.

⇒⊹ ⊹⇐

Mother required us to practice proper table manners: no chewing with our mouths open and no elbows on the table. There were not enough chairs for everyone. Johnny and Randy sat on wooden crates. I sat in a chair, even though Johnny as the older brother could have claimed it. But, for whatever reason, he preferred the box, and I was glad to let him have it. Johnny became very accomplished at tilting his crate backward on its edge and balancing while seated at the table. One night he was performing this acrobatic trick while tilting his head back to drink a glass of milk. As he took a sip, he fell all the way back to the floor. The glass of milk nearly drowned him on the way down. There was a loud crash.

"What the hell just happened?" my mother screamed, running over from the kitchen. "Are you all right, Johnny?"

"Yes, Mother, I just lost my balance," Johnny replied as he got up, soaked.

Mother began cleaning up the milk. "Damn it! You need to be careful," she scolded.

⚊⟊ ⟊⚊

One night when supper was ready and we had all gathered at the table, Daddy announced, "Young'uns, beginning tonight and every night hereafter when I'm home, we'll have scripture reading before we eat." He started reading the Bible. Deborah, Dawn, and Phillip, my youngest siblings, began to cry. The smell of food made them hungry, and they didn't want to wait. The rest of us fidgeted but said nothing, not willing to challenge Daddy and risk his anger.

After supper, Mother said, "John, tomorrow night, read the scripture after we eat. These babies get too hungry, and the food gets cold if you have the devotion first."

The next evening, after we had eaten, Daddy continued the Bible reading, but this arrangement didn't work well either. The younger children couldn't be still, and the older ones were glum and disinterested. After a few nights, Mother said, "John, I don't believe the scripture reading is working out."

"They'll just have to get used to it," Daddy replied. To liven up the devotional, the next night, Daddy read the Song of Solomon from the King James Version of the Bible. "Let him kiss me with the kisses of his mouth, for thy love is better than wine," he read.

"Solomon kissed a girl!" Johnny said.

"Ugh!" Randy and I said in unison.

"Did Solomon drink wine?" Elaine asked.

Not answering this question, Daddy said, "Because of the savour of thy good ointments thy name is as ointment poured forth, therefore do the virgins love thee."

"What are virgins?" I asked innocently. Daddy ignored my inquiry.

"I am black, but comely, O ye daughters of Jerusalem, as the tents of Kedar, as the curtains of Solomon. Look not upon me, because I am black, because the sun hath looked upon me."

"Solomon's wife was black!" Gloria gasped in disbelief.

"A bundle of myrrh is my well beloved unto me; he shall lie all night betwixt my breasts."

"Breasts? What's she talking about?" Johnny said.

"John, do you think it's a good idea to be reading that passage of scripture to these kids?" Mother asked.

Undeterred, Daddy said, "Behold, thou art fair, my beloved, yea, pleasant. Also our bed is green."

"Solomon had a green bed!" Randy exclaimed. All of us screamed with laughter.

By now Daddy had become somewhat irritated, but he continued to read. "Stay me with flagons, comfort me with apples, for I am sick of love."

"What's a flagon?" I asked.

"I'm sick of love, too!" Johnny interjected. We all laughed again.

"My beloved is like a roe or a young hart: behold, he standeth behind our wall, he looketh forth at the windows, shewing himself through the lattice," Daddy read.

"What's a roe?" someone asked.

"What's a hart?" another asked.

Mother, now joining the fun said, "Are you sure Solomon wasn't a Peeping Tom?"

Annoyed, Daddy read on: "How beautiful are thy feet with shoes, O prince's daughter! The joints of thy thighs are like jewels, the work of the hands of a cunning workman. Thy navel is like a round goblet, which wanteth not liquor: thy belly is like a heap of wheat set about with lilies."

"Is a navel the same as a belly button?" Randy asked.

"Belly like a heap of wheat? Was she fat?" Johnny asked.

"Was she naked?" I asked.

"Did Solomon drink liquor?" Elaine said.

Again ignoring our questions, Daddy persevered. "Thy breasts are like two young roes that are twins."

"Daddy, you still haven't told us about breasts," Johnny reminded him.

"And we still don't know what a roe is either," someone else said.

"Johnny, shut up!" Mother demanded.

Daddy ignored all this commotion too. "Thy neck is as a tower of ivory; thine eyes like the fish pools in Heshbon, by the gate of Bathrabbim. Thy nose is as the tower of Lebanon which looketh toward Damascus."

"Solomon's wife sure was ugly!" I said, and everyone again burst into laughter, this time Daddy included.

At last, Daddy stopped reading. "Golly-bum, you blame young'uns. Dad gum! A body can't even read a little scripture around here!" he said. Afterward, suppertime scripture readings dwindled and then ended, as crying youngsters and bored adolescents eventually got their way. Daddy gave up on the nightly devotionals, but we always remembered the Song of Solomon.

CHAPTER 15

THE CHICKEN MOTHER FRIED

Mother usually bought the chicken she fried for supper at the grocery store, but sometimes we got fresh chicken from a farm. Mr. Stamey was one farmer who supplied us with many chickens during our years at Mount Hope. While he wasn't a member of our church, Mr. Stamey liked Mother and Daddy and occasionally asked us to come to his home for dinner. Because our family was so large, we rarely got such invitations. Having the Willises over for dinner or supper meant feeding an extra ten mouths. I liked to visit the Stamey farm because the family had a barn filled with hay and other interesting things. I also loved all the farm animals—horses, chickens, cows, and pigs. I enjoyed playing around the barn and watching all the activity.

One day, Mr. Stamey's son, Marion, took Johnny, Randy, and me out into the pasture to explore. While I was excited about the adventure, I was somewhat apprehensive and fearful of the cows. "They won't hurt you," Marion reassured me. "They usually move on when they see people coming. You'd be better off worrying about all these cow patties. If you step in one, the manure will get all over you."

"Yes, I know. I fell into one once," I said. While we were talking, I saw a large white block sticking up on the end of a post. "What's that?" I asked Marion.

"It's a salt block."

"Why is it there?"

"The cows lick it. Salt helps them to stay healthy and produce milk," Marion said.

"Do you mean salt like in a saltshaker?"

"Yes, it's just in a big hunk. Go ahead and have a taste." This suggestion seemed a good idea to Johnny, Randy, and me. The three of us were much younger than Marion.

"Who's going to try it first?" I asked.

"Not me!" said Johnny.

"I'll lick it," said Randy.

"Be sure to lick on the bottom where the cows haven't," Marion said. Randy bent underneath and licked the salt block at the bottom. Johnny and I followed, each tasting the large block underneath in different spots.

"Daddy, we licked a salt block!" Randy announced as we returned from the pasture.

"You did? Where did you lick it?" Daddy asked.

"At the bottom!" Randy said.

"Did all of you lick it at the bottom?" he asked.

"Yes," we all said.

Daddy started laughing, and so did Mr. Stamey. "Marion, did you warn these boys that's where the cows lick?" Mr. Stamey asked.

"No, he didn't. That's where he told us to lick it," I said before Marion could answer.

"Marion, you ought to be ashamed of yourself," Mr. Stamey said as they continued to laugh. Marion grinned with pleasure, knowing he had completely fooled us.

The Stameys grew sugarcane to make molasses. In the fall, at harvest time, it was interesting to watch as the entire family worked to manufacture this thick, dark syrup. First, they cut the sugarcane. They then squeezed the juice into large tubs. After this task, they strained the liquid through clean white cloths, which were then wrung out.

The liquid was then poured into boiler pans and cooked over a wood fire for several hours. A green substance was skimmed with a strainer from the top of the juice as it boiled. The molasses was poured into sterilized canning jars while it was still hot to keep the syrup from cooling and turning hard. The jars self-sealed as the molasses cooled. Finally, the Stameys packaged the finished product and sold the jars of molasses for cash.

Mr. Stamey gave us some of his sorghum molasses every year. I enjoyed the unique flavor of this syrup, which was perfect on a hot, buttered homemade biscuit.

At the end of every visit, Mr. Stamey gave us a chicken. We had our choice. We could take it either dead or alive. If Mother was going to prepare it right away, we took a dead one. Otherwise, we got a live chicken. A chicken first had to be caught, which was not easy. Mr. Stamey had Marion do the job. Marion quietly made his way to the chicken coop to find one while it was off guard. He then grabbed a chicken by the legs, lifted it off the ground, and held it upside down. The chicken flapped around trying to get loose, but Marion's grip was firm. On the rare occasion that Marion did lose his grasp, it was hard to catch the chicken again.

Next, the chicken was killed, which was accomplished by one of two methods. The first was to lay the chicken on a chopping block and cut off its head. This technique was the bloodiest but the best way of knowing the chicken was dead, and it was Mr. Stamey's preferred way.

Johnny, Randy, and I crowded each other to get the best spot to watch Mr. Stamey as he killed the chicken with his ax. Before the event, Marion or Mr. Stamey tied the legs of the chicken together. "Why are you tying the chicken's legs?" I asked.

"So, it won't run around when its head is cut off."

"A chicken can run with a chopped-off head?" I asked in disbelief.

"Yes, it can. That's why I tie the chicken's legs together. That way, it can't run."

After someone had placed the bird's neck on the chopping block, in one swift motion, the ax head came down, and its head rolled off the chopping block. The body of the chicken then thrashed about on the ground. Blood spurted from its neck. Mr. Stamey was right—the headless chicken tried to run, and it would have if they had not tied its legs. Once it stopped moving, Mr. Stamey strung the bird up to let the blood drain.

Mr. Stamey sometimes let Marion shoot a chicken with his twenty-two rifle. Marion preferred to use his gun because he wouldn't have to catch the chicken first.

"Marion, you take good aim," Mr. Stamey warned. "Shoot her in the head. We don't want the Willises to have bullet fragments in their chicken."

When we left, Daddy took the dead chicken and put it in the trunk of the car. If we took a live chicken, Mr. Stamey lent us a small chicken coop to transport it. The live chicken also went into the trunk of the car.

The other method of killing a chicken was to wring its neck, which was tidy, but it was necessary to know exactly how to do it to avoid torturing the bird. Mother used this technique at home. To wring a chicken's neck, Mother held the chicken by the legs upside down with one hand and with the other, pulled down on the neck and then bent it upward very quickly. When the bird's neck snapped and the wings began to flap, she dropped the chicken to our dirt basement floor and let it flop around until it stopped moving.

Next, she hung the chicken upside down over a pan, took a sharp knife, and cut its throat. The chicken stayed there until the blood drained out into the pan.

Plucking and dressing the chicken was the messiest part of the whole process. Before the plucking began, Mother first boiled hot water on the stove. She then took it downstairs to the basement, where she poured the hot water into a larger tub. Next, she took the chicken by the feet and dunked it into the water for several seconds using a stick to hold it under before drawing it out. Mother then placed the chicken upside down and began pulling off the feathers, discarding them in another pan and producing an almost unbearable smell. She gagged, and so did I. Heaving continued until the chicken was fully dressed. Mother didn't eat chicken when she prepared it this way.

Live chickens were stored in the basement and kept in the small coop we had borrowed from Mr. Stamey. They were there for only a few days until Mother had time to prepare them. In the meantime, she fed and cared for the chicken. Mother didn't want us to spend time around them because she knew we would get attached.

Once we kept a chicken much longer than usual, and I did get fond of it and named her Clucky.

"Mother, can we keep Clucky?" I asked.

"Hell, no. I'm not letting that damn chicken out around this church property. I don't want to keep feeding it, and besides, they're nasty creatures. Anyway, some dog almost surely would kill it," Mother said. The next day, when I got home from school, Mother was preparing fried chicken for supper. I went downstairs to the basement and found Clucky gone.

I didn't eat chicken that night. "I can't eat Clucky. She was my pet chicken," I told Mother. No one else at the supper table had any sympathy for me. They ate every bite of Clucky.

It wasn't too long after Clucky died that Mother gave us another chance to have pet chickens.

Randy was down by Cartoogechaye Creek when he saw them. He came running to the house. "Mother, there are chickens in the woods!" he exclaimed. Johnny and I went to the woods and saw two hens and a rooster making their way through the underbrush.

"How are we going to catch them?" Randy asked.

"Let's surround them in the brush," Johnny said.

After we caught them, we headed to the house with the three birds nestled in our arms. "Be careful, they're awfully small," I said.

"I'll be!" Mother said, as she surveyed our find. "That's a first. No one has ever set chickens out around the church before. They're Banty chickens!"

"Can we keep them? Please?" I implored.

"A Banty chicken isn't good for much of anything. They're too small to eat, and their eggs are about half the size of a regular hen's," Mother said. "I don't think they'll last very long since a dog or some wild animal is likely to get them, but if you want to keep them, we'll try."

Having the Banty rooster and his two hens around the house was delightful, and contrary to what Mother had predicted about their fate, they thrived. The little cock was the fiercest bird I had ever seen. He attacked any dog or other animal that came near the hens. Over time, Mother came to like the chickens and fed them every day. Once, the rooster jumped on the back of a hen and started pulling its comb. Mother was outside hanging wet clothes on the clothesline.

"Mother, what's the rooster doing? Why is he pulling her comb?" I asked excitedly.

"That's nothing. Don't pay any attention. The rooster won't hurt the hen. Pulling the comb is the way he helps a hen have eggs that hatch into chicks." Several weeks later, when the birds came out of the underbrush at the edge of the backyard where they nested, they had an entire clutch of chicks. We had more chickens than any of us could have imagined. Later, when we moved, they went to live on the Parker Dairy Farm.

CHAPTER 16

ALL KINDS OF ROUTINES

Aside from all the church activity, mealtimes, and visits with the Stameys, our household was full of all kinds of routines. The telephone was an important part of our lives. When we moved into the parsonage, we went from a call system that utilized a live operator to a party line shared among eight households. We had to listen to the ring cadence carefully to know if the call was for our family. Our ring pattern was two short rings followed by one long ring. Anyone on the party line could listen in on other people's conversations and often did. You could hear the click of each telephone as neighbors picked up their receivers. One had to be careful what was said, or it could become the topic of conversation throughout the community.

Mother warned Daddy, "John, Old Lady Taylor, has nothing better to do than pick up on everybody's calls. That's all she does all day long. You'd better be watching what you say, or it'll be everywhere by tomorrow." She didn't like the constant ringing, especially if the call wasn't for us. "That telephone's wearing me out. I wish we didn't even have the damn thing!" she said.

Daddy never stayed on long-distance calls for very long since they were very expensive. The sound of a long-distance call was very different from a local call. The quality wasn't as good, and there was a distinct hollowness that made the person on the other end sound far away. He raised his voice on long-distance calls. I could always tell when he had made or received one when he shouted into the receiver.

⇥ ⇤

Laundry was a daily task for Mother. After the clothes had been washed and then dried on the clothesline, she ironed them with a rotary ironing-board press machine. Daddy bought it for her at a bargain price. She liked this appliance and used it to do much of her ironing. She sat in a chair and pressed shirts, pants, dresses, skirts, blouses, underwear, sheets, and towels. Mother ironed everything in our house. What she couldn't finish on the press machine, she ironed on a regular ironing board with an electric steam iron. Before ironing Daddy's white shirts, she had to dip them in starch.

Mother also sewed dresses for my sisters, using paper patterns she purchased from a store along with the fabric. My sisters wore these homemade clothes to school and church. She was proud of her modern electric Singer sewing machine that she used to sew these outfits. She never attempted to make clothing for the boys, instead buying us blue jeans and button-down shirts for school. We also had at least one good pair of dress pants and a button-down dress shirt for Sundays. We wore everyday shoes for school and a different pair for church. After Easter was over, our outfits were used only on very special occasions.

Mother bought me husky-size jeans, but Johnny and Randy wore regular size. I didn't like wearing husky pants and was glad when I slimmed down. After that, Mother bought me regulars too. She cuffed the blue jeans four to six inches. When we wore holes in them, Mother purchased patches at the store to iron over the tear. She also stitched the edges of the patch to keep them from coming loose. A pair of blue jeans was meant to last an entire school year. Johnny, Randy, and I had two or three pairs each that Mother washed over and over to make it through a full week. The dark blue of the new jeans faded to a light blue by the time they were worn out.

House cleaning was an important activity for Mother, and even with eight children at home, she maintained a meticulously clean home. The parsonage had hardwood floors that required periodic waxing and buffing. While occasionally every room in the house got this treatment, she took great care to keep the living room, the hallway, and the kitchen and dining areas in top shape, which required frequent waxing.

Floor waxing was the only time she allowed the boys to help, but we didn't consider it work. After Mother and my older sisters had gotten down on their hands and knees to apply the paste wax, my brothers and I buffed the floors with old rags.

⊷⊱ ⊰⊶

Field mice came into the house from the cornfields and the hay fields surrounding the parsonage. They were a constant nuisance. Mother was terrified of mice and ran screaming out of any room in which she found one. "Shit. There's a rat in the kitchen! Someone kill it!" she would yell as she ran from the room. To rid us of these pests, Mother set out mousetraps and rat poison. Removing a mouse from the trap was almost more than she could bear, and the rat poison resulted in a smelly odor that was present until we found the dead mouse. It was also a task to clean up. There were no easy solutions to the mouse problem for Mother.

This rodent-killing method proved to be tragic for our hamster, which we had talked Daddy into getting us for a pet. We kept the hamster in a cage in the living room. Mother didn't like the creature because it reminded her of a rat, and she also had to clean its cage. Occasionally, the hamster got out because, as we played with it, we sometimes forgot to latch the door securely. We usually found the pet and returned it to the cage. One day the hamster was gone, and we couldn't find it. We searched and searched until finally it was discovered behind the refrigerator. We then returned the hamster to its enclosure.

Johnny was standing next to the cage when he observed the hamster puffing up and bloating. "Mother, the hamster looks like it is about to..." The hamster exploded before he could get the final word out of his mouth. It was dead, having eaten rat poison.

"Goddamn it! That's the nastiest thing I have ever seen," Mother complained as she cleaned up the mess, gagging as she did it. She then made us take the cage to the basement. "There'll be no more hamsters in this house. Do you understand me?"

Haircuts were an important part of everyday life in our home. Mother arranged for the girls to have their hair cut by a skilled neighbor, if possible, to save money. She went to the beauty shop. Likewise, Daddy went to a barbershop on a regular basis, but Johnny, Randy, Phillip, and I never went to a barber. Instead, Daddy cut our hair with a set of electric clippers and its accompanying attachments. He cut our hair very short, next to the scalp. Sometimes he attempted to cut flattops with the clipper's attachments, but these were often unsuccessful. Frequently, he gapped our hair. If a flattop was gapped, the only solution was a buzz cut. If the clippers were not sharp, prickly pain shot through the head.

"Ouch, that hurts!" I would protest.

"I guess I'll need to sharpen the clippers before I finish," Daddy would reply. He would then remove the blade and use a sharpening tool to take care of the problem. His haircutting skills were limited.

⇒ ⇐

Since we lived in western North Carolina, we all had southern accents, but that wasn't an excuse for using poor English. Mother insisted on its proper use. Out of literally hundreds of mountain words and phrases, only a few colloquialisms were allowed, such as "young'uns" for *children*; "ya'll" for *you*, used mostly in the plural form; and "fixin'" for *getting ready*. Most others were not allowed. Daddy frequently used terms of surprise or exclamation like "dad-gum," "dad-gem," "tom-thunder," "golly-bum," and "great day in the morning." We used them, too. Mother didn't allow the use of "you'uns" for *you* or "ain't" and "hain't" for *am not, are not, is not, has not*, or *have not*. We could not say "nary" for *not one*, "mater" for *tomato*, "tater" for *potato*, and other similar words. All such words were out, even though many of our church members and neighbors used this terminology all the time.

"Don't you be using those words. They make you sound like hicks and rednecks," Mother warned. At school, I often used this mountain dialect to blend in with my peers, but at home, I knew I'd get in trouble for using the forbidden words. Mother did occasionally use an old southern saying, the meaning of which I never understood at the time.

"What have you got, Mother?" I would ask when she quickly put an item away.

"It's a layover to catch a meddler," she would reply.

"What's that?"

"Never mind."

The phrase "layover to catch a meddler" was an expression used by adults to evade a direct answer to children. Mother might just as easily have said, "It's none of your business." The term came from the use of animal traps called layovers. A layover was a pit dug into the ground in the woods and covered over with branches to catch bears or other wild animals. Thus, a "layover to catch a meddler" was a trap intended to grab a meddler, which was the inquisitive child. Mother used this phrase all the time.

⇌ ⇋

One Christmas, Deborah and Dawn got Chatty Cathy dolls. I wanted a go-cart but didn't get one because it was too expensive. Each Christmas Mother received in the mail a Sears and Roebuck catalog with all the company's latest sales items. It had clothes, toys, appliances, and many other things—including go-carts. I carefully looked at each go-cart and imagined it was mine, but the cheapest one was almost $300. "Mikey, son, they're just too expensive. We can't afford to get you a go-cart. You'll have to pick something else," Mother said. Still, I imagined right up until Christmas morning that I would get it. I was very disappointed.

Deborah's and Dawn's Chatty Cathy dolls were different from any dolls I had ever seen because they could talk. All you had to do was pull a ring attached to a string located on the doll's back. One day I talked my younger sisters into letting me open the backs of their dolls. I wanted to see what made them talk. "If you let me open your Chatty Cathy dolls, I promise I'll fix them right back, just as good as new," I said.

"Okay," both Deborah and Dawn said as they innocently handed them over. I dissected the dolls and discovered each had a small vinyl record inside. When someone pulled the ring, it played a little utterance such as "I love you" or "Please take me with you."

"These small records are a marvelous invention," I said. Once I was finished and tried to put the Chatty Cathy dolls back together, I was in trouble. I couldn't get them to work again even though I tried very hard.

"Mikey, you shithead. Damnation! Why the hell did you destroy the babies' dolls?" Mother asked as she whipped me.

⚡ ⚡

When fighting at home, Johnny, Randy, and I wrestled and didn't use our fists as we did at school. To avoid hurting one another, we grabbed on to pin the other down. For Christmas Daddy bought us boxing gloves. He was a big fan of boxing and thought the sport might be fun. Since Johnny and I had never boxed before, we set some rules before our first match to avoid getting hurt. "There will be no hitting in the face or below the belt," I said. Johnny agreed. These rules left only the arms, chest, and stomach as targets.

"I'll referee this match," Daddy said.

"Come on, Mikey, let's fight," Johnny said. Those were the last words I remember before waking up on the floor. I was knocked out cold with one punch. Johnny had hit me in the stomach, sucking the air right out of me. It was the first and last boxing match we ever had.

⚡ ⚡

As Elaine got older, Mother and Daddy left her in charge when they went shopping or to some other place. Once they left, Johnny, Randy, and I set out to defy any authority Elaine might try to exert over us. We played in all the bedrooms that were forbidden when Mother was home. We opened dressers, chests of drawers, and closets and did all we could to make Elaine's job miserable. But we didn't mess up the beds, since doing so produced undeniable proof of our mischief.

In Mother and Daddy's bedroom, I found hidden candy. "They never bring candy home for us but hide candy for themselves. I can't believe it!" I said. Then Johnny, Randy, and I explored Daddy's study. It had a musty smell from all the old books he had about theology and the Bible. Daddy also had an old manual typewriter he used to prepare his sermons. He had several notebooks full. We looked through all of them.

"I'm going to tattle on you when Mother and Daddy get home," Elaine warned. We ignored this admonition since we knew a whipping was a foregone conclusion from the moment Mother and Daddy left Elaine in charge.

Once when Mother and Daddy were gone longer than usual, we got hungry.

"When will Mother be home to cook supper?" I asked.

"I don't know, but *I'll* fix supper," Elaine said.

"Ugh. Not you!" Johnny, Randy, and I said.

Elaine went into the kitchen and began cooking. Flour dust went all over the kitchen.

"What happened?" I asked.

"Nothing. Don't worry; supper will be ready soon."

Elaine finally presented her concoction, but we refused to eat it. "I'm not going to eat that stuff. It looks awful," I said, and Johnny and Randy agreed.

"Then just go without," Elaine said. Gloria and the younger siblings sided with Elaine and ate.

Another time Elaine was in charge, she was adamant that we not mess up the house. "Mother strictly said everything had better be just the way she left it or *I'll* get a whipping," she informed us.

Seizing on this opportunity, Johnny, Randy, and I went over to the stove in the living room where old newspapers were stacked. The paper was used to mix with kindling, which was then lit with a match to get a fire started. Once the blaze got going, they added coal from a bucket that sat nearby. Mother and Daddy subscribed to the *Asheville Citizen-Times* and the *Franklin Press*. There was always plenty of newspaper available to start a fire. In defiance of

Elaine, we took the pile of newspapers, shredded them, and scattered the pieces throughout the house.

"No, don't do that!" Elaine screamed, but it was too late. In a few minutes, we had shredded newspaper everywhere.

"Mother's going to kill me!" Elaine moaned as she began picking up all the paper before Mother and Daddy returned. When they did return, it was Johnny, Randy, and I who got the whipping.

⇥ ⇤

In 1959, Johnny and I asked Mother and Daddy for permission to join the Cub Scouts. At first, they said no, due to the cost of the uniforms. Later, they relented and let us join as a means of getting us out of the house. I looked fine in my brand-new blue Cub Scout uniform. Meetings were held at the community center a mile away. Since Daddy was gone much of the time, Mother let us walk to our scout meetings. Sometimes we took our BB guns to shoot cans and other things during our walk. We also pretended to protect ourselves from outlaws, even though we knew there was no such thing in Cartoogechaye. Almost no residents in Macon County locked their doors. Their homes were left wide open when they went to town or to visit other people. Everyone felt safe and secure. We only locked the parsonage doors when Daddy was at the seminary. Mother was scared during these absences and secured all the entrances, but the church doors were never locked.

Taking our BB guns to the Cub Scout meeting was a bad idea since we ended up getting into a fight with one of our pack members. When Jimmy saw that Johnny and I had brought our air rifles, he brought his to the next get-together. After the meeting had ended, we competed to determine who was the best marksman. When Jimmy discovered we could shoot as well as he could, things turned sour, and he began shooting at us. He didn't intend to hit us—just shot over our heads and near our feet. We returned fire, imitating Jimmy, intentionally missing one another as we skirmished along the road. Finally, we squared off, abandoning our BB guns on the school playground. Jimmy was as fierce a fighter as Johnny and I were, and after a while, we called a truce. After that, Johnny and I got along with Jimmy just fine, but we never again took our air rifles to the Cub Scout meeting.

During our Cub Scout treks, Johnny and I began picking up soft drink bottles, which we then sold at Kiser's Store, located a short distance from the parsonage. Drinks were ten cents, but if you returned the bottle, you got three cents back, or you could sell bottles and get three cents each. Once we discovered this potential for profit making, we began to hunt along the highway for bottles.

Two gasoline pumps were in front of Kiser's Store. Above the pumps was an oval sign that read ESSO, which indicated the brand. Bud Kiser was both the owner and operator. Outside Bud pumped gasoline, cleaned windshields, and checked the oil and tire pressure.

Since Mother regularly sent us to Kiser's to buy things she needed, we had plenty of opportunities to cash in our bottles and to spend the money. We usually bought candy, peanuts, crackers, and soft drinks.

One year gypsies set up camp in the parking lot of Kiser's Store and stayed all summer. This turn of events was a matter of concern to many in Cartoogechaye, especially Mother. Their small campers parked at the side of the store were an eyesore, and Mother was more than suspicious of their activity.

"Boys, keep away from those dirty, nasty gypsies. They're thieves and will steal you blind. Don't go near the bastards!" she told us. My brothers and I were watchful every time we went to Kiser's Store that summer.

Wallace's Grocery was another store we frequented. Occasionally, Daddy stopped here to treat us to a soft drink. Reverend Lane, the pastor of the Methodist church in Cartoogechaye, also stopped at Wallace's to let us buy drinks after our baseball games. In the summertime, Preacher Lane gathered up as many Cartoogechaye boys as he could find, put them in the back of his truck, and traveled to Franklin High School, where we played baseball all afternoon on the school's practice football field. He took us once a week. Johnny, Randy, and I always spent the dime Mother gave each of us. Sometimes Reverend Lane bought treats for us. Once everyone had finished his soft drink, we cashed in the bottle and bought penny candy.

CHAPTER 17
OUTINGS AND TRIPS

Our family often went swimming and had picnics at Arrowood Glade, where, despite my best efforts, I often got sunburned. We also took a week's vacation at Lake Chatuge in Hayesville, North Carolina. We stayed in two rustic cabins situated along the shore of the lake. Swimming, fishing, and boating were the main attractions. It was a mountainous wonderland surrounded by the Nantahala National Forest. Once Daddy rented a rowboat and took Johnny, Randy, and me out. After rowing hard for a while, he let us try our hands at the task. It wore us out very quickly. Finally, we put down the anchor and began to fish, but the fish were not biting. Soon, the sun came up, scorching and bothersome, and Daddy decided it was time to return to shore. Since neither Johnny nor I had been successful at rowing the boat, Daddy had to row all the way back by himself. He was wringing wet with sweat when we arrived.

"Dad-gum, that rowing business is much harder than it looks," he said.

"Let's rent a motorboat tomorrow," I suggested.

"No, they're too expensive."

Daddy didn't take us out in the rowboat again. We had to fish from the shore or the pier.

Mother wasn't very happy with the two-cabin arrangement, and for her, the trip to Lake Chatuge wasn't a vacation at all since she had to continue to cook and clean. "Hellfire, I don't need to come to a goddamn lake to work as a slave. I can do that just fine at home," she said. The only way Daddy talked Mother into coming to Lake Chatuge the next year was by promising to stay only three days.

⚞⚟

On rare occasions, Johnny, Randy, and I went to visit relatives. One time we stayed the weekend with Grandmother and Granddaddy Willis. Their home in Canton was a relatively small house, but it had an upstairs, where we slept. Spending the night in this bedroom was spooky. During our stay, Granddaddy Willis threatened to whip me if I didn't stop fighting with Johnny and Randy.

"You can't whip me, Granddaddy. You're not my parent!" I protested.

"Yes, I can, and I will if you continue fighting."

I thought he was too feeble to whip me. Still, I complied, concluding it was best not to test whether Granddaddy's threat was real. That evening Johnny, Randy, and I accompanied Granddaddy out to the backyard to feed his chickens. Here he had a small barn, and next to it was a little coop where he kept the chickens. When Granddaddy opened the gate leading to the barn, he slipped and fell, landing squarely on his buttocks.

"Granddaddy, look! You just missed falling on that stub," I said, pointing to a small post.

"An inch is as good as a mile," Granddaddy said as he picked himself off the ground.

That Sunday, Grandmother Willis got us up early to attend church at Calvary Baptist. "When you're getting ready this morning, remember not to cut your fingernails."

"Why's that, Grandmother?" I asked.

"Don't you know what the Bible says? 'Better that a man had never been born than to cut his nails on Sunday morn.'"

"Grandmother, that's not in the Bible."

"Yes, it is, Mikey. I'll have to find the verse," she replied.

"I've never heard a Bible verse that rhymes before. I don't think it's in the Bible, and the word *Sunday* is not in the Bible either."

"After church, I'll show it to you, but in the meantime, don't cut your nails," Grandmother said. After church, she was too busy to find the scripture verse, even after my repeated requests.

Another time we stayed with Uncle Doyle, one of Daddy's older brothers. He had a house full of stepchildren, whom we got along with very well. Johnny, Randy, and I stayed for an entire week. Uncle Doyle lived in the Haywood County backcountry, which was very primitive by our standards. The house had electricity, but only for lighting. Naked bulbs hung from the ceilings on exposed electrical cords. In the kitchen, a wood-burning stove was used to prepare all the meals. Water was taken from a nearby spring in buckets and brought to the house for use. Drinking water was drawn from a bucket, using a shared dipper. A springhouse located out back served as the refrigerator to store milk, butter, and other perishables. A smokehouse stored meats.

All the boys slept in the same bed diagonally. When the lights were turned off, it was pitch-black. Since I slept with a night-light at home, it took some effort to get accustomed to the darkness. The night creatures called out from the surrounding woods, especially the frogs, hoot owls, and katydids. At daylight, you could hear the roosters crow. Being at Uncle Doyle's felt more like camping than staying in a home, but I loved being there. I enjoyed everything about this rural lifestyle—except the outdoor toilet. It was smelly and nasty. It took all my bravery to use it. I quickly learned how they used the Sears and Roebuck catalog in an outdoor privy.

"Where's the toilet paper?" I asked Uncle Doyle, as I headed out the first time to use the outhouse.

"Just use the Sears and Roebuck catalog that's in there," he replied.

"No, I don't want to read or look at pictures; I need to do number two."

"That's what I mean. Use the pages from the Sears and Roebuck catalog. Either that or you can use some of those corncobs piled up in there," he said.

"Corncobs? What do you mean?"

"You have a choice: use a page or two from the catalog, or use a few corncobs. It's up to you," Uncle Doyle said. I chose Sears and Roebuck, skipping over all the go-carts.

I also didn't like some of the foods. One night we had blood pudding, a type of sausage made of animal blood and filler, but I couldn't eat it, and neither could my brothers. Just the thought turned my stomach, but Uncle Doyle and his family ate every bite. I did like the rhubarb pie. I had never had it before, but this pastry proved to be very delicious. The naturally sour rhubarb, combined with sugar and thickened with cornstarch, made for a delightful pie filling.

I liked playing with Uncle Doyle's stepsons, Dale and Jessie. We had an excellent time hiking up the side of a mountain full of pine trees, climbing to the tops, and swinging from one tree to the next as we came all the way back down. We also chased a pig through the woods after it got loose from its pen. Catching a squealing pig was a tall order, but Uncle Doyle's stepsons finally cornered and wrestled it under control, returning it to its enclosure.

Even though I had a lot of fun at Uncle Doyle's, by the end of the week, I was ready to return home and back to civilization.

In 1961 Daddy took Johnny, Randy, and me with him on a trip to Asheville, North Carolina. I was in awe of this city. It was the largest I had ever seen. As we entered Asheville by way of Patton Avenue, we came upon a Burger Chef, the first fast-food restaurant I had ever seen. I had only heard about fast-food chains from others. We begged Daddy to stop. Since it was noontime, he agreed.

"Wow, we're going to eat fast food. I can't wait!" I said.

"You each can have a hamburger, french fries, and a Coke," Daddy said.

"I'd rather have a hot dog," Randy replied.

"That'll be okay too," Daddy said. Johnny, Randy, and I went with Daddy to the window to order.

"Can we have a cheeseburger instead of a hamburger?" I asked.

"They're ten cents extra, but yes, you can have cheeseburgers," Daddy said. He completed our orders, but when it came to his, he said, "I just want a *plain* hamburger." He paid for the food, and we returned to the car to eat our meal.

"Great day in the morning, this hamburger has nothing on it. It's just a patty and a bun!" Daddy said.

"You ordered it plain, and that's how you got it," I replied.

"Yes, but I meant I just wanted a regular hamburger, not a cheeseburger."

"Take it back. The attendant will still put ketchup, mustard, and a pickle on it," I said.

"No, I'll just eat it the way it is. Next time I'll know better."

After Burger Chef, we went to Woolworth's and several other five-and-dime stores in downtown Asheville. Daddy was looking for dress shirts and ties for his suits. Since he wore a white shirt and a tie every day, he was in constant need of these items. I was embarrassed when Daddy asked for the "preacher's discount" and moved away from the sales counter. While we were at Woolworth's, I heard sirens as police cars raced through the city.

"What's going on?" Daddy asked one of the store clerks.

"They said a construction worker was trapped in a collapsed trench somewhere downtown," he replied. Later, the store clerk came by to tell Daddy the man had died from his injuries. "They couldn't get him dug out quickly enough. He suffocated," he said. This tragedy became the news of the day everywhere we went. From Woolworth's and the five-and-dime stores, we went to Sears and Roebuck.

"Sears and Roebuck is a store, too?" I asked in astonishment. "I thought it was only a catalog!" There I saw an escalator; the first I had ever seen. I also saw, for the first time, an elevator. Daddy let us ride them over and over. In the downstairs section of the store was a luncheonette. Since we had already eaten at Burger Chef, I asked Daddy, "Can we sit at the counter and have a Coke?"

He said yes.

"Would you rather have a cherry Coke?" the attendant asked. "They're the same price."

"Yes, please. I'll have a cherry Coke," I replied.

The server dispensed the Coke from the fountain into a glass filled with ice. He then squirted in cherry juice. The taste was excellent. As we were leaving, I asked, "Daddy, why is it so cool in here? It's hot outside, but there's a cold breeze blowing inside."

"That's air conditioning. Many of the department stores and other large buildings have it now," Daddy replied.

"What's air conditioning?" I asked.

"It's something new. A big electrical system that pumps in cold air, keeping a building cool," Daddy explained.

"Wow, I can't believe it. Do you think homes will ever have air conditioning?"

"Probably not. It would be too expensive."

After we had left Sears and Roebuck, Daddy gave us a grand tour of the rest of downtown Asheville. We drove all over, including Pack Square.

"I love the big city, Daddy. Can we move here?" I asked.

"Yes, can we live in Asheville?" both Johnny and Randy pleaded.

"You just can't pull up and move on a whim. I'd have to have a church to pastor first. But who knows what God may have in store for the future," he said.

Our trip to Asheville was both beautiful and magical. I now wanted to live in this big city in the worst way.

CHAPTER 18

TELEVISION AND ROCK
AND ROLL

Television and rock and roll music became an increasingly important source of entertainment after we moved into the Mount Hope parsonage. At this location, we got better television reception, and with it, more station options. Daddy put up a large antenna on a very tall pole, just outside the front door. You manually turned it in the direction of the station you wanted to watch: NBC, CBS, or ABC. When the wind was blowing, it moved the antenna, requiring frequent adjustments to avoid a snowy picture. A stiff breeze was a perplexing problem that sometimes interfered with our favorite television programs. The technology of the day required each TV to connect to an individual antenna. Multiple sets in a home were virtually unknown.

In the daytime, while Mother did her housework, she watched the soap operas *As the World Turns* and *The Edge of Night*. In the summertime, when we were allowed in the house, I saw these programs, but I never admitted to anyone I watched soap operas. Mother had other favorite daytime programs I viewed also. Game shows included *Truth or Consequences*, *Concentration*, and *The Price Is*

Right, but *Queen for a Day* was Mother's favorite. She readily identified with the plight of each woman who discussed her financial or emotional difficulties as each competed to win the title of "Queen for a Day" and all the prizes that went with it. "With all you young'uns and John not here most of the time, I deserve to be queen for a day. There's nobody on that show who lives a harder life than I do," Mother said.

After school and on Saturdays, Mother let us watch cartoons. We also loved *The Roy Rogers Show, Zorro,* and *Adventures of Superman.* One day I donned a cape (a towel Mother pinned around my neck), stuck out my arms as if flying, and ran outside around the house. While playing, I saw Daddy had left a wooden ladder on the side of the house.

"Mother, I'm going up on the roof and fly off just like Superman," I announced as I headed up the ladder.

"You get the hell off there, you idiot. Nobody can fly. You'll break your damn fool neck," she scolded.

Emulating the Little Rascals also became a passion for Johnny, Randy, and me. On one of the shows, we saw some of the gang go down a hill knotted up inside an old tire. "Wow, that's a good idea!" I said.

"Let's try it," Johnny said. We headed to the basement to retrieve one of Daddy's old tires and then to the backyard, which had a very steep slope. Johnny tried to wedge himself inside the tire, but he was too big. I tried, but I also was too big. I was disappointed I couldn't roll down the hill in the tire. Finally, Randy got into the tire, and he fit fine. The only problem was that Randy didn't want to go down the hill.

"Let me out. I'm afraid," Randy protested as Johnny and I stuffed him into the tire against his wishes. "No, no!" he screamed at the top of his voice all the way down the hill. All I could see as Randy went down were his arms, which were the only part of his body outside the tire, turning over and over as he rolled. The tire hit a ditch and landed on its side. Randy was crying hysterically. Mother and Daddy came running from the house, thinking one of us was dead. Instead, they found Randy still wedged in the tire, now on its side in the ditch.

"What the hell did you boys think you were doing?" Mother said. "If that tire had gotten over the ditch, it could have rolled into Cartoogechaye Creek!"

By then, Daddy had freed Randy from the tire. Red marks were visible on much of his body from the ride down the hill. Daddy gave Johnny and me a beating right there on the spot. It was one of the few we got that we probably deserved.

Not to be thwarted, some time later, we tried again, but this time with a new fifty-five-gallon steel drum Daddy had obtained for burning trash. I took the drum to the top of the slope, got into the barrel, and away I went—all the way down the hill. The barrel came to rest in the ditch that had saved Randy from rolling into Cartoogechaye Creek. The ride was painful, and I was dizzy from the experience, but that didn't keep Johnny and Randy from trying it. They, too, were scratched and bruised after the ride. We didn't try that again.

Daddy's favorite sport was boxing, which all the television networks carried. *Friday Night Fights* was a must-see at our house. Daddy never missed any of these telecasts when he was home.

"Daddy, are we for the one in white trunks or the one in black trunks?" I asked.

"I'm for the one in white trunks tonight."

"Then so am I."

In 1960, the network canceled *Friday Night Fights*, but later in the year, *Fight of the Week* started airing on Saturday evenings. Daddy's favorite boxing champions from the past were Joe Louis and Rocky Marciano. He didn't believe any of the current fighters compared to them. Still, he pulled for Sugar Ray Robinson, Floyd

Patterson, Joe Brown, Archie Moore, and others. Johnny, Randy, and I also liked professional wrestling. We were in awe of all the striking, grappling, and body-slamming that occurred in the ring.

"Boys, don't be fooled by that stuff; it's all fake, and the winner is predetermined," Daddy warned. "It's just a bunch of theatrics, so don't be trying any of those moves on each other. You'll get hurt," he said. I didn't want to believe him. On television, professional wrestling seemed very real to me. Over time, I came to agree with Daddy—it was all fakery.

Mother's favorite primetime show was *The Lawrence Welk Show,* broadcast on Saturday night. She listened to the music and watched the program as she gave us our baths and ironed our clothing for Sunday morning.

My favorite programs were westerns. *Bonanza* was perhaps the most popular program of the era. Since it played on Sunday evenings at nine o'clock, it had a dramatic impact on the evening worship service at Mount Hope. Members no longer stayed around to mingle after church, since it was more important to get home to avoid missing an episode.

The limited choices of television networks and programming created an instant connection among all social groups. When striking up a conversation, the latest episode of any program was usually sufficient to get it going.

By the time Elaine started Franklin High School in 1960, rock and roll music had already permeated our home, a change that had begun a few years earlier. This music genre, exemplified at the outset by Elvis Presley, proved to be a transformative influence in our lives in the same manner as television. My siblings and I believed country and western music was detestable, a style of music listened to only by old people and "rednecks." We held this view notwithstanding the fact that both Mother and Daddy occasionally listened to it. When they did, we made fun.

The radio was our primary source of music. While we had a record player, Daddy used it almost exclusively to play hymns and southern gospel music. The record player played 78 rpm vinyl discs. He always had a stack of 78s. Daddy kept a stash of new needles to replace the ones that became dull with use. It was important to be careful when lowering the stylus onto the turntable to avoid scratching the record. A scratch usually rendered the phonographic disk useless. Many of Daddy's records met this fate.

After riding the bus home from high school, Elaine sat by the radio, located in the kitchen, and listened to rock and roll until suppertime, helping Mother as needed. Elaine's most beloved musical artist was Elvis Presley.

One time she got excited when she heard the local disk jockey announce, "We've received a special request! This song goes to Elaine Willis. Hope you're listening out there."

"Oh my, someone's called in a special song just for me. I wonder who," Elaine said.

"And now here it is, the 'Beer Barrel Polka'! It's time to roll out the barrel," the announcer said. Elaine was in shock. She gasped, "Who'd request 'Roll Out the Barrel'? I'm going to kill someone if I can find out who did it." She never discovered the prankster.

I screamed with laughter.

"Mikey, don't be coming into this kitchen to torment Elaine! Now get your ass out of here," Mother demanded.

The Highwaymen hit it big in 1961 with a song titled "Michael." It began by telling Michael to row the boat ashore and then went into a chorus of hallelujahs. I didn't particularly like the song, preferring ones with a faster tempo. Johnny began singing a slightly altered version of the song. "*Mikey* row the boat ashore, hallelujah. *Mikey* row the boat ashore, hallelujah," he sang.

Furious, I yelled, "Quit singing that song!"

Johnny and I wrestled to the floor. He was stronger than I was and held me down and sang right into my face, "*Mikey* row the boat ashore, hallelujah. *Mikey* row the boat ashore, hallelujah."

Mother finally intervened. "Johnny, get off Mikey, and don't be singing that song to him anymore. Can't you see it makes him mad?" Johnny pushed me as he got up, laughing with delight. "Mikey, you got a little taste of being tormented. So, don't torture anybody else!" she said.

Elaine liked *American Bandstand*, but Daddy didn't allow her to watch it. When he was gone, Mother allowed Elaine to watch and served as the lookout. "Here comes your Daddy, you'd better turn the channel," she would say. On *American Bandstand* I first saw a dance called "The Twist," popularized by Chubby Checker. We would swing our hips back and forth to the music in our living room just like the dancers on television. *American Bandstand* also showcased teenage fashion. Still, Elaine and all her high school friends wore very conservative clothing—skirts and dresses to the knee, cardigan-style sweaters, knee socks, and such. Girls couldn't wear pants to school. Boys wore dress pants and button-down shirts.

Daddy believed the changes in music and dress were an evil force in America. "Young people are a disgrace. Beatniks, greasers, rockers, and such are the devil's work. It's all fueled by rock and roll music. America needs to get right with God!" he said.

While we didn't see any beatniks or rockers in Macon County, we did have a greaser, or at least a greaser imitator. Donald Southards raced up and down the highway every day in a 1957 Chevy. Occasionally, he stopped by the parsonage to chat with Daddy. Daddy believed the real reason for his visits was to get a glimpse of Elaine. Donald Southards, in his twenties, had jet-black hair slicked back with Brylcreem or a similar product. He wore a tight white T-shirt with the sleeves rolled up and a pack of cigarettes tucked in the left sleeve. Donald also wore tight-fitting blue jeans, double cuffed one inch. White socks and black penny loafers, including brand new pennies, rounded out the attire.

"I'm going to dress like that when I grow up," I announced.

"Hell, no, you're not!" Mother said.

Daddy said, "Donald Southards isn't the kind of man you want to dress like!"

"I like his car," Elaine said.

"You stay away from him!" Daddy responded. Still, he was always kind to Donald when he stopped by to visit.

Daddy's obsession with moral decay in America had a negative impact on Elaine during her high school years. Once she was old enough to go out, Daddy followed Elaine and her date, spying to make sure she didn't go somewhere he disapproved. One time he went to the roller-skating rink in Franklin, pulled Elaine out, and brought her home, leaving the date behind.

In June 1962, when I was ten years old, Daddy gathered the family together for a major announcement. "Young'uns, I've been called to pastor Oakley Baptist Church over in Buncombe County. We're moving within the next few weeks."

"Where's Oakley?" I asked.

"It's inside the city limits of Asheville."

I couldn't believe my ears. I was ecstatic. We were moving to the big city! "There will be no more country life for Mikey Willis. From now on, I'm a city boy," I said.

Everyone in the family except Elaine was excited about the impending move. She was upset about having to leave Franklin High School and all her friends.

CHAPTER 19
OAKLEY

Daddy's bachelor's in theology from Southeastern Baptist Theological Seminary made a move to Asheville possible. Without this degree, Daddy had advanced as far as he could go in the preaching profession, which was a small rural church. Now, new opportunities were available, and he seized the chance. He was almost thirty-nine years old. Mother was soon turning thirty-four. With his degree in hand, Daddy was headed for a new and greater challenge, a church with an attendance almost six times larger than Mount Hope's.

Asheville, the county seat of Buncombe County, was the largest city in western North Carolina, with a population of sixty thousand in 1962. It was known for its art deco architecture, which dated from the early twentieth century. Asheville was a beautiful city amid the majestic Blue Ridge Mountains. Perhaps best recognized for the Biltmore Estate, built by George Vanderbilt III in 1895, tourism was an important part of the city's economy. The Grove Park Inn also drew many visitors.

On the morning of our move to Asheville, the Oakley church sent a large truck and two movers to assist with the packing and loading. Several Mount Hope church members stopped by to wish us good-bye. Many had not taken the news of our impending departure very well. They were sad to see their popular pastor and his beloved family move away.

We drove to Asheville in the 1960 Dodge Matador that Daddy had bought. He got a good deal since the car was the previous year's model. It was a white, three-seat station wagon. For the first time, all ten family members could ride comfortably in the same vehicle. The back seat, where Johnny, Randy, and I rode, faced backward, allowing us to see out of the back window as we rode along. The purchase of this car wasn't without controversy. Mother didn't think we could afford it. Daddy surprised everyone—including Mother—when he brought it home.

"John, we can't afford the payments on a new car. We can barely afford the groceries," she protested. This argument didn't faze Daddy. He was very proud of this Dodge, the only new car he ever owned.

That day I announced to the family something I had been thinking about from the time I learned we were moving. "When we get to Oakley, I want to be called Mike, not Mikey. Mikey is a name for little boys, and I'm not little anymore."

Johnny immediately began saying, "I'm going to call you *Mikey*. I'm going to call you *Mikey*!" All the others chimed in and said the same thing.

"Yes, I'm with Johnny; I'm going to call you *Mikey*, too," Elaine said.

"No, you're not," Mother said. "If he wants to be called *Mike*, then that's what we'll call him, and I'll whip the first one who calls him *Mikey* again." No one dared to call me *Mikey* from that time forward.

By the time we arrived at the Oakley Baptist Church parsonage, the moving truck had already come. As the movers began to unload, the neighborhood children gathered to watch the unpacking. Among those who showed up that first day were Gene

Hollingsworth, fourteen years old; his brother Jack, eleven years old; and David Garland, ten years old—my age. David and I were destined to become best friends. Because of all the activity and the growing number of children, Daddy said, "Young'uns, come back later in the afternoon once we finish the unpacking. I'm afraid one of you will get hurt. Once the truck is gone, feel free to return."

That was just what Gene, Jack, and David did. After we had eaten supper provided by the women of our new church, Daddy, Johnny, Randy, and I went outside just before nightfall. Sitting next to the parsonage was an old church bus that was no longer running. Apparently, it had been left there until the church could get rid of it. Daddy, my brothers, and I went over to look at the bus. We opened the doors and went inside. As we sat there chatting, Gene entered the bus, and not realizing in the dusk that Daddy was there, said, "Here we are, big daddy; here we are! Here we are, big daddy; here we are!" Jack and David were behind him.

Daddy said, "You are, are you?" Embarrassed, Gene started to exit the bus, but Daddy said, "Boys, don't leave. Get on in here." Reassured by Daddy's words, Gene entered sheepishly, along with Jack and David. Shortly after that, Daddy left my brothers and me alone with our new friends.

Gene was a tall boy with brown hair and fair skin. He had pimples. Jack also had brown hair, but a slightly darker complexion. David was blond haired with fair skin. He was a big, strong boy, much larger than I was. Gene was clearly in charge because he dominated the conversation. Because Gene was much older and wiser than the rest, my brothers and I readily submitted to his superior knowledge and insight, just as Jack and David had done.

As it got dark, we retreated from the bus to the streetlight at the end of Cypress Drive, next to our driveway. It was the first streetlight I had ever sat under after dark. That evening, Gene solidified his leadership over the group by educating us about sex. "Do you know how babies get here?" was his first question.

"No, tell us," we said. So, during the evening, Gene gave us the first sex education class of our lives.

"Wow, I just can't believe all that," I said when Gene had finished pouring out all his knowledge on the subject. Johnny and Randy agreed.

"Don't tell your mom and dad I said it," Gene said.

"Don't worry. Our parents would kill us if they thought we knew. We'll never tell," I said. Johnny and Randy agreed. In this instance, the pack held. There was no chance that one of us would tell. We didn't want Mother and Daddy to know we knew about sex!

The next day we all headed to Oakley Methodist Church. We stopped to play in the parking lot, although Gene said the church had forbidden any activity on its property. "If we see someone from the church coming, we'll have to run," he said.

Randy set off to explore the area while the rest of us stood and talked. After a while, Randy returned with what appeared to be a transparent balloon he had blown up and tied. "Look at my balloon," Randy said. The inside contained a white milky substance that coated the entire surface of the interior. Gene, Jack, and David laughed so hard they were rolling on the ground. Johnny, Randy, and I just stood there, not knowing what had happened.

"Ugh, Randy, what's in the balloon?" I asked.

"I don't know. I found it over behind the bushes," Randy replied.

By now, Gene had regained his composure. "Do you not know what a rubber is?" he asked.

"No, tell us," Johnny replied.

Gene proceeded to educate us about condoms and their use. "And Randy blew up a used rubber!" Gene said, as Jack, David, and he once again began laughing hysterically.

"That's nasty!" Johnny and I said.

"I need to wash my mouth out," Randy said as he threw the rubber away.

Gene was our sole source of sex education. For the most part, Gene got the story right, but there were a few glaring errors. I didn't know about these mistakes until I was eighteen and read the book, *Everything You Always Wanted to Know about Sex (But Were Afraid to Ask)* by David Reuben, MD

The Oakley Baptist Church parsonage was on a parcel of land that included the entire left side of Cypress Drive as you entered the cul-de-sac, an area of several wooded and open acres. A long graveled driveway to our house extended from Cypress Drive and continued to the basement garage. The parsonage was a two-story red-brick bungalow with white-trimmed windows. It had a front porch enclosed with wire-screen mesh and a door. A visitor had to first open the screen door before reaching the front door. The porch had a red-and-white-striped aluminum awning. Shrubs lined the exterior front porch area. These and the rest of the landscaping around the house were somewhat overgrown.

The interior walls of the parsonage were off-white. The floors were hardwood. The dining room was an open area, visible from the living room as one opened the front door. The kitchen was behind the dining room, the door of which you could see from the front door. From the living room, if you were looking from the front door, the bedrooms were located to the right and were joined by a hallway that extended the length of the house beginning in the living room.

The boys were assigned the first corner bedroom. It had two sets of large windows; one set was visible from the front of the house, and the other set was visible from the side. Randy and Phillip were assigned the bunk beds, while Johnny and I shared a double bed. Mother and Daddy took the middle bedroom next to the only bathroom. Their room had two large windows. The girls were assigned the back corner bedroom, located on the other side of the bathroom. At the very end of the hallway, there was a fourth bedroom, which Daddy used as a study. The hallway then opened back into the dining room. The upstairs was unfinished, so we used it as storage space. There was a full basement with plumbing fixtures for a washing machine. The stairway to it descended from the dining room near the hallway and through a heavy wooden door. A clothesline was in the backyard.

The large windows were opened in the summer to cool the home. In the winter, the parsonage was heated by a coal-burning furnace. It, along with its coal bin, took up a considerable amount of basement space. The container was filled using a chute that was accessed when needed by the deliveryman. He flipped open a door set at the base of the house and poured in the gravel-sized stoker coal.

I was excited about our new home. It was much larger than the Mount Hope parsonage, but more importantly, it was surrounded by other children, most of them my age.

⊷⊷ ⊶⊶

Oakley Baptist Church was located a half mile from the parsonage on Fairview Avenue. I thought this was odd since I was used to a parsonage being right next to the church, but Daddy reassured me it wasn't unusual at all. "Many parsonages are located separately from the church. It just means I'll have to drive over to the church each day."

The large church was cross-shaped, just like Mount Hope, but was built on a much greater scale. A magnificent staircase led upward to the outside porch area, which was secured by four massive columns. A large, majestic steeple towered over the gray-shingled roof of the redbrick structure. The arched windows were stained glass. I had never seen stained glass in a Baptist church before. The large sanctuary contained all oak furnishings—including the pews, the communion table, the pulpit, and the chairs on the podium. The edge of the podium served as an altar since there was no rail. It had the appearance and feel of a more traditional one because of its decorative wood paneling and a single step on which people knelt. Red carpet covered the central and side aisles, the front of the church, and the podium. It was the first carpet I had ever seen inside a church building. Behind the rostrum and the choir loft was a baptismal pool with a beautiful landscape mural painted above it.

"Getting baptized in a baptismal pool would have been much better than getting baptized in Cartoogechaye Creek," I told Daddy when I first saw this wonder.

"People have become too comfortable. I like the old ways myself," he replied, referring to outdoor immersion in a stream or lake.

Attendance for the Sunday morning worship service sometimes approached six hundred, with Sunday school attendance about half that. At Oakley Baptist Church, we quickly resumed the familiar routine of Sunday morning, Sunday night, and Wednesday night prayer meeting. I was also involved in all the programs I had experienced at Mount Hope, such as Sunday school, Training Union, two-week Bible school, and the Royal Ambassadors, but obviously now on a bigger scale. I also joined the youth choir, something we didn't have at Mount Hope. A significant change and something I enjoyed was socializing after church. On many Sunday nights, a group went out to eat. At first, we went to McDonald's on Tunnel Road and later to Burger King, which opened a competing store across the street. These were the early days for both franchises.

"Things can't get any better than this," I said. "I love living in Asheville. City life was made just for me." Sometimes we came home on Sunday evening instead of going out.

Mother began a Sunday night tradition of either making a pizza from a box or frying canned oysters, neither of which I had ever had before. They were excellent additions to our menu.

Youth social events were a regular feature at Oakley Baptist Church. One highlight of the evening was competing to win the limbo contest. A phonograph played over and over a 45 rpm vinyl disc of Chubby Checker's number-one hit of 1963, "Limbo Rock," as the competitors bent underneath a small pole held by two adults. After each round, they lowered the bar until finally, only one contender remained and was declared the winner.

Oakley also had an annual homecoming, which included dinner on the grounds provided by all the women, who brought their best covered dishes. There was a traditional dessert several of the women prepared, a red velvet cake made from a specific recipe. One woman had seen the recipe in a magazine and liked the picture and description of the cake so well that she ordered it. When the recipe arrived, there was an invoice for $100 included. Startled, she mailed the recipe back, but the company returned it, indicating the bill was still owed because she could have copied the recipe. Taking her cue from the cake company, she made and sold copies of the red velvet cake recipe for a dollar each to pay the bill. Almost every woman in the church bought one, including Mother. Her scheme raised more than enough funds to pay the bill in full. It was the best red velvet cake I ever had.

Various church members asked our family over for Sunday dinner. It didn't appear to be as big a hardship on these members as it was for those at Mount Hope. During one of these Sunday dinners, I first saw a color TV. I couldn't believe my eyes. I marveled at the brilliant colors of the new technology. Still, it was years before we had one.

Social outings and activities were the norms at Oakley Baptist Church. It was a very community-minded group. Being the pastor of a large church meant Daddy had to make some significant adjustments in how he performed his duties. For one thing, he was required to keep regular office times, something he had never done before. He didn't like set hours. He also had a full-time, paid secretary who made appointments for him and completed his correspondence. The music director also had a paid, part-time position.

Daddy didn't like having to prepare sermons and give them titles in advance so that they could print the titles in the bulletin. The formality of written order of service and preselected hymns bothered him. He didn't like putting in writing when there would be prayers and when the offering was to be taken up. Daddy held this opinion even though his unwritten order of service at Mount Hope had rarely deviated from a set pattern. "A printed order of service causes staleness in a service, and I don't like it at all," he said. He didn't even like the hymnbook used at Oakley, the *Baptist Hymnal*, preferring the *Broadman Hymnal* or the *Church Hymnal* instead, because they contained all his favorites. The *Baptist Hymnal* omitted some of these while publishing others Daddy didn't prefer. He didn't object to their messages but rather to the formal sound of songs such as "All Creatures of Our God and King" and "This Is My Father's World."

He also didn't like the way the deacon board exerted control over the affairs of the church, much more so than at any other church he had pastored. He was taken aback when the deacons restricted the number of revivals he could conduct during a year. Still, he had arrived at the top of his profession, and he made the best of it.

As for me, I had many other interests besides church that competed for my attention. While I was still involved, the church took a backseat to many of these things.

CHAPTER 20

CYPRESS DRIVE

As far as I was concerned, Cypress Drive was where the action was. Besides the eight Willis siblings, a dozen other children lived nearby. At the top of Cypress Drive was Gene and Jack Hollingsworth's house. They lived with their single mother, who struggled to make a living.

On Cypress Drive, next to the Hollingsworth home, lived Linda Nelson, an only child who resided with her white-collar parents. At the next residence, directly across from the parsonage, was Mr. Sprinkle, an older man who took it upon himself to make all the neighborhood children miserable. We, in turn, made his life miserable.

In the next house lived Nanny and Papaw Wyatt, grandparents of David Garland and his sister, Gail, and younger brother, Tim. The Garlands lived next to Nanny and Papaw. Next to them at the end of Cypress Drive lived Sparkplug, his wife, Mavis, and their small daughter, Allison. Their house was next to Woodlawn Cemetery, which was owned by Oakley Baptist Church. It stood at the head of the cul-de-sac turnaround. Sparkplug lived in a small shack-like structure. He was David's cousin.

Just across the street lived the Lees—Debbie, Johnny, and Gary. Debbie and Doug Taylor lived a few houses down from them. Doug was nicknamed Radar because his ears stuck out very prominently from his head. He was teased mercilessly by the other children, but not by the Willis boys. We knew our parents didn't approve of such behavior. Still, Radar was what we called him when he wasn't around.

There was a neighborhood drunk who often got out in the middle of the street in the evening to yell and stumble around. Except for Nanny and Papaw Wyatt and Mr. Sprinkle—who were retired—the drunk, and Sparkplug—who didn't work—all the parents were working-class people who did their best to provide for their families.

The parsonage was the nicest home in the neighborhood. Most of the others were small with some in need of repair. Our family attracted all the children to our yard almost every day. For the most part, the boys played with the boys, and the girls played with the girls, but there were times we all played together. For the boys, the pecking order was established by age, with Gene at the top. Since Johnny and Jack were the same age and each proud of his fighting prowess, it quickly became apparent a clash between them was inevitable. Their fights went back and forth over the years, with Jack first prevailing, but Johnny eventually got the best of Jack. On the other hand, David and I got along from the outset and became fast friends. There was no need for us to fight. Still, I engaged in more contests during the years we lived in Oakley than I ever did in Cartoogechaye. As it turned out, nothing could have prepared me better for life on the city streets of Asheville and at Oakley Elementary School.

Johnny and I were from the country, but it became evident to all the other boys we were hardnosed fistfighters, and we couldn't be bullied or intimidated. Gene, Jack, Johnny, David, and I established a loose-knit group that stayed together for the next four years. Randy and Johnny Lee, who were a few years younger, were also part of the Cypress Drive boys but were treated more like understudies.

Our interests were fighting, talking about sex, cursing, and playing baseball. It took only a short time for Johnny and me to prove our fighting abilities. The others also related stories of their fighting skills. As to the second curiosity, Gene had provided sex education on our first day in Oakley and afterward kept us updated on the latest information as it became available. Concerning the third interest, we adapted to the art of cursing well. Swearing for us wasn't a problem; after all, Mother was an excellent teacher. We already knew most of the choice words. Still, we had never used them very much until we arrived in Oakley. We also became good at not slipping up at home. This tactic was like Mother's ability to use profanity in our home but never at church. We learned additional words and phrases—ones that Mother never used.

Cursing wasn't without its consequences. At a high school football game, Johnny and I were running around and playing. We got in the way of one fan, and he couldn't see. We inadvertently blocked his view when we moved forward toward a fence to get a better view of the game. "Hey, you two, get out of the way; I can't see!" the man said in anger. This fan's outburst didn't set well with Johnny and me. We released a volley of curse words toward him as we moved away from the fence and shot him our middle fingers. We didn't think any more about this incident until the next day when Daddy called us into his office at the parsonage.

"Boys, did you enjoy yourselves last night at the football game?" he asked.

"Yes, we did."

"Do you have anything to tell me about last night?"

"No, why?" we both said.

"I came to look for you last night when I overhead all the swearing the two of you were hurling at that gentleman." Daddy had remained calm and had shown no anger at all. Suddenly, his face turned red as he screamed at the top of his voice, alternately hitting Johnny and then me, over and over. "I'll not have boys in my house who curse. Don't ever let me hear words like those come from your mouths again. Do you understand me?" Bruised from our injuries, Johnny and I determined to be more vigilant and to know our surroundings before cursing in the future. Daddy never caught us again.

Baseball was probably our biggest interest. We watched the major leagues on television, went to games of the Asheville Tourists (a local minor-league team), and participated on Little League teams. Many summer days we gathered in a field next to Woodlawn Cemetery and played baseball until noon. At noon, we took a break for dinner, which these boys called lunch, each going to his house to eat. We then returned and continued to play baseball all afternoon. We didn't keep score. Since there were not enough players to field a whole team, we employed a pitcher and catcher, a batter, a first baseman, a shortstop or second baseman, and a left or right fielder. The location of these last two positions depended on whether Johnny or me, both left-handed, were batting. All the posts were periodically rotated, so all the boys played every position during the day. When a batter got a hit, he ran the bases, and the fielders tried to throw him out. By this method, we practiced every part of the game.

Playing all the time meant it didn't take long for Johnny and me to become very skilled, just like our new friends. While we arrived too late to play Little League the first year, Johnny and I were assigned to the Elks team the next year, in 1963. Randy played on a different team.

"Elks, now that's a real name," I said.

"Wow, the uniforms look great!" Johnny said. They were white cotton uniforms with maroon letters. The cap was maroon with a white *E*. The stirrup socks were also maroon with white stripes.

"I want number seven, Mickey Mantle's number," I told Coach Jacobs, who obliged.

"No, that's my shirt," said Jerry. "I had it last year."

Coach Jacobs made me give it to Jerry. "So, is there another number you'd like to have?" he asked me.

"How about number three. Has anyone claimed it?" I asked. No one replied. Coach Jacobs gave me Babe Ruth's number—number three, but I had hoped to get Mickey Mantle's.

We played our games at Biltmore School. The team was made up of three nine-year-olds, three ten-year-olds, three eleven-year-olds, and three twelve-year-olds. Every member had to earn his starting position on a field of nine players. Otherwise, he "rode the pine" as the boys called it and maybe got to play in the last few innings of a game if the score wasn't close. As we began practice at the beginning of the season, Coach Jacobs made an announcement. "Boys, a couple of players will be here shortly. I thought I'd better tell you about them before they get here. Tommy and Jessie are Negroes. They'll be the first to play here at Biltmore, and this will be the first team to have colored boys on the roster," he said.

Almost every player gasped.

"No, we won't have it," one player said.

"I don't want to play with niggers," another agreed.

The whole team erupted in an outrage. I was taken up in the anger, influenced by my teammates, and slammed my hat down in disgust.

"Boys, that's just the way it's going to be, so you'll have to get used to it," Coach Jacobs stated emphatically.

Daddy, who had brought Johnny and me to practice and had stayed to watch, approached me, picking up my hat. "Son, that's the last time I ever want to see you act like that. Remember what

I've said. The color of a man's skin doesn't matter, but rather what's in his heart. Everyone is equal with God."

"You're right, Daddy. I won't ever do it again." I kept my word.

Tommy and Jessie joined the team and became valuable additions, a pitcher and catcher duo. I became good friends with them. Also, by the end of the season, many of the other boys had learned the same lesson I had learned on that first day.

With the Elks, Johnny got to start right off. I had to play my way into a starting position, but by the end of the year, I was a starter too. The Elks went undefeated for the season, but at the end, we had to forfeit all our games because the team had one ineligible player. Forfeiting all our games was a great disappointment. The Elks Lodge dropped their sponsorship of the team the next year. In 1964, Johnny moved on to play Babe Ruth baseball at Skyland, because he turned thirteen, while I returned as a twelve-year-old to my old Little League team at Biltmore, now renamed Gerber.

"Gerber, that's baby food. It's no name for a baseball team. Can I get on another team?" I asked Coach Phillips.

"No, Mike, you'll have to play for Gerber or no one."

I chose to play for Gerber. Our uniforms were gray cotton with navy blue lettering. A navy-blue cap with a white *G* and solid navy-blue stirrup socks rounded out the outfit. I thought they were ugly. All season, the team took a great deal of teasing over its name, and we won only a few games. For me, it turned out to be a good year. My center field play was superior, and I was one of the leading hitters. At the end of the season, I made the all-star team. The Biltmore All-Stars played only one game in the citywide tournament before being eliminated.

Each year my brothers and I made several trips to McCormick Field, home of the Asheville Tourists. It was a wooden stadium near downtown Asheville situated on the flat portion of a hill. In addition to the Asheville Tourists, we also saw the Pittsburg Pirates play the Philadelphia Phillies in an exhibition match at McCormick Field. These were the first major leaguers I had ever seen. At the end of the game, I got an official major league baseball given to me by one of the Pirates coaches. I had it autographed by as many players as I could find. When I got home, I put my trophy on the dresser in my bedroom, but the temptation to use the baseball in our daily games was too much. We played ball with it, and the names eventually faded as the baseball turned from white to dark brown.

Going to McCormick Field was always an exciting adventure. My cousin David Hall, a grandson of Aunt Dorcas, came to visit from Sylva, North Carolina, and we took him to an Asheville Tourists game. David, a few years younger than I was, had never stayed with us in Asheville before, and for him, the trip was overwhelming. He was overjoyed to be at a minor-league baseball game. "Can we go to the concession stand? I have money," David told me.

"Sure, I'll take you. Come on!" I replied. "We'll take a short-cut underneath the grandstands." Off we went to the concessions. Just as we were about to exit from our underside path, a group of about a dozen African American boys surrounded us. I thought we might be in trouble when I first spotted them, so I told David, "Keep quiet. Don't say a word and let me do the talking." I knew by experience that some of them were probably carrying knives.

"You boys coming around here to make trouble?" one of them said.

"No, we're just going to the concession stand," I replied.

"Have you got money? Give me some money!" another one said.

As the group closed in, I said, "Everyone calm down! There's no reason to be pushy. We'll just head along. We don't want any trouble."

Suddenly David yelled, "Leave us alone, you black niggers!"

159

"Run!" I yelled. I grabbed him by the collar, and we ran back underneath the grandstands, which was the only way unblocked. We reached full running speed in just seconds. The African American group was in hot pursuit. Just when it looked like they were going to overtake us, we turned a corner, and there stood a policeman. I was never so happy to see one. David and I fell at his feet. At the same moment, the African American boys rounded the corner, only to face the policeman. Instantly, they turned and ran.

"Those boys were trying to get us," I explained to the policeman as I huffed and puffed. "We were just going for concessions."

"Boys, it can be dangerous under these grandstands. Next time, take the outside route," the policeman warned as he went off in search of our pursuers.

I followed his advice. It was the last time I ever went that way to the concession stand. "David, you can't talk like that here in Asheville. That kind of language will get you killed!" I warned.

World Series time was the best time of year. We eagerly anticipated this event each season and rushed home to watch the games after school. All of us were New York Yankees fans, and Mickey Mantle and Roger Maris were our favorite players. We were all proud of the fact that Roger Maris had broken Babe Ruth's record by hitting sixty-one home runs in the 1961 season. Still, we were respectful of Babe Ruth because, after all, he was a legend. But no one understood why some thought Roger Maris didn't deserve the record.

We were overjoyed in 1962 when the Yankees won the World Series against the San Francisco Giants in a seven-game thriller. The games featured Mickey Mantle and Roger Maris against Willie Mays. In 1963, the Yankees lost to the Los Angeles Dodgers in four games, a great disappointment, since the Dodgers were our hated enemy. While I didn't like the Dodgers, I still respected their two pitching aces, Sandy Koufax and Don Drysdale. Mother was a big Dodgers fan. The Yankees returned to the World Series in 1964 but lost to the Saint Louis Cardinals. In 1965, the Yankees didn't make it to the World Series, the first time since I had been watching. I was very disappointed. Instead, we saw the Dodgers beat the Minnesota Twins. Again, Mother was pleased with the outcome.

———

When my neighborhood friends and I were not engaged in the sport of baseball, there were plenty of other things to do in Oakley. The entire community was our playground. Occasionally, the group camped out in the open lot next to the parsonage. One of the boys had an old tent we used for that purpose, and sometimes more than half a dozen crowded into it. We ate snacks and told scary stories. One night, as we settled down to sleep, we heard growling sounds outside.

"It's a wild animal!" someone yelled.

"Let's get out of here!" another boy said. Each trampled over the other to exit the tent, resulting in its collapse.

"Hey, boys, it's just us," Jim Crayton, a neighborhood teenager and member of our church said, as we finally emerged from the flattened tent. "We were just having fun. We didn't mean for your tent to cave in," he said.

Jim and his cousin Jim Honeycutt had seen our camp and had decided to scare us, but they hadn't anticipated the hysteria their joke provoked. Jim Crayton helped me with my gear as I headed home for the night. "I'm sorry to cause all that trouble for you. We had no idea you were scared!" Jim said.

"That's all right. I was tired of camping out anyway," I said. Neither of us knew it then, but in a few years, Jim was to become my brother-in-law.

———

All the boys had bicycles except for Johnny, Randy, and me. We had not thought of them at Mount Hope. Out in the country, there wasn't much use for a bicycle since it was too dangerous to ride on the highway. Besides, there were plenty of woods and the creek to keep us occupied.

Once we moved to Oakley, a bicycle became a necessity. During that first summer of 1962, the Willis boys walked while our friends rode. Mother, just as she had done at Mount Hope, let us wander, not knowing what we were doing, where we went, or when we returned. The only difference in Oakley was there was no way for Mother to whistle us home as she had done at Mount Hope.

One of our favorite places to visit was the Sayles Biltmore Bleachery Village, a neighborhood next to ours. Gene and Jack had many friends who lived there including Alan Jenkins. Another friend was One Ball Paul, or One Ball for short. "Gene, how'd One Ball Paul get his name?" I asked.

"That's obvious! He only has one ball!" He laughed hysterically.

Remembering the admonition from Mother and Daddy to respect those with disabilities, I was kind to Paul, not teasing him as the other boys did. But just as with Radar, I referred to him by his nickname when he wasn't around.

David, Randy, and I headed to the village one day. David, impatient with our slow pace because we were walking, said, "Mike, get on the back of my bike, and Randy, you get on the handlebars. I'll ride you down this hill." I got on the bicycle's carrier while Randy straddled the handlebars as David instructed, and away we went. At the bottom of the hill was a wooden bridge shaped like the top portion of an octagon. It rose sharply on each side before flattening across the top. Railroad tracks ran underneath. We raced down the hill as fast as David could pedal. As we approached the bridge, the front tire hit the edge where the pavement and bridge met.

"No!" we all yelled as the bicycle went out of control. We went up the steep bridge, headed for the railing. As the bike hit the side rail, I fell off the rear of the bicycle. Randy hit the top of the fence. David and his bike crumpled onto the flattened portion of the bridge.

"What happened?" I said as I got up, checking my bruises.

"I lost control," David said.

Crying, Randy said, "I almost went over the rail!"

"You'd have ended up at the bottom, in the middle of the railroad tracks," David replied, as we looked down below, approximately a hundred feet.

"Randy, you were lucky!" I said. Since David's bicycle tire rim was bent, we returned home, sore but much wiser.

For Christmas in 1962, Johnny, Randy, and I finally got our bicycles. Even though it was sleeting and snowing on Cypress Drive that day, I couldn't wait to ride. The inclement weather conditions contributed to my first accident. When I crashed, I bruised my tailbone.

It didn't take long for the Willis boys to become as proficient at bike riding as the others. We also became superb at fixing them. Whether the problem was with a flat tire, the chain, the brakes, or something else, we made all the repairs. I could take my bike apart completely and put it back together, if necessary. Johnny, Randy, and I were not alone in this ability; all the Cypress Drive boys could fix their bicycles too. In fact, we all learned from one another. In a short time, I became very talented on my bike. I rode down Cypress Drive with no hands on the handlebars.

"That's nothing. I can stand on my seat," David said and demonstrated his skill. As he came down Cypress Drive, David got up on the bicycle seat with his feet, legs bent, holding the handlebars with his hands as he went along. Not to be outdone, I copied David's maneuver until I became skillful at it, too. With practice, I eventually went one step further. Getting up enough speed, I could stand up on the bicycle seat, freestyle, my hands held out for balance, like an acrobat. Before the bike slowed, I then got down while maintaining control. David never duplicated that accomplishment.

"Mike, you'll break your fool neck, you idiot!" said Mother, one day while observing my achievement.

Streaking down Cypress Drive on our bikes was just one of many grievances Mr. Sprinkle had against all the neighborhood children, but there was little he could do about it. One day, quite by accident, I ran over his small poodle with my bike. Mr. Sprinkle usually guarded his dog carefully, but apparently that day it had wandered across the street and into the vacant lot next to the parsonage. As I raced down Cypress Drive, I saw the furry little creature running across the street and into my path. Before I could react, I hit him. My front tire rolled over the middle of the dog's body. "Arf, arf, arf!" the dog cried as I went head over heels into the midst of Cypress Drive. Bruised, cut, and bleeding, I picked myself up out of the middle of the street.

I've killed the dog! Mr. Sprinkle will have me arrested, I thought. Looking over into Mr. Sprinkle's yard, I saw him attending to his wounded poodle. The dog lived, but the incident hardened Mr. Sprinkle's attitude toward me and the rest of the Cypress Drive boys.

One summer day in 1963 David and I rode our bicycles over to Raleigh Road, just a short distance from Cypress Drive. It was a very famous street for many of the neighborhood boys because of a steep dip between two hills. On a bicycle, a boy could go down one hill, reaching great velocity and hitting bottom at maximum speed, and then brake gently while ascending the other side to the stop sign. "I bet you can't go down this hill," David said as we looked down from on top of the highest side.

"I want to see you do it first. Then I'll follow," I told David. Down he went to the bottom and back to the top of the other side. I saw David had difficulty with his ride, but I still went. As I raced to the bottom, it took all my strength to keep the bicycle upright. I almost lost control. I took a quick glimpse at my speedometer as I hit bottom and before I began the ascent. It recorded a speed of fifty miles per hour. I barely got the bike stopped as I rode up the other side.

"Wow! That was incredible. We'll have to do it again sometime," I said to David.

"Yeah, we'll do it again sometime," David replied. We never tried a second time.

We played basketball on a goal using a net set up in the driveway. During football season all the boys played in the front yard of the parsonage. In fact, we played there so much the grass was eventually worn away, exposing the bare dirt. Playing football here meant that sometimes the ball ended up in Mr. Sprinkle's yard. One of us always made a mad dash to retrieve the football since Mr. Sprinkle kept it if he got there first. Gene, Jack, and David assured us that Mr. Sprinkle had a box full of baseballs and footballs they had lost. This knowledge made us even more diligent to be on the lookout for Mr. Sprinkle.

Some of the older neighborhood boys liked to get in on the football games. Eighteen-year-old Jim Crayton was one of them. One day when he was playing with us, someone punted the football. It crossed the street and landed in one of Mr. Sprinkle's trees.

Mr. Sprinkle, who was standing right by the tree, said, "You can't come into my yard and get the football. It's mine now."

Jim said, "Mr. Sprinkle, it won't hurt the tree for me to climb and get it."

"You can't do it," Mr. Sprinkle insisted. Jim, frustrated by Mr. Sprinkle's obstinacy, climbed the tree and retrieved the football anyway. The next day, a policeman served Jim with a complaint Mr. Sprinkle had sworn out on him.

All the parents were incensed. They signed and circulated a petition asking the judge to dismiss the charge. On the day of the court hearing, all the Cypress Drive boys went to see what would happen. It was the first time I had ever seen a courtroom. After reading the petition and hearing Jim's testimony, the judge dismissed the case and admonished Mr. Sprinkle for bringing such a frivolous action. We all felt vindicated—especially Jim.

We also played cemetery football. This activity was the same as regular football, but the game was in Woodlawn Cemetery. When running with the football or when going out for a pass, we had to make sure to dodge the tombstones. Likewise, the tacklers and pass defenders had to watch out for them, too. For the most part, we negotiated the headstones just fine.

At dusk, we also played hide-and-seek in the cemetery. This game was open to anyone, both boys and girls of all ages. Those hiding took shelter behind the tombstones or in sunken graves while the seeker prowled the cemetery. Very often the seeker was spooked by the hider.

At the top of Cypress Drive, we also played ball with a plastic Wiffle ball and oversized bat. Mother and Daddy had gotten the set for my younger siblings, but Johnny, Randy, and I took it over. Everyone played: young and old, boys and girls.

"Gene, come and play ball with us," I implored one day after seeing him watching from his yard.

"No, that's for little kids. I'm not playing," he said.

"That's fine, but we're still playing," I said. Gene laughed at us. As we played, it soon became apparent to him we were having a lot of fun. First base was the big tree on the right. Second base was in the middle of Cypress Drive where it met Merchant Street and was marked by an old rag. Third base was a rock positioned across the street from the big tree. Home plate was a glove we put down in the middle of Cypress Drive. When a car came by on Merchant Street or turned onto Cypress Drive, we moved out of the way to let it pass.

"Hey, I think I'll play after all," Gene said.

"Come on, you're up to bat now," I said. A home run was anything hit all the way across Merchant Street. Gene blasted the plastic ball, hitting the window of a house but not breaking it. Everyone started to scatter, as we thought the owner would come out to complain, but she never did. From then on, the house became a target when playing with the plastic ball and bat.

The wooded area behind the parsonage was part of the Oakley Baptist Church property. We played in these woods often. Since we liked this area so much, our group decided to build a clubhouse in the very center of the woods in a small thicket. It was the perfect spot, for the rest of the trees shielded it from view. We gathered brush, boards, and tree limbs to cover over the thicket. We secured some of these to the nearby trees with nails and ropes to make a sound structure. Next, an entryway was punched through, and the inside was cleaned out, leaving a beautiful interior. Our clubhouse was then ready for business. It was an excellent place to play.

One day we went to the clubhouse, but someone had been inside and had messed it up. We repaired the damage, but it happened again. After it had happened a third time, I said, "Let's set some booby traps."

"What can we use?" Randy asked.

"I know, I'll ask Mother for some mousetraps," I said.

"That's a marvelous idea," Johnny said. I went to the house and asked Mother for the mousetraps. She gave me a whole bunch once I explained the situation. Back at the clubhouse, we set the traps.

"Wait a minute. We'll have to camouflage these traps," I said. "Let's cover them with leaves. That should do the trick."

The next day we went back and just as we suspected, the clubhouse had had unwelcome guests. The strangers had gotten a rude surprise from several of the mousetraps. It looked like the intruders had made a hasty exit. While inspecting the clubhouse, we realized we now had another issue—the remaining booby traps were still under the leaves.

"How will we know where they are?" Johnny asked.

"We'll have to take sticks and poke around until we find them all," I said, which we did. The unknown intruders never returned after the booby-trap incident.

＝<＋ ＋>＝

Mother didn't permit any of the Cypress Drive boys to come into the parsonage. "You keep all those kids out of this house, Mike. I have the hardest time keeping this place clean with all you young'uns in here. I don't need a bunch of other children messing around too."

"Can I let David in the basement when I need to fix my bike?" I asked.

"For something like that, it will be all right, but keep it to a minimum. You never know what those boys will get into."

While the neighborhood kids couldn't come into the parsonage, we were allowed into their homes. Gene and Jack's house had a full-size pool table that filled an entire room. The pool table was too large for the room, which meant the pool sticks often hit the walls as we played. It didn't take long for me to become an accomplished pool player.

In the summers, I went to David's house to get him out of bed. Without my assistance, he slept until noon, since both of his parents worked. Once he was up, we headed over to his grandparents' home to get something to eat. Nanny and Pawpaw were adamant that all the neighborhood children call them by these names. Nanny fried eggs and bacon served with toast and jelly or apple butter. She always insisted that I eat too. I obliged, even though I had eaten breakfast long before. At lunchtime, she served us fried potatoes, pinto beans with cornbread, and fried baloney sandwiches on toast with mayonnaise. She also dished up fresh, homemade chocolate or coconut pie.

"Mike, you're a good boy. I like you and all your brothers and sisters. You can come to my house anytime and make yourself at home, just like my grandchildren," Nanny told me. "I can't say that about most of the other children in this neighborhood. I'd just as soon some of them stay away—especially Alan Jenkins."

She meant what she said about Alan. One day he opened the door and entered.

"March your ass right back out that door just like you came in," Nanny said. He left more quickly than he entered.

Nanny and Pawpaw had experienced rural life similar to the what most people in Cartoogechaye were accustomed to, but the city had gradually surrounded them. By the time we moved to Cypress Drive, the only remainder of their earlier agrarian lifestyle was the chickens they kept. Nanny and Pawpaw collected the eggs and occasionally killed a chicken, a procedure with which I was very familiar.

One day while we were playing at Nanny and Pawpaw's, we noticed a rattlesnake in the front yard. David and I came near for a look, but I recognized it as poisonous and kept a safe distance. The snake moved toward Deborah.

"No!" she screamed, as she went running in terror. It appeared the snake was in hot pursuit. Pawpaw intervened just in time. He crushed the snake with a shovel he found nearby.

The days I spent at Nanny and Pawpaw's reminded me of my country life at Mount Hope, but I much preferred my new city life.

⋙ ⋘

We often played in the woods across the railroad tracks. We also walked the railroad tracks. Going south, they went toward Skyland. Going west, they took you to Biltmore Village. Now and then the group also hiked east on railroad tracks near Sayles Biltmore Bleachery Village to swim at the public swimming pool near Oteen. At Cartoogechaye, I had learned to swim a little bit at Arrowood Glade, but at Oteen I became experienced. Roger Wyatt, David's teenage cousin, forced me to become a good swimmer by throwing me into the deep end repeatedly and requiring me to swim out on my own.

Just as I did at Mount Hope, I got money by collecting soft drink bottles and turning them in for cash. Occasionally, I also talked Daddy into giving me money. All these excursions were fun and for the most part, without incident, but there were exceptions.

CHAPTER 21

THE CYPRESS DRIVE BOYS

The Cypress Drive boys were involved in many other adventures—some were innocent while others were more mischievous. Halloween was a great holiday. For our group, it was an evening to have some naughty fun. At Mount Hope, Halloween had never been a big holiday, for a couple of reasons. For many years, Daddy was away at the seminary on the night of the event, which meant we had no means to go trick-or-treating. Also, we lived in the country where such activity was limited. We had only celebrated Halloween a few times when Daddy was home.

Mother and Daddy bought each of us plastic Halloween masks and took us into Franklin, where there were many houses. We went door-to-door collecting candy and fruit. In Oakley, it was pranking that drove the evening, not trick-or-treating. Water balloons were the primary means of fun. Early in the afternoon of one Halloween, before it was dark, Gene and David filled a long balloon. They had to be careful not to break it on themselves. They took it to Merchant Street, where they ascended a bank overlooking the street and waited. When a car finally approached, it took both to throw the balloon. Randy and I were watching from across the street in the woods. The balloon burst on the windshield of an older man's car as it passed. The long, water-filled balloon hit near the driver, wrapped around, and splashed into the open driver's-side window, drenching him.

The car came to a halt as Gene and David ran away through the field immediately behind them. The old man parked his car and began a slow chase. Gene and David ran so hard they soon became winded, allowing the man to catch up to them. He marched them back through the field and to their homes to tell their parents. The old man thought telling on Gene and David would take care of the problem, but after he left, everyone including their parents had a good laugh.

Laughing, I asked Gene and David, "Why did you let him catch you? Couldn't you run any faster?"

"We just got tired of running," David said defensively.

"Getting caught by an old man doesn't say much for your running ability," I observed.

"Just shut up," Gene replied.

After it had become dark, we took the rest of the water balloons and pelted children as they walked along Merchant Street to trick-or-treat. Once we depleted our arsenal, we headed over to Sayles Biltmore Bleachery Village for more fun. In this neighborhood, many of the homes were set back from the street on the side of the hill. Here we became the targets of boys throwing water balloons from their porches. We didn't stay in the village for long. We ran as water balloons whizzed by our heads, some hitting the mark.

We returned to the entrance to Cypress Drive, where there was a caution sign. It faced north to warn southbound traffic of a curve ahead. Through much practice and because of the sign's flexibility, David and I had previously learned how to run into this sign at full force without getting injured. Just as we hit it broadside, we put up our hands to protect our heads and to prepare for the fall. The sign bent forward but quickly sprang back. The recoil tossed us onto the shoulder of the street, uninjured. Passing drivers thought they had witnessed a serious injury to a boy running aimlessly into a street sign. As vehicles approached, David and I took turns running into the sign. Each time we heard screeching tires and someone exiting his or her vehicle to find out how seriously we were injured.

"Are you all right?" the motorist would ask.

"Yes, I'm fine. I'll have to watch out for that sign next time," I would say.

Every Halloween in Oakley was an eventful one.

At Gene's house, we pretended to be radio disk jockeys and used the telephone book to call people at random. When an individual answered, we would say, "This is James Fox with WIEB Radio here in Asheville, and you are our grand prize winner of the day."

"Wonderful! What did I win?" the voice on the other end of the line would ask.

"Your grand prize is two pots of piss and a barrel of shit!" we would say.

At this, the person would usually slam down the receiver.

Gene told me an old joke that some played on grocery store clerks. He assured me it wouldn't work since it was a very common trick. The prank involved asking about the availability of a Prince Albert pipe tobacco that came in a can. I decided to give it a try anyway and called Oakley Store across from Oakley Elementary School.

"Hello," the clerk from the store said as he picked up my call.

"Do you have Prince Albert in a can?" I asked.

"Why, yes, we do!" the store clerk said.

"You'd better let him out before he smothers!" I then banged down the receiver.

One day David and I were exploring the brushy area behind Woodlawn Cemetery when we saw a hunter across the railroad tracks in the woods. It was unusual to see one in the area. It didn't take us long to decide to play a prank. "Let's throw rocks in his direction, just for fun, but don't hit him," I said to David. We picked up stones and began to pelt the area to his left and right. The hunter reacted quickly, and soon I felt the percussion of a bullet as it whizzed past my head. David and I started running back toward the cemetery through the undergrowth. More shots followed as we moved. Once we got safely out of sight, I asked, "David, did you feel the shots going past your head?"

"Yes, I did. I thought we were dead," David said.

"Let's not do anything like that again. Throwing rocks at a man with a gun is a bad idea!" I observed.

Another incident involving a gun happened while we were at the swimming pool near Oteen. David knew where to find cattails—reeds that grew in a nearby marshy area. We used the cattails to make torches by dipping the ends in kerosene, which we then lit at night. David and I left the swimming pool and traveled along a well-worn path through the woods to reach the marsh. The trail followed along the bottom of a hill. The ridge was visible above. As we walked along, suddenly David and I were under fire, shots hitting the ground all around us. Disoriented by what was happening, we ran toward the marsh instead of backtracking. As David moved in front of me, I could see shots hitting the ground just behind his feet. We found shelter around the bend, up ahead of us.

"Who is that?" David gasped.

"I don't know. Did you tell anybody we were coming over here?"

"No, I didn't tell anyone," David said.

"I know about BB guns. I don't think it was one, but it could be a pellet gun."

"What are we going to do now?" David asked.

"I don't know. Let's hunker down and wait. Maybe we'll see or hear someone." We waited and waited, but the woods were silent. We didn't see or hear anything. Finally, after a period of hiding, I said, "We can't stay here all day. Maybe they're gone. Let's run back. Otherwise, we could be here forever."

David ran as fast as he could. I was close behind. As we crossed the area where we had been shot at, there was no activity. Apparently, the attacker had moved on. David and I didn't get cattails that day. We returned later with a large contingent of boys to show them the location of the attack. We never found out who had fired the shots.

The homeless were a problem throughout Oakley. They came by way of the two railroad lines that crossed through the community. Most were just smelly nuisances, some were scary, and others were dangerous. You never knew what you were getting when you saw one. A homeless man got killed on the railroad tracks nearby where the tracks crossed Crayton Road. Someone speculated that he had fallen asleep on the tracks. The Cypress Drive boys went to inspect the site. To our disappointment, by the time we arrived, new gravel had already been laid down to cover the mess caused by the impact.

In the winter, homeless men crept into the parsonage basement to spend the night near the furnace. We could tell when they had slipped down the coal chute. It was the boys' job to fill the coal hopper when it got low, a task always performed in the early evening.

One night as we descended the stairs to the basement, we saw a hand exposed from the shadows of the furnace. In unison, all three of us screamed, "It's a hobo!" as we fled the basement. By the time Daddy got downstairs, the man had fled. Sometimes we encountered homeless people when walking the railroad tracks, but they never bothered us. We found hiking the rails too much fun to be stopped by the sight of one.

━═╋ ╋═━

Gene, Jack, Alan, and David liked to hop slow-moving trains, an activity I refused to do. "Come on Mike. You're just a big chicken. Hopping a train is the easiest thing in the world," twelve-year-old David said.

"I don't care what you say. I'm not doing it. You could get killed."

"No way," David said. He jumped up on the ladder of a moving car but just as quickly fell. David might have avoided injury had his foot not gotten caught on the bottom step of the attached ladder. The train dragged David, flipping and twisting him down the railroad tracks. Finally, his shoe came off, freeing him from his dreadful ride. His parents took him to the hospital, where he spent several days mending from a punctured lung. Railway officials visited David and chastised him for hopping the train. They told him it was illegal and warned him not to do it again. The hospital returned David's coat, which nursing staff had removed upon his arrival.

"Look at my jacket," David said when I saw him. "See where the train wheel ran right over it." It was true. A visible line in the shape of a train wheel creased the back of his coat.

"David, that wheel could've cut you in half. I hope you've learned your lesson," I said.

Because of the accident, the Cypress Drive boys' train-hopping activities came to an end, but we still walked the rails.

━═╋ ╋═━

David's great uncle, Thomas, went missing. No one knew where he was, and no one could remember the last time he had been seen. Nanny, his sister, reported him to the police as a missing person.

Months went by until one day in the spring a hunter found a body in the woods near the railroad tracks. Evidence on the body indicated it was Thomas. Nanny and Pawpaw's whole family mourned the loss.

"What happened to your brother?" I asked Nanny.

"No one knows for sure. Thomas had been out in those woods for a long time. Hobos could have killed him. We just don't know."

"David, do you have any idea where they found his body?" I asked.

"Yes, I believe I can find it," he said.

"Let's go see."

We traveled by way of the railroad tracks behind the cemetery. After some distance, we turned off at a spot that had been marked by investigators.

"The police were just here this morning," David said.

"Where'd they find the body?" I asked.

"Under that thicket over there," David replied as we peeked into the undergrowth. All I could see was a small greasy spot.

"Is that it?" I asked skeptically. "I thought there was more to see than that."

"We'll poke around and then leave. This place makes me nervous," David said.

"David, look—it's a bone!" I exclaimed.

"No, it's one of my uncle's!" David said in disbelief.

"What do you think we should do with it?"

"We can't leave it here. I'll take it home to Nanny," he said. Off to Nanny's we scurried with the bone of David's great uncle.

On the way, I took a closer look at it. "David, it's one of your uncle's upper arm bones. Yuk, it has armpit hair on one end."

"Quit making fun of my uncle's bone," David said. When we got home, he deposited it in Nanny's mailbox and went inside to tell the news. Authorities arrived later and took the bone away.

While on our excursions throughout Oakley, it was routine to meet up with other groups of boys. These matchups were almost always random and happened at a moment's notice. While most encounters were cordial, you never knew what to expect. We were always on guard.

Oakley Elementary School was one such place we saw lots of boys. The school's playground and gymnasium were open each summer and on Saturdays throughout the year for all the neighborhood children to use. For the most part, we had no trouble at the school. We gathered, chose teams, and played baseball, basketball, or football, depending on the season. Although not allowed by the rules to do so, some children ran the halls of the school building when it was open for basketball. If there was a fight, it almost always occurred on the playground.

Some of these boys carried knives, a new element in fighting I had not previously encountered. I didn't carry a knife because I knew they could be deadly. I believed any boy who brought a knife was a coward—a dangerous coward—but a coward nonetheless.

I was at one of these summertime outings at Oakley Elementary School when I happened upon Billy. He confronted me in the school's driveway as I was departing the school on my bike.

"You want to fight? You asshole," Billy said.

"Why do you want to fight me? I haven't done anything to you," I said.

"I'm going to show you how tough I am," Billy said as he pulled out what appeared to be a knife. Upon further inspection, I could see it wasn't a knife but a soft-drink opener. One end was blunt and used to open bottles, while the other end was pointed and used to open cans. He had sharpened the pointed end of the opener as fine as a razor. I felt sorry for Billy and didn't want to fight him. He was filthy and penniless and was mocked by all the other boys. Billy's bike had no tires. He rode on the bare rims.

"You goddamn son of a bitch, I'm going to beat the hell out of you!" Billy yelled as he moved toward me with his weapon. Before he said another word, I hit him so hard the sharpened soft-drink opener fell from his hand as he hit the pavement. Seeing the weapon gone, I pummeled Billy until he begged me to stop.

"Billy, don't you ever pull another knife on me. Get your ass out of here now!" I demanded. He mounted his bike and rode away as fast as he could go. I heard the naked rims grinding the pavement as he rode out of sight. Then I picked the weapon up and threw it into the weeds. The sight of the obnoxious object infuriated me.

⊫+ +⊨

Tommy, who lived a few streets over, came by to make trouble. His object of scorn was Jack Hollingsworth. I didn't know what their issues were, just that there was bad blood between them.

"You son of a bitch, I've wanted to whip your ass, and now's the day," Tommy yelled as the fight began.

Jack grabbed Tommy, wrestled him to the ground, and started throwing punches. Familiarity had taught me the best fighting method was to move in lightening quick, land a few punches, and then move back. After the first blows, if your opponent wanted to continue the fight, you repeated the tactic. I never wanted to get tied up in a wrestling match while fighting. Jack's decision to wrestle proved to be almost fatal, for Tommy pulled a knife that no one saw until he cut Jack.

"Ouch!" Jack screamed in pain as blood gushed from his head. Tommy had stabbed him in the temple.

When Jack went down, I stepped forward and instantly hit Tommy with the hardest blow I had ever delivered. Tommy fell back. It was the first and only time I hit a boy hard enough to knock him out cold. Tommy went down like a tree trunk. As Tommy fell onto Merchant Street, the knife dropped limply from his hand. I took the knife and threw it into the woods next to the road. It was the sight of a knife that had again incensed me enough to leap into action.

Someone retrieved a towel to catch the blood still pouring from Jack's head, and off to the hospital he went.

The police came and took a report. "Son, they say you stopped the fight. Is that right?" the cop asked.

"Yes, I knocked Tommy out."

"What did you do with the knife? We'll need it for evidence," the officer said.

"I'm sorry. I was mad, and I threw it over there in the woods."

Two policemen scoured the underbrush until they found the weapon.

At the hospital, the doctor told Jack he was a very lucky boy. "If that blade had gone a fraction of an inch deeper, you would have died," the doctor said.

In Oakley, the resilient country boy from Mount Hope had become a hardened street fighter.

CHAPTER 22

OAKLEY ELEMENTARY SCHOOL

Oakley Elementary School was a half mile from the parsonage. It was an all-white school and not yet integrated. The school was a campus of four buildings, including a newly constructed cafeteria. The playground consisted of two softball fields, a large open area, swings, a high steel slide, and a set of steel monkey bars. I wore dress pants with my button-down shirts to class, dispensing with the blue jeans I had worn at Cartoogechaye. I walked to school every morning, usually with David and others, but sometimes by myself.

From the parsonage, I frequently left as late as 8:20 a.m. and arrived at 8:30 a.m. before the tardy bell. A fast walking pace and the use of a shortcut made the brief walk possible. When school let out in the afternoon, I made a more leisurely return trip with friends. There was a cherry tree located along the shortcut where we picked and ate the delicious fruit in the summertime.

During my fifth-grade year, walkers were dismissed first and given several minutes to disperse before the bus departures began. When I was in the sixth grade, the school reversed the procedure because the walkers hung around too long, getting in the way of the buses. Some of the children alleged they were superior to bus riders because of their status as walkers. This boast was never substantiated. The departure change allowed the walkers a new opportunity that had previously gone to the bus riders.

Each afternoon, student volunteers picked by the teachers cleaned the hardwood floors on each level of the school building using an oily floor cleaner poured onto a push mop. There was always competition to see who got to run the mop, while other volunteers moved the chairs. After cleaning the classroom floors, one had to be careful not to slip on the newly oiled surfaces. There was a similar competition to see who got to clean the chalkboards. Teachers handed out the privilege to those students who demonstrated the best behavior, which sometimes left me out of the running due to my many fights.

When we first moved to Asheville, Mother and Daddy warned us about Oakley Elementary School. "Now Oakley is not like Cartoogechaye. It's much larger, and the schoolwork will be harder," they told us. Their counseling helped set the stage for my near-failing grades to come.

At the beginning of the school year in 1962, I went into to Mrs. Pressley's fifth-grade class. She was a white-haired, older woman who cared deeply for all her students. David Garland and I were fortunate enough to become classmates. While we were thrilled at the news, the school principal, Mr. Nesbitt, and Mrs. Pressley belatedly came to see it as a mistake. There were more than forty students in my fifth-grade class. We learned reading, English, spelling, writing, social studies, health, physical education, science, arithmetic, music, and art the best way forty-plus pupils could with one teacher who had no assistant.

Our first major current events topic centered on the Cuban Missile Crisis, which unfolded in October 1962. Thanks to my interest in current events, I was following this issue not only in our discussions at school but also at home on television. It was the third serious Cold War predicament in the span of just one and a half years. Just as with the Berlin crisis, the Cuban Missile Crisis again evoked heightened fear about the prospect of World War III. It was much more intense this time as the world faced the threat of nuclear war. After coming to the very edge of war, President Kennedy and Soviet premier Nikita Khrushchev reached a compromise that brought about the dismantlement of the nuclear missiles in Cuba and their return to the Soviet Union. With this agreement, the crisis ended.

In fifth grade, David and I sat next to each other, but this arrangement didn't last long. Mrs. Pressley soon separated us because we couldn't stop talking. Moving me didn't solve the problem. I continued to speak to the other pupils and never finished my assignments on time.

From almost the first day, I began fighting on the playground and sometimes in the boy's bathroom. It appeared every schoolboy wanted to challenge the new lad, whom they considered to be an outsider. It didn't take long for them to learn I was more than their match. Still, these challenges continued to flare up from time to time.

Behavioral issues and fighting earned me many paddlings from Mrs. Pressley—thirty-three, to be exact—during the year. David and I started a competition to see who could get the most. By the end of the year, I had beat out David to win the challenge. My response to Mrs. Pressley after each paddling was to be friendly and cheerful toward her and always to be courteous. This mild reaction puzzled her. "Mike, you're a good boy, and you're polite. Why is it you're always fighting, talking, and causing me so much trouble?" she asked.

"I don't know, Miss Pressley."

Still, Mrs. Pressley tried to get me involved. "Mike, I want you to take the lead part in our school play. Will you do it?"

"No, Miss Pressley, it would scare me too much."

After repeated attempts to get me to take the play assignment, Mrs. Pressley finally gave up on the notion because of my adamant refusal.

I couldn't wait for the school day to end. After heading home to Cypress Drive, David and the rest of the boys and I played until suppertime. We usually returned afterward to play some more.

Homework, something I had always done at Cartoogechaye, went unfinished. There was simply no time for it.

One afternoon after school, Mrs. Pressley showed up at the parsonage to talk to Mother and Daddy. After she had left, Mother said, "Mike, Mrs. Pressley tells me you're not doing as well as you should. She tells me you're brilliant, but it's not reflected in your grades. Why are you doing so poorly? You're not going to amount to anything!"

"I don't know. Oakley is hard, just like you told me it would be."

"You need to make sure you complete all your schoolwork."

For the next few days, Mother made me sit in the house to do homework while the other boys played outside. The effort didn't last very long, since Mother soon forgot about Mrs. Pressley's concerns, and I returned to my playtime. At the end of the school year, I had a poor average—a severe drop from my As and Bs at Cartoogechaye Elementary School. Still, my grades weren't enough to fail me, and I would have moved on to sixth grade had it not been for Daddy.

Earlier in the year, Johnny had gone to Baptist Hospital in Winston-Salem, North Carolina, for an operation and had stayed there six weeks. Daddy took Randy and me to see Johnny at the hospital. He was in a small bed in a large ward filled with men and boys of all ages. By the time Johnny returned to school months later, he was woefully behind in his schoolwork, and the best solution was for him to repeat the sixth grade. Daddy didn't want Johnny and me to be in the sixth grade together, so he proposed to have me repeat the fifth grade. My repeating the fifth grade created a ripple effect. To keep the rest of the siblings in sequence, Daddy planned for Randy to repeat the fourth grade and for Deborah to repeat the second. Dawn and Phillip had not yet started to school. Daddy took his idea to Mr. Nesbitt, who at first soundly rejected it.

"While all your children performed below average, I'll only be retaining Johnny," Mr. Nesbitt said.

"Mr. Nesbitt, I insist on the implementation of my idea. I know what's best for my young'uns." Daddy's opinion prevailed, and the plan began at the start of the school year in 1963.

That summer I taught Dawn, who was scheduled to start first grade in the fall, how to read. One day I saw her pretending to read a storybook.

"Do you want to read?" I asked.

"Sure, but how?"

"I'll show you," I said, and with that, I began the lessons. First, I taught Dawn the alphabet. Once she could recognize and pro-nounce all the consonants, I then showed her the vowels and how they sounded. From there, I had her sound out different words I showed her, using her storybooks. By the end of the summer, Dawn was reading very proficiently.

⇥ ⇤

In the fall of 1963, I began my second stint in the fifth grade at Oakley Elementary School, in Mrs. Coleman's class. She was a young teacher with brown hair and glasses. I enjoyed her class because I was bigger than most of the other boys, so I didn't have to fight. The schoolwork, too, was very enjoyable. I was making straight As. The learning, in fact, was so effortless I began answering questions before Mrs. Coleman could ask them, and in the process, I inad-vertently became disruptive of the learning environment.

"Mike, I understand you already know all these lessons, but the other pupils do not. Please allow them the opportunity to answer, too," she said. After several weeks in which I displayed my new-found academic skills, one morning Mrs. Coleman said, "Mike, gather all your things from your desk and come with me."

I was frightened, thinking I had done something wrong. In the hallway, Mrs. Coleman said as we walked along, "It's clear some-how you absorbed all the teaching from last year, even though your grades didn't show it. It would be a disservice to keep you in the fifth grade any longer. The school has transferred you to Mrs. Singleton's sixth-grade class."

Mrs. Coleman introduced me to Mrs. Singleton. She was a mid-dle-aged woman with graying brown hair. "Students, you have a new classmate, Mike Willis," Mrs. Singleton announced to the class upon my arrival.

"He's not new; I was in class with him last year," one boy said.

"He's new to this class," Mrs. Singleton replied.

At home that evening, I said to Daddy, "They moved me to the sixth grade today!"

"What? No one called me. We'll see about that in the morning." The next day Daddy went to see Mr. Nesbitt. He was determined to have me returned to the fifth grade. Daddy's plan didn't work; Mr. Nesbitt refused even to discuss it.

"Mike should have never been retained in the first place. He's much too smart, even if his grades were bad last year," Mr. Nesbitt said. Losing the argument, Daddy had no recourse but to let the decision stand.

I had mixed feelings about moving to Mrs. Singleton's class. I had enjoyed my superior status in Mrs. Coleman's fifth grade but was glad to be back with my age group. But I was now several weeks behind the other students in my schoolwork, a problem that caused me to lag the rest of the year.

Mrs. Singleton taught one of three sixth-grade classes. I was placed in her class because Mr. Nesbitt had issued a directive stat-ing that David Garland and I could never again be in the same class and that Johnny and I could not be together. Each of us went to a separate classroom. Some of the boys wanted to make an issue of my having begun the year in fifth grade, but it didn't take too many fights to resolve this matter—no one would taunt me. That issue went away, but fighting continued over other problems.

Unlike Mrs. Pressley, Mrs. Singleton didn't paddle. Instead, she recruited Mr. Nesbitt to do the job. On numerous occasions, Mr. Nesbitt administered three licks with the paddle. Each time he warned me not to fight anymore. Mr. Nesbitt had no clue how tough I was. His paddlings were tame compared to the whippings I got at home. They had little effect. My response to him was the same as it had been toward Mrs. Pressley. After each paddling, I was kind and cheerful and always courteous, but it was never too long before I was back in Mr. Nesbitt's office again.

Before the end of the school year, tragedy struck. Mr. Nesbitt died suddenly of a heart attack. The news of his passing was devastating to the entire school—students, teachers, and parents. The community eulogized Mr. Nesbitt as a man who had stood firm for education and had dedicated his whole life to helping students achieve their best. It took a while for me to sleep at night after his passing. After all, because of the many paddlings, I knew Mr. Nesbitt very personally, more so than anyone else I had known that had died.

Mrs. Sellers was appointed to replace Mr. Nesbitt as the principal of Oakley Elementary School, the first woman I had ever heard of to become the head of a school.

⇒⇐

On Friday, November 22, 1963, I was sick and stayed home from school. It was highly unusual for me to be sick and out of class on a school day. In fact, most years I had earned perfect attendance certificates. On that day, I was home and lying on the couch in the living room sleeping while the TV was on. Mother was watching a soap opera, *As the World Turns,* on CBS. I awoke to an announcement that President Kennedy's motorcade in Dallas, Texas, had been fired upon, and the president was wounded. The news bulletin asked viewers to stay tuned for further details.

I became fully awake with the reading of this statement. I was staring at the television screen that showed only "CBS News Bulletin." A live broadcast had not yet begun. At the same time, I realized Mother was in the living room watching the notice too. We sat in stunned disbelief. Shortly after that, CBS News anchorman Walter Cronkite came on live TV, and in less than an hour, the official announcement came that President Kennedy was dead. All three networks—CBS, NBC, and ABC—immediately canceled all their regular programming and on a continuous basis covered the events of the tragedy for the next four days.

The whole nation went into mourning. The assassination of our young president was inconceivable. For four days, I hardly left the television screen—nor did anyone else in our family. That evening Daddy left to attend a Cliff Barrows revival meeting in downtown at the Asheville Civic Auditorium. Reverend Barrows, the music and program director for the Billy Graham Evangelistic Association, was conducting his separate meetings, but I was too distraught to attend. When Daddy returned, he told us Billy Graham had come from his home in Montreat to speak about the tragedy to those assembled. I regretted missing Billy Graham.

Tiring of the continuing television coverage, on Sunday I decided to go to church, although in a rare decision because of the tragic events, Daddy allowed us to decide if we wanted to go or not. When I arrived home from church, I learned that Lee Harvey Oswald, the alleged assassin of President Kennedy, had been shot by Jack Ruby. I was disturbed by the news, but I was also upset because I had missed the killing, which had occurred live on national television. Schools were canceled the next day so everyone could watch President Kennedy's state funeral on television. It was the saddest day ever. After these troubling days, however, life for everyone moved on, and soon things got back to normal.

In sixth grade, the best part of the school day was lunch and recess. At lunch, we walked in single file to the cafeteria following a blessing prayed over the food by Mrs. Singleton. The prayers continued, just as they had in Mrs. Pressley class, despite *Engel v. Vitale*, the Supreme Court ruling on June 25, 1962, holding that prayer in public schools violated the Establishment Clause of the US Constitution. In fact, schools ignored the decision throughout all my years in school.

In the cafeteria, peanut butter cookies were served for dessert almost every day. The aroma was almost more than one could stand, but first, we were required to eat our lunch. We went through a line where several servers placed food on our plates. Even though the school wasn't integrated, one of the cafeteria workers was African American. The first time I saw her serving food, I had a dilemma. Mother had always said African Americans were dirty and nasty and I was to stay away from them.

Since I was in line, I wondered what to do. I observed that none of the other children seemed to mind her serving them. I stayed in line and paid close attention to this woman's hands to see if they were dirty. They were dark on top, while the palms were almost as light as mine, but more importantly, her hands were spotless. *I'll be! Mother was wrong about that. I'll have to tell her,* I thought, as the worker placed food on my plate.

While we got one giant peanut butter cookie as we went through the line, sometimes there were leftovers, and we could return for a second one. These cookies were the best.

One week David Garland suggested we pack our lunches and save the money to buy things at the store. Believing this was a good idea, I agreed. I sneaked and made a peanut butter sandwich at home before leaving for school. Our plan went as scheduled for a few days until Mrs. Singleton noticed my brown-paper-bag lunch.

"Mike, you eat a big meal, but your mother is sending you only a peanut butter sandwich. Does she know you're packing your lunch?"

"Yes, Mrs. Singleton. She says it's okay."

"Then bring me a note from her tomorrow."

Mrs. Singleton's inquiry ended my sneaking a sack lunch from home and none too soon. I had almost starved during the few days I had brought it.

At recess, for the boys, softball and flag football ruled the playground. For either sport, there were enough kids to assemble two teams from a single class. Sometimes, teams were chosen to compete against the other classes. Also, in the gymnasium, we divided up for basketball. The playground and gym games were the highlights of recess every year I attended Oakley Elementary School.

By the end of the school year, my scores for sixth grade were better than those from the fifth grade. I had made some progress.

At the beginning of the new school year in 1964, I had Mrs. Symington for seventh grade. She was a young, blond-haired woman who always seemed to be miserable. Our classroom was located on the first floor of the main building, next to the principal's office. After the first few days of school, we learned Mrs. Symington was very unpleasant. The whole class felt her unkindness, but at times she singled out individuals too. Mrs. Symington had difficulty maintaining control, so there were many disturbances in the classroom. She easily became frustrated when teaching, particularly with those who had trouble comprehending.

One day she asked Danny a simple question, but he couldn't answer her even after she gave him the answer. "Danny, you mean to tell me you don't know? The answer is simple, but you don't know? I told you the answer, but you still don't know? I quit. I quit. I quit!" Mrs. Symington screamed as she went running out of the room in tears. In a few minutes, Mrs. Sellers, an old white-haired sage of the North Carolina educational system, dragged Mrs. Symington back into the classroom, still crying.

"Now get back to your work here, Mrs. Symington! You have students counting on you," Mrs. Sellers said as she marched out of the room. Mrs. Symington stayed, but the scolding from the principal did no good. She was as hateful as ever.

The 1964 presidential election was a topic of discussion in our seventh-grade class. We followed it and other current events in the *Weekly Reader*, a news magazine for school children. This election pitted the incumbent, Democrat Lyndon B. Johnson, who had succeeded John F. Kennedy when he was assassinated, against Barry Goldwater, the Republican challenger. The presidential election was also a hot topic at home. This time both my parents were for Johnson. "Barry Goldwater is a right-wing extremist. If elected, he could get us into a nuclear war with the Soviets!" Daddy argued. All my friends were for Johnson too. It appeared the choice was unanimous.

"I'm for Johnson. Who are you for?" David Garland asked.

"I'm for Johnson, too. Daddy says Goldwater is dangerous."

Lyndon B. Johnson won in a landslide on November 3, 1964. After the election, I came to class sporting a new Beatles hairstyle. Being very self-conscious, I came sheepishly into the classroom that morning. Enraged by what she believed to be a ridiculous hairdo, Mrs. Symington said, "Mike, go to the bathroom right now and comb your hair."

"I won't do it, Mrs. Symington. I can wear my hair any way I choose."

Grabbing her paddle, she took me into the hallway. "Now, I'm going to give you one more chance to comb your hair, and if you don't, I'm going to use this paddle," she said.

"It's none of your business how I wear my hair. If my parents allow it, there's nothing you can do."

Furious, Mrs. Symington took the paddle with both hands and hit me repeatedly in the buttocks as hard as she could until she tired from the exertion. "Are you going to comb your hair now?" she asked.

"No, I will not," I replied.

"We'll see about that. You go back to the classroom. I'm going to talk to Mrs. Sellers," Mrs. Symington said.

I went into the class and sat down. By now, I was determined not to comb my hair—regardless of what the principal said.

Upon returning, Mrs. Symington said, "We have no policy that prevents you from wearing your hair that way, but I think it looks awful."

Mrs. Sellers's ruling ended my standoff with Mrs. Symington and forced me to wear my hair in the style of the Beatles for the next few weeks. Mrs. Symington never knew I had almost combed my hair back to its old look before arriving at school that first morning. After the paddling, I couldn't back down. I didn't want Mrs. Symington to think she could intimidate me.

After the controversy had passed, I finally came to school with my hair combed the old way. Mrs. Symington looked at me and smiled. She probably believed I had changed it back because of her objections. I knew her wish had only postponed the decision.

Despite the chaos in Mrs. Symington's class, by the end of the year, I had again improved my grades.

In 1965, I had Mrs. Williams for eighth grade. She was an older woman with gray hair and was a strict disciplinarian. Her classroom was on the second floor of the main building. The order maintained in Mrs. Williams's classroom was in stark contrast to what I had experienced in Mrs. Symington's seventh grade, but it was a much better environment.

Mrs. Williams was the only teacher I ever had who emphasized dance. She particularly liked square dancing and taught the steps every time we had use of the gymnasium. I didn't mind learning the steps, but when it came time to partner off and dance, I didn't want to do it.

"Mrs. Williams, I'm not allowed to square dance. It's against my religion!" I said.

"What? You've never told me that before. Are you sure, or are you just wanting to get out of dancing?" she replied.

"No, ma'am. I promise you it's against my religion. Why, what would the members think over at the church, if the preacher's son was square dancing?" It was the first time I had invoked such an argument, but I was desperate. It worked, even though I lied. Daddy had never expressed an opinion about square dancing.

"All right then, you may sit out, but remain seated in the bleachers," she said. I was the only student in my class excused from dancing.

By the eighth grade, the necessity of fighting had tapered off somewhat, but there were still occasional challenges with which I had to deal. David Garland and I reunited as classmates in the eighth grade. It was almost certainly the passing of Mr. Nesbitt that had allowed this to happen. The new principal, Mrs. Sellers, was unaware or had forgotten about our history together. Still, now that we were older, our reunion was not as disruptive as it had been in the fifth grade, although we were constant companions in the classroom and on the playground.

After the first fight of the new school year, which happened on the playground, Mrs. Williams took my side, concluding that the other boy had wronged me. Later she turned against me as other fights occurred. "Mike, the first fight you had, I believed Terry caused it. Now, after you've continued to fight, I think you're the problem," Mrs. Williams said and then gave me a good paddling. She didn't believe I didn't start fights and only fought after other options had failed.

One day, a group of boys who were afraid to challenge me themselves instigated a fight between me and Tony. Tony had a speech impediment. I felt sorry for him and didn't want to fight. Tony also occasionally rode the church bus to attend Oakley Baptist Church, which was another reason not to fight him.

In the bathroom, after being goaded to do so by these boys, Tony came up to me, pumping his arms and fists in a boxing motion, and said, "Want to thight? Let's thight!"

"No, Tony, I don't want to fight you," I replied.

"You're a thicken!" Tony replied.

"No, I'm not a chicken. I'm not afraid of you," I said.

The boys who had encouraged Tony chimed in, "Mike's a chicken. Mike's a chicken!"

Tony continued to pump his arms and fists, while the other boys began laughing.

"Let's thight. Let's thight," Tony said.

With one swift left hook to the mouth, I sent Tony to the floor, bleeding profusely. He got up and headed to the sink to wash the blood off. I had cut my left middle knuckle on his front tooth, which amazingly had stayed in his skull. My hand was bleeding too. The boys who had persuaded Tony to fight took off to tell Mrs. Williams.

"Mike Willis, you've gone too far this time. I'm taking you to Mrs. Sellers," Mrs. Williams said as we headed to the principal's office. Mrs. Sellers paddled me as hard as she could, but it was nowhere near the level of Mr. Nesbitt's paddlings.

"Mike, since you've moved out of this zone, you're a guest here at Oakley now. So, if you fight one more time, I'll have you transferred to Sandhill," Mrs. Sellers warned. Since there were only a few weeks of school left, I was very careful not to fight from that time on.

Academically, the eighth grade was my best year at Oakley Elementary School. Toward the end, Mrs. Williams began preparing her pupils for high school, which we were to start the next year. Besides discussing the differences between high school and elementary school, she also had each student sign up for a career track—agricultural, general education, or college preparatory. Mrs. Williams passed out all the forms for each student to complete. I signed up for general education classes, concluding I certainly didn't want an agricultural career, and I gave no thought at all to the college-preparatory track. After completing the form, I returned it to Mrs. Williams, who looked over each student's decision.

"Mike, please come to my desk," Mrs. Williams said. As I got up and headed toward her, I wondered what I had done wrong. "You signed up for general education classes, but you're a smart boy. You should consider the college-preparatory track. You're capable of college work." It was the first time anyone had ever told me I was intelligent enough to attend college, and Mrs. Williams was the first person ever to encourage me to go. Until that moment, the idea had never occurred to me. In fact, I had believed I was incapable of college work.

I returned to my seat with the form Mrs. Williams had handed back to me. I sat there for a while to think about the decision. "College preparatory must be harder than general education classes," I said as I pondered what to do. Slowly, I began erasing my general education selections and checked college-preparatory classes. *If I go to college, I'll prove Mother wrong. Maybe I can amount to something. Maybe I won't have to dig ditches*, I thought. I returned the form to Mrs. Williams, who said, "Mike, I believe you've made the right decision."

CHAPTER 23

ENTERTAINMENT

After our move to Oakley, my primary source of entertainment came from all the activity on Cypress Drive and the
surrounding area. From that first day, the amount of television I
watched declined dramatically. The regular interaction with all
the other children made me the happiest I had ever been. Still,
television, music, and the movies were influential. Sometimes I
still watched the Saturday cartoon programs, if nothing else was
happening that morning.

Mother watched these primetime shows: *Ben Casey*, *The Andy
Williams Show*, *Peyton Place*, *Dr. Kildare*, *The Red Skelton Hour*, and
The Dean Martin Show. Daddy didn't watch many of these programs
since he was gone much of the time, but when home, he had negative things to say about *Peyton Place*.

"That show's too worldly. There's too much talk about sex. I
can't believe such trash is on television," Daddy said. Still, his opinion didn't keep Mother from watching the program. I didn't watch
Peyton Place because it was a soap opera.

About the only TV Daddy saw on a regular basis was boxing.
While he watched any match that came on, he mainly followed the
heavyweight division. Floyd Patterson was Daddy's favorite fighter.

He was disappointed when Sonny Liston knocked Patterson out to gain the heavyweight title on September 25, 1962, and again on July 22, 1963, in a rematch. Daddy disliked Cassius Clay even more than he did Liston. Thus, when Sonny Liston defended his title against Clay on February 25, 1964, Daddy was for Liston.

In that fight, Cassius Clay knocked out Liston in the seventh round to become the heavyweight champion. In the rematch on May 25, 1964, Muhammad Ali, who had changed his name from Cassius Clay, beat Liston in the first round to retain the title. This fight was very controversial since no one saw the knockout punch. It wasn't visible to television viewers or spectators at the arena.

Daddy said, "Someone fixed that fight. They paid a lot of money for Liston to go down like that. Cassius Clay or Muhammad Ali—or whatever his name is—is a fraud!"

My favorite shows included *The Andy Griffith Show*, *The Beverly Hillbillies*, and *McHale's Navy*. Late on Friday nights, Mother also let us watch *Twilight Zone* and *The Alfred Hitchcock Hour*. "I don't care if you watch those scary programs, but don't be coming to my bedroom door telling me you can't sleep afterward," she said.

Bonanza also continued to be a Sunday night staple, if we got home in time from McDonald's or Burger King. Other Sunday night shows I liked but rarely saw because I attended evening church services included *The Jetsons*, *Dennis the Menace*, *Lassie*, and *Walt Disney's Wonderful World of Color*. *The Ed Sullivan Show* was another one of these programs. On many Sunday nights, the show featured singing groups and artists I had come to enjoy. The Beatles were the greatest group to appear. On February 9, 1964, I missed the Beatles' American debut singing their number-one hit "I Want to Hold Your Hand" on *The Ed Sullivan Show*. It marked the beginning of the British Invasion in American music. I also missed their follow-up performances on February 16 and February 23. I heard about them from Gene, Jack, and David.

They immediately went out and purchased 45 rpm vinyl records of all the Beatles' songs.

Daddy didn't like the Beatles. He complained that their music was ruining the country, just as Elvis Presley's was. Still, he wasn't as vocal in his opposition as he was with Elvis. Daddy never prohibited us from listening to this group or, for that matter, any other rock band or artist.

When we had the money, we bought the Beatles' records and other singles. We also watched *American Bandstand* without having to be wary of Daddy, as he began to see the futility of his opposition. Rock music became an increasingly important influence in the lives of the Willis boys.

Music in the early part of the 1960s had a different sound from that ushered in by the British Invasion of 1964. Hits before 1964 included songs such as "He's So Fine" by the Chiffons, "Go Away Little Girl" by Steve Lawrence, and "The End of the World" by Skeeter Davis. "The Stripper" by David Rose and His Orchestra was popular when we first moved to Oakley. Daddy thought the song was decadent even though it was only an instrumental. "Any music played for women to strip off their clothes is not fit for the ears," Daddy said, as the song played on the radio, but he didn't turn it off, even as we laughed and pretended to strip off our clothes.

Also, just before Halloween in 1962, "Monster Mash" by Bobby "Boris" Picket & the Crypt-Kickers hit the top of the chart. This song played over and over in my head as our group set out that Halloween evening.

The Beatles were the first in a wave of bands from Britain, including Herman's Hermits, the Animals, the Birds, the Mindbenders, and the Rolling Stones. American groups like the Supremes, the 4 Seasons, the Four Tops, the Temptations, the Impressions, and the

Beach Boys remained popular also, but the British Invasion had become the predominant force in American music. Individual artists from past years such as Elvis Presley, Rick Nelson, and Bobby Vinton also remained popular but clearly began to fade, although Elvis eventually staged a comeback. Bob Dylan, a musical force of his own, recorded "Like a Rolling Stone."

For Christmas in 1963, Mother and Daddy got Johnny, Randy, and me transistor radios. They arrived just in time for us to hear a steady diet of all the British Invaders' songs and those of the other favorite musical groups and artists of the era. Gene, Jack, and David had already acquired these portable devices. Our radios finally brought us up to their standing. I tuned my transistor radio, which had a nine-volt battery, to any of the local AM stations. In case I dropped it, the radio included a leather carrying case to protect it from damage. I took my radio everywhere and listened to it all the time, especially as I rode my bicycle throughout Oakley. Having a transistor radio strapped to one's bike was considered a status symbol.

Daddy also bought a new stereo, which replaced our aging record player. With its arrival, we could listen to our favorite music singles and 33 LP albums. The new technology produced a much better sound quality than the old record player, and the stylus was made of a diamond chip, meaning it never had to be replaced. The stylus also had a spring-like quality that allowed the head to bounce up and down on the record if it was accidentally dropped, without scratching the vinyl. The spindle could be stacked to allow several singles or albums to be played mechanically and consecutively without having to change them out.

⟻⊹ ⊹⟼

Before we moved to Oakley, I had not given much consideration to going to the movies. It never occurred to me that this form of entertainment was for children too. After our move, I soon discovered that all my new friends were into movies. Now and then they boarded a City of Asheville bus that stopped at the intersection of Merchant Street and Cypress Drive and rode downtown to the Plaza Theater located on Pack Square.

We always wanted to go with Gene, Jack, and David, but Daddy said no. "Going to the movies is a sin. I'll not allow my children to go into a den of iniquity," he said. Daddy's attitude was hardened even more on August 5, 1962, with the death of Marilyn Monroe. I heard the news from David Garland. "Did you hear? Marilyn Monroe died today!" he said.

"Who's Marilyn Monroe?" I asked.

"You don't know who Marilyn Monroe is? Why she's the most beautiful actress in Hollywood!" David informed me. "She was only thirty-six years old."

All the boys on Cypress Drive went into mourning. They couldn't believe this beautiful young actress had died. I was upset too, although I had just learned about her.

Marilyn Monroe's death from an apparent suicide validated all of Daddy's suspicions about the movie industry. "That's what happens to a person when they don't have God in their life," he said.

We didn't take Daddy's "no" about the movies for an answer, as we kept asking every time our friends departed for the Plaza Theater. "Daddy, all the boys are going to see *The Sword in the Stone*. It's a Walt Disney cartoon movie. Can we go too? Please!" I asked. Disney released the animated film to theaters on December 25, 1963.

"You know what I think about going to the movies," Daddy replied.

"John, it's a Walt Disney children's film!" Mother interjected.

Taken aback by Mother's support for our cause, Daddy finally agreed, "Okay, this time. But don't be thinking it will become a regular habit." We were given money for tickets, popcorn, and

Cokes. We went on the bus with Gene, Jack, and David. They were very familiar with the Asheville bus system and knew where to board and exit. We had an enjoyable time at the movies. It was the first time I had ever seen a moving picture in color. I sat in awe. After seeing *The Sword in the Stone*, we got to return to the theater to see others. All the boys liked to go and stay all afternoon, watching the featured movie over and over. Moviegoing was a great new experience, but it was a rare, special treat for the Willis boys due to the cost.

CHAPTER 24

ROAD TRIPS

Once we moved to Oakley, our family road trips diminished dramatically. With all the time and pressure involved in pastoring a large church, Daddy simply didn't have the time for this kind of activity. My siblings and I also had less interest in traveling the mountainsides. Instead, we preferred to spend the time with our friends near home. We still occasionally went on day-trips, but not as often as we had at Mount Hope.

In Buncombe County, we traveled atop Beaucatcher Mountain for a hilly ride right in the heart of Asheville. We then came down and went along Tunnel Road through Beaucatcher Tunnel, which was the only way city traffic could get through the mountain. Next, we drove over to Black Mountain and Montreat, the hometown of Billy Graham.

In the outlying counties, we visited Chimney Rock, Lake Lure, Grandfather Mountain, Mount Mitchell, and Linville Caverns. At Grandfather Mountain, I tried to traverse the mile-high swinging bridge but found the swaying overpass too treacherous to cross. Driving from town to town was still the only way to get to these majestic sites since the construction of Interstate 40 and Interstate 26 had just commenced. Also, the Blue Ridge Parkway was still under construction.

We also visited Mother's and Daddy's families, with trips to see Grandmother and Granddaddy Willis and Aunt Winifred in Canton and to see Aunt Dorcas in Sylva. They sometimes visited us also at the Oakley Baptist Church parsonage. We drove across town to West Asheville, where we visited with Daddy's sister, Aunt Ardith; her husband, Zenith; and cousins Gary and Danny Keylon. Cousin Vickie from Virginia occasionally came to stay with us. She was Aunt Naomi's daughter, Daddy's sister. Vickie was closer in age to Elaine and Gloria than to Johnny, Randy, and me. Daddy also had family in Baltimore, Maryland, and during our first summer in Oakley, Aunt Clara and her family, including Cousin Billy Fisher, came down to visit. They stayed with Grandmother and Granddaddy Willis but came to visit us at the parsonage. Billy was close to my age. I had not seen him since 1956 at our grandparent's fiftieth wedding anniversary. When I introduced Billy to Gene, Jack, and David, they made fun of his Yankee accent. At the time, I didn't know just how upset this teasing had made him. When Aunt Clara left, she invited us to visit them the next summer in Baltimore, an invitation Daddy accepted.

In July 1963, we began our trip to Baltimore. It was fortunate Daddy had bought the 1960 Dodge Matador since it took every inch of its space to carry our family of ten and all our luggage. In fact, Daddy had to tie the luggage to the top of the car in a rooftop cargo carrier he had borrowed. We also made use of several borrowed suitcases to hold all the clothing. We traveled east into the North Carolina Piedmont before turning north into Virginia. We had to make numerous gasoline, food, and bathroom stops. After one of these breaks, we loaded up and headed out. Once we got down the highway a little distance, someone asked, "Where's Dawn?"

"She's not here. Stop the car!" Elaine yelled. Daddy slammed on the brakes and pulled off the road to turn around, but before he could reverse direction, we saw little six-year-old Dawn running down the highway toward the car. She was screaming and in tears. From then on, Daddy took a headcount after every stop.

In Virginia, when we stopped at restrooms, restaurants, or water fountains, I saw signs that said, "Whites Only," "Colored," or "Colored at This Window." Such markers were around Asheville too, but I had never paid attention to them before. I asked Daddy, "What do the signs mean?"

"Colored people and whites are not allowed to use the same facilities. The law says they have to be kept separate," he replied.

"I've never seen signs like that at home," I said.

"Well, they're there, but every state is different, and even one city is distinct from another when it comes to segregation," he explained. "Virginia happens to have some of the strictest laws in the country."

"What about Little League? Our Elks team had colored boys on it this year. Do they have baseball teams with both colored and white kids here?" I asked.

"It's not likely."

"I like Virginia's laws. I like segregation. I don't think niggers and whites should be together!" Mother said. "Martin Luther King Jr. and that bunch are about to destroy this nation with all their marching and protesting. They ought to send them all back to Africa."

"As I've said before, I disagree with how these civil rights people are going about things—all that civil disobedience and such. It's dangerous for the country," Daddy replied. "Some say the Communists are behind King, and maybe they are. I can't support what he's doing. He does have a point, though. Everyone, regardless of the color of their skin, is equal in the eyes of God. After all, God created us all."

Mother was referring to earlier in the spring, to April 16, 1963, when police had put Martin Luther King Jr. in jail during anti-segregation protests in Birmingham, Alabama. She was also referring to May, when, as the protests continued in Birmingham, police had used brutal tactics such as fire hoses and police dogs on African American demonstrators. While these tactics were popular among many white Southerners like Mother, the images of brutality shown on television engendered support for the civil rights movement throughout much of the rest of the country and the world. Mother also had in mind an event in June, right before our trip, when a Mississippi NAACP field secretary by the name of Medgar Evers was murdered outside his home. All these events had created fear among many Southern whites, including Mother, who were intolerant, and concern among others, like Daddy, who had a more moderate stand on racial issues but thought the unrest was risky.

Added to this worry was anxiety about an upcoming protest in Washington, DC, in August, a march against discrimination. Martin Luther King Jr. and his supporters were determined to overturn Jim Crow laws, prominent throughout the south and in other parts of the country. The term *Jim Crow* came from an old minstrel show in which a white actor blackened his face and danced a jig to an old tune that contained the name. Over time, the expression began to be used to refer to African Americans in general. These laws had mandated *de jure* racial segregation in all public facilities for almost a hundred years, and they required a supposedly "separate but equal" status for African Americans. Instead, the laws led to treatment and accommodations that were inferior to those of whites. My mother believed there should be no change and that the civil rights movement was going to tear down the fabric of our society. Daddy was more measured, thinking a change was necessary but should come without disrupting civil order.

205

When we got to Washington, DC, we met Uncle Rudolph, one of Daddy's brothers, and ate at a restaurant he had chosen. "Now you children can order anything you want," Uncle Rudolph told us.

I ordered, but Mother said, "Mike, you can't have that. It's too expensive."

"Now, Mildred, let him have what he wants. I wouldn't have brought you here if I couldn't afford it," he said. I got what I wanted. After lunch, we took a short tour of Washington, DC, where we saw the White House, the Capitol, and most of the prominent monuments. We also stopped at the Smithsonian Institution, where we saw dinosaur bones, space rockets, and space capsules.

When we arrived in Maryland, the family split up. Half stayed with Uncle Robert Lee, Daddy's oldest brother, while the other half stayed with Aunt Clara. They both lived in the Baltimore area. Johnny, Randy, and I stayed with Aunt Clara and Cousin Billy. Billy was very interested in playing with us but first arranged a surprise for Johnny, Randy, and me to settle an old score. A group of his friends had gathered to make fun of our southern accents. Billy intended to retaliate for the teasing he had endured the previous summer from Gene, Jack, and David, which we hadn't tried to stop. When Johnny and I became aware of these boys' intentions, we warned them not to do it. "Don't you say anything else about how I talk," Johnny said.

"Yes, we don't want any trouble here, so don't be making fun," I warned.

Billy and his friends, sensing a fight was about to commence, stopped joking. From then on, we had no more trouble during our stay in Baltimore. In fact, we had fun.

Near Aunt Clara's was a beach situated along the Chesapeake Bay. "Let's go swimming," Billy said, and off we went. "This is a private beach. Only members and the guests they bring are permitted here," Billy said as we arrived.

"Why is it private?" I asked.

"To keep colored people from swimming," Billy replied. "According to the law, that's the only way we can prevent them from coming. No one wants to swim with colored people!" We had a wonderful time swimming in the salty water, although as usual, I got sunburned. I found it easier to swim in salt water than in fresh water.

The next day, the family took a driving tour of the Baltimore area, including a ferryboat ride across the Chesapeake Bay. At first, the ride was fun, but as the waves churned and the time passed, I became sick. "Daddy, I feel like throwing up. What's wrong?" I asked.

"You're seasick. The motion of the waves is causing it," Daddy replied.

I vomited by the time we got to shore. "I don't ever want to ride on a ferryboat again!" I said after my recovery.

On our trip home, we stopped in Jamestown and Williamsburg, Virginia; we also visited Newport News, Virginia, where we saw Mother's brother, Uncle Joe Parks, who worked at a ship dock. He had settled there after serving in the navy. It was the first and last time I ever met Uncle Joe. After a whirlwind week, we finally arrived back in Oakley. It was the only out-of-state vacation the family ever took. Following our trip, on August 28, 1963, the March on Washington was held to express support for civil and economic rights for African Americans. As many as two hundred thousand or three hundred thousand attended the march as Martin Luther King Jr. delivered what became a famous speech. In it, he said, "I have a dream that one day this nation will rise up and live out the true meaning of its creed: 'We hold these truths to be self-evident, that all men are created equal.'"

The effect of the speech and the march were electrifying and helped lead to support for passage of the Civil Rights Act of 1964, which banned all Jim Crow laws and prohibited discrimination. It also propelled the passage of the Voting Rights Act of 1965 banning discriminatory voting practices, which had been responsible for denying many African Americans this right.

This piece of legislation had previously been given momentum by the ratification of the Twenty-Fourth Amendment to the US Constitution on January 23, 1964. It abolished the poll tax, which had made it difficult for poor African-Americans to vote. Mother wasn't happy with these changes, while Daddy believed they were necessary.

CHAPTER 25

THE OAKLEY PARSONAGE

At the Oakley parsonage, some things changed, and some things remained the same. Instead of an eight-party line, we had a private telephone line, and instead of burning the trash in a fifty-five-gallon steel drum, we set out trash twice a week for a garbage truck to pick up. Streetlights dotted all the streets as opposed to the pitch darkness of the Mount Hope countryside, and all the streets were paved, unlike many of the back roads in Cartoogechaye.

Snow days from school continued, but they were much more enjoyable since we had a whole neighborhood of children with which to play. One year we missed an entire month of school because of snow. It was great fun to be out of school that long, but when spring arrived, I didn't like the Saturday make-up days or the extension of the school year into the middle of June.

Our backyard became the gathering place for children to bring their sleds, as we trampled a flat track down the hill for everyone's use. Those winter months also brought a severe outbreak of the flu. In fact, Mother became so ill Daddy called a doctor, who made a house call. The doctor came carrying a black leather medical bag. After announcing that Mother had influenza, he gave her some medication. Still, the disease had to run its course. After Mother had become sick, almost all my siblings got the flu too. Fortunately, I didn't.

When we first arrived in Oakley, Daddy was still giving the boys haircuts at home with his clippers. Gene, Jack, David, and most of the other boys got their haircuts at a barbershop located on Fairview Road. One day I went with David to the barbershop. It was the first time I had ever been inside one. After that day, I begged Daddy to let me have my hair clipped there.

"No, son, I can't afford to pay to have your hair cut when I can do it at home for free."

"What if I use my money? Can I get it trimmed by the barber then?" I asked.

"Sure, but where are you going to get the money?"

"I'll pick up soft drink bottles!" I said. I combed the nearby streets until I had accumulated enough cash to pay the barber.

"Dad-gum, you did it!" Daddy said when I came home sporting my new haircut. After that, he gave the Willis boys money to go to the barbershop.

One day our washing machine stopped working. This appliance was essential to a family of ten, and Mother soon had laundry stacked up, since she washed several loads a day. The solution was to go to a nearby Laundromat. "Mike, I need you to come and help me with the laundry. I want you to watch it while I return to the house to do chores," Mother told me. I agreed to go. She loaded many washing machines and gave me instructions. "When you see the washers begin to agitate, place a cupful of detergent in the machines." Mother and Daddy left me alone with the laundry. When the machines filled with water, I put a cup of detergent in each. I then sat back and waited for them to stop. Once they finished,

I thought my job was complete, but to my surprise, the machines began to fill with water again and agitate. I poured detergent in each machine a second time. After the second cycle, the machines stopped and didn't start again.

I was proud of myself for completing this job. When Mother returned and started taking the clothes out of the washers, she discovered they were still very sudsy.

"Mike, what have you done?" she asked.

"Nothing. I put the detergent in the machines just as you told me."

"Did you put soap in once or twice?"

"Twice. Remember you told me to put the detergent in after the washers filled up, and they filled up twice."

"The second one was the rinse. It wasn't supposed to have detergent!" She took the clothes out of the washers. Because she didn't have enough money to run the machines again, Mother took the clothes home and hand rinsed each garment. I didn't get into trouble since Mother blamed herself for not giving me better instructions.

I began to pay attention to the neighborhood girls, and one caught my eye. When I was twelve years old, Debbie Lee became my girlfriend. We had been friends from the time I moved to Oakley. She was blond and cute, and we got along well. Debbie began attending Oakley Baptist Church with me, and even though I was the preacher's son, I rode the church bus each Sunday morning just to be with her. As the bus picked up the other neighborhood children, Debbie and I held hands and talked. We had an excellent time.

Her father didn't like me at all. When I went to see her, he always became angry and threatening. At first, I ignored his intimidations, but over time, they became unbearable and wore me down. "I've got enough trouble at home without having to deal with your Daddy, too," I told Debbie. "We'll have to break up, but we'll remain friends." She agreed since we had always been friends anyway. She was a sweet girl.

Just as they had done at Mount Hope, from time to time, my parents left Elaine in charge and went shopping. Each time, Johnny, Randy, and I did our best to torture Elaine, a custom we had started at Mount Hope. One day, while Mother and Daddy were gone, Elaine was especially insistent we obey her commands. She became very upset when we destroyed an old doll, tearing it limb from limb.

"You boys ought to be ashamed of yourselves for tearing up that doll," Elaine protested.

"It was old, and Deborah and Dawn don't even play with it anymore," I replied. After Elaine had gotten through reprimanding us, I said, "Hey, Randy, I've got a plan."

"What is it?" he asked.

"See these doll eyeballs? Let's play a trick on Elaine." The eyeballs were half-spherical, hollow objects, a little smaller than Ping-Pong balls. When you placed the plastic eyeballs over your eyes and squinted, they stayed in place. The blue eyes stared out in a horrific manner. I showed Randy how they worked.

"Ooh! It looks like your eyeballs have bugged out of your head," he said.

"Great! Now put them over yours, and I'll cause a commotion like we're fighting. It'll get Elaine in here, and when she comes, act like you're crying. Keep your hands over your eyes, and say, 'Mike hit me in the eyes.' Keep repeating that and crying until she sees the eyeballs," I instructed.

"That's a good plan," Randy said. He pretended to cry, and Elaine came running.

"What's going on here? What's the matter, Randy?" she asked.

"Mike hit me in the eyes! Mike hit me in the eyes!" Randy bellowed.

"Let me see!" Elaine said as she pulled Randy's hands away from his face. "Oh, God, no! Oh, God. Oh, God, no!" she screeched in horror. "You've blinded him; you've blinded him!" she yelled. Just as it looked like Elaine was passing out, Randy took off the doll eyeballs, and the two of us rolled in laughter.

"You're the meanest boys that have ever lived. I'm telling Mother and Daddy when they get home!" Elaine said as she stomped off.

Turbulence continued in our household. The pressure of a large church was too much for both my parents, creating madness and uncertainty at home. They were miserable. Exacerbating this turmoil were financial pressures that grew as the years went by. When we moved to Oakley, Daddy's weekly salary rose from $60 to $100. During the four years we lived there, it went up to $125 per week. But while it seemed to be quite an increase, the family was barely getting by since the church had limited the number of revivals Daddy could conduct, which in turn reduced his earning potential. There was also an increasing demand for more of every-thing because the Willis siblings were growing older. Daddy sold the 1960 Dodge Matador and replaced it with an old 1956 Dodge Custom Royal. It was embarrassing to go from a modern-looking station wagon that seated all the family comfortably to an older and smaller automobile that we all had to pile into. Daddy was frustrated at church, as he was pulled in all directions trying to perform all his pastoral duties. He felt suffocated and restricted by all the responsibilities. Mother felt the pressure too.

"I wish I were dead," Mother moaned and cried as she went about her housework. Their abusive behavior toward my siblings and me, which had always been bad, intensified as these pressures continued to mount. If it was possible for Mother to whip us more, she did. At the same time, Daddy's whippings became more violent. His brutality was demonstrated to me one day when I returned from the store without a ten-dollar bill that he had given me to buy an item for supper.

"Now this is the only ten dollars to my name, so make sure you bring me the change," he said. David Garland and I headed to the closest store on Fairview Road, using a shortcut. We took a trail through a field behind Nanny and Pawpaw's house. Once we had gotten through the area, I realized I had dropped the money somewhere along the path.

"David, I've lost the ten-dollar bill. Daddy will kill me if I return home without it! Help me look," I said. We did a desperate search for the money, looking along the path over and over to no avail. I was panic-stricken. Finally, giving up, I returned home to face Daddy. "Daddy, I lost the money! I've looked everywhere for it. I looked and looked and looked," I said.

"Yes, I bet you looked for it! Let's go into your bedroom," he said. "Now, I'm going to give you an incentive to go back and get that ten-dollar bill." He told me to stretch out against the foot of the bunk beds with my arms and legs held far apart. At first, he used his belt, whipping me across the back and legs, but as his anger grew, he dispensed with the belt and began punching, hitting, and kicking me repeatedly. Then he started throwing me all over the room and slamming my head against the wall. "Now get out of here and don't come back without that money!" Daddy demanded.

Crying profusely, I headed out the door looking for David. "We've got to find the ten-dollar bill, or I can't go home again," I told him in tears. David was quite startled at the sight of me. Besides the bruises and bleeding, he had never seen me cry before.

"I'll help you look again," David said as we headed off into the field. We retraced the path once again, looking in all the places we had looked before. Finally, I saw a green piece of paper hidden in a clump of grass. It was the ten-dollar bill. Perhaps panic during the earlier search had prevented me from seeing what now seemed so obvious. "Thank God. Now I won't be killed!" I said to David. When I got home, I handed the ten-dollar bill to Daddy.

"That's just what I thought. Don't ever try to steal money from me again!" Daddy said with a slight smile of satisfaction coming over his face.

This beating wasn't an isolated incident. It seemed as though Daddy was determined to beat the hell out of me. In one incident, I received a fractured finger. He didn't take me to the doctor, and it took several weeks to heal. In another encounter, Daddy severely bruised my tailbone. I could hardly walk for several days. After that, Daddy was more careful with his beatings, stopping if he thought he had seriously injured me. Noticing this change of behavior, I began to fake an injury to stop a whipping. Still, I was careful not to overuse the strategy to avoid tipping Daddy off to what I was doing. Instead, I reserved a feigned injury for the most severe attacks.

The madness at home drove seventeen-year-old Elaine, who was a senior, to elope in November 1963, just before President Kennedy's assassination. After we had moved to Oakley, Daddy had tried to prevent Elaine from dating, just as he had done in Franklin. He followed her in his car as she walked to Oakley Elementary each morning to catch a ride on the bus to Reynolds High School.

"Daddy, why don't you just give me a lift to school rather than follow me every morning?" Elaine said, which only made things worse for her. At church, the embarrassment of Elaine's leaving home to marry was almost too much for Mother and Daddy to endure. The next year, sixteen-year-old Gloria announced she intended to be married. To avoid a repeat embarrassment, Daddy gave his consent.

Jim Crayton and Gloria exchanged vows in December 1964. At first, Jim and Gloria tried to make it on their own, but the expenses of maintaining a home were far greater than their income. By the end of 1965, Jim and Gloria, who was now pregnant, came to live with us at the parsonage, taking Daddy's study as their bedroom. The tension was thick after they arrived. Mother resented them being there, and she didn't appreciate Gloria not helping with the housework.

"Gloria, get up and give me some help," Mother would implore.

"I'm too ill to help. It must be morning sickness."

Mother got mad and vented her anger to Daddy saying, "Gloria refuses to help me!"

"I'll just see about that," he said as he headed to Gloria's room. "Get out of that bed and help your mother!" he demanded.

"I can't. My stomach is too upset," Gloria said.

"Get out of the bed now!" Daddy said as he took his belt off and began whipping Gloria. "No young'un of mine is going to disobey me if they live under my roof, married or unmarried, pregnant or not."

Jim was working at the time, but when he returned, he and Gloria packed up their things and left. News of the incident went swirling through the church congregation, and for the next several months, Daddy engaged in a huge endeavor of damage control. The charm and warmth Daddy displayed toward his congregation made it difficult for most to believe what they had heard regarding the episode, preferring the more sanitized version offered by their pastor. In the end, Daddy had gone too far. His pastorate at Oakley Baptist Church came to an end. His supporters were in the majority, but it was the more vocal minority that prevailed. When the uproar subsided, Daddy called for a vote of confidence to be conducted at a business meeting held for that sole purpose. He won it overwhelmingly. Following the election, Daddy promptly resigned, telling the congregation he was called to pastor Edgewood Baptist Church.

The four years we lived in Oakley, my group of friends was unchanging. Gene was our leader, just entering high school as a freshman upon our arrival. When we left, he was still the head of our group, a graduating senior. The rest of us kept our places in the pecking order too. It seemed that time had stood still. No one new had joined our group, and no one had left. For me, Oakley proved to be a critical period in defining who I was and what I was to become in the future. I had moved to Oakley as a country boy, excited about the prospect of life in the city. I left as a streetwise, experienced teen whose worldview had changed forever.

CHAPTER 26

EDGEWOOD

Edgewood Baptist Church was in Enka, a few miles west of Asheville. Even though our new home was in the county and not in the city of Asheville, I felt good about the move once I knew we were still in Buncombe County, as I didn't think there was much difference between the two. Instead of attending Reynolds High School, home of the Rockets, I was to attend Enka High School, home of the Jets. We moved in June 1966 before the school year was finished, which meant Daddy had to get permission for us to finish out at Oakley Elementary School. Once the go-ahead came, he drove us all the way across town for the last few weeks until the school term ended. I was fourteen years old and finishing up the eighth grade.

The church stood atop a hill, north of the Enka Plant. The parsonage was a wood-framed, odd-shaped structure resulting from additions to the back and side. On the hillside between the church and the parsonage was a terraced cemetery, owned and maintained by the church. To attend services, Johnny, Randy, and I walked straight up the hill through the cemetery, while the other family members rode the short distance with Daddy in his car.

Edgewood Baptist Church was half the size of the Oakley church, with upward of three hundred attendees at the Sunday morning worship services. The architecture was cross-shaped with red brick and white trim and included a tall steeple that rose high in the sky due to its location atop the hill. The church didn't have a baptismal pool, which meant Daddy performed this ordinance in nearby Enka Lake, the way he preferred. The church services were less formal than they had been at Oakley and there was no written order of service, which Daddy was glad to discard. Edgewood used both the *Broadman Hymnal* and the *Church Hymnal* in their song services, another improvement from Daddy's perspective. He always thought the *Baptist Hymnal* used at Oakley was too proper.

Daddy's salary was unchanged at $125 per week. It was a smaller church, but more importantly for Daddy, Edgewood didn't impose a limit on the number of revivals he could conduct, and he didn't have to maintain regular office hours.

For Daddy, the pressures of Oakley Baptist Church were finally off him. Mother, in turn, seemed to be happier at Edgewood too. Their happier moods then made life a little easier for my siblings and me, at least for a time.

At Edgewood, I became more involved in church activities, something I had gotten away from at the Oakley church. My interest was due in large part to Mr. Lingelbach, the youth Sunday school teacher. He presented lessons in an interesting way. He dispensed with the *Southern Baptist Quarterly* my teachers had always used before and prepared original teachings. His stories were full of life. I thought I could listen to him all day. Also, the process of getting to know a whole new group of friends was exciting to me. My interest in Mr. Lingelbach's daughter also significantly contributed to my renewed interest in church.

Mr. Lingelbach's family was full of talented singers. His two daughters and one of his sons sang as a trio. They were marvelous. Denise, the youngest daughter, was a year younger than I was. I was smitten by her charm, good looks, and dark hair and eyes, and I began to pursue her to be my girlfriend, a chase I briefly won. I had not had a girlfriend since Debbie Lee, two years prior. With

Debbie, maintaining a relationship had not been difficult. After all, she lived nearby; we were more like friends. It was always easy to talk to Debbie.

Denise was wonderful. I became intoxicated by her presence, and her scent was incredible. No, it wasn't perfume! It was a pleasant, appealing, delightful aroma that I could never figure out. I never noticed it on any other girl. With Denise, I didn't have the luxury of her living close to me. The only time I saw her was at church. The problem with our relationship might have been overcome using the telephone, but I found talking on it to be awkward. There was a deeper dilemma, too. I simply found it complicated to communicate with Denise. Speaking to her was uncomfortable, a new problem I had never had before. I wanted to connect, to share, but I couldn't express myself, a situation I found perplexing. This awkwardness produced lots of anxiety for me, which only made matters worse, and apparently, the uncertainty was too much for Denise. It wasn't very long before she broke up with me, which was a crushing blow. My trouble with Denise was a precursor to my dilemma with girls throughout my high school years.

At the Oakley church, southern gospel music had played little role in the services, since the members preferred more traditional hymns and inspirational songs. At Edgewood, the congregation embraced southern gospel music, which made Daddy jubilant. On Sunday nights, Edgewood frequently hosted local southern gospel groups. The Kingsmen Quartet from Asheville and the Inspirations from Bryson City were the two most famous groups that performed. It was into this more conservative, fundamentalist church environment that the Jesus controversy erupted in August 1966, when one of the Beatles, John Lennon, said his group had become more popular than Jesus.

Some members of Edgewood advocated burning all the Beatles albums and records. They were outraged. The anger continued even after John Lennon apologized for his remarks, explaining that others had quoted him out of context. I was upset, fearing Daddy would forbid me to listen to my favorite rock band. Surprisingly, he was restrained in his opinion, believing like a minority of other ministers did that Lennon's statement was, unfortunately, correct.

That summer at Edgewood Baptist Church, Daddy went back to his roots by participating in an open-air tabernacle revival, an annual event held by the Baptist churches in the area. He required that we also attend. I had never been to one of these meetings before, although I had heard Daddy talk about them. The music was loud, the crowd was emotional, and the singing went on for a very long time. I had witnessed a milder version of this kind of service years earlier at the Mount Hope Baptist Church revivals. The open-slatted benches were hard and reminded me of the ones in James Chapel, which I had attended with Daddy when I was a child. The whole place was dusty from the fresh sawdust that had been put down for this yearly event. Shouting, weeping, and many other forms of emotion were displayed. Daddy was taken up in this whirlwind of passion too, enjoying every minute of it. Before the evening was over, many perspiring Baptists were rolling in the sawdust—something Daddy had told me only Pentecostals did. My siblings and I sat back in amazement.

When we were not at church, there were plenty of other activities around the Edgewood parsonage. The neighborhood in which we lived was full of children, and it didn't take long for our yard to draw in most of them. When we moved, I missed Gene, Jack, David, and the others at Cypress Drive. The loss, though, was offset by all the new friends I acquired from the church and neighborhood. We played with kids in our yard from sunup to sundown.

That summer Grandmother and Granddaddy Willis celebrated their sixtieth wedding anniversary, an occasion that prompted all their children to come together for the first time in ten years. Unlike their fiftieth held at Plains Methodist Church, this anniversary was at my grandparents' home in Canton. It was great to see first cousins whom I had seen only a few times before. At this event, Uncle Robert Lee gave Daddy a deep freezer that required him to make plans to travel to Baltimore to pick it up.

"Jim, I'll have to borrow your pickup truck," Daddy said to my brother-in-law.

"Preacher, I'll just take you," Jim said.

"I want to go too. Can I?" I pleaded.

"Sure, but you may have to ride in the back. That truck cab is awfully small," Daddy said.

Shortly after the anniversary, Daddy, Jim, and I headed off to Baltimore to get the freezer. Daddy and Jim alternated driving, while Jim and I alternated riding in the truck bed. Except for a stop at the White House, we quickly drove through Washington, DC, in the old 1952 International pickup, looking at all the monuments. At the White House, we took our time gazing through the fence from every angle possible.

In Baltimore, we stayed only a few days. In addition to visiting Uncle Robert Lee, we also visited Aunt Clara. At her house, Jim and I decided to go swimming in the Chesapeake Bay—the same place where Cousin Billy had taken Johnny, Randy, and me three years earlier.

"What happened to the gate? Why is no one checking your membership?" I asked Billy.

"It's an open beach now. The law changed. They won't allow private clubs here anymore," he said.

On our trip home, Jim and I again switched out riding in the truck bed, and he and Daddy again switched out driving.

At the Edgewood parsonage, I resumed my mowing chores. I found this new parsonage yard uneven and difficult to mow. It was important for me to take my time. One week, without warning, I hit a rough spot. Gravel and rocks flew everywhere, and lots of dust was stirred up. I also felt a blow, as if someone had slapped me in the stomach. At the same time, the mower stalled from what I thought to be the object I had hit. Looking around, I wondered what it was. When I pulled up my shirt, I observed a bright-red stripe about two inches wide marked across my stomach. Lying at my feet was the mower's blade. I picked it up and compared the broad side of the blade to the mark on my body. It was the identical size.

"Daddy, the mower's blade hit me in the stomach."

"Now, how can that be? How could the blade get out from under the mower?"

"Compare the mark with the flat part of the blade. What else could it be?" I said. He didn't have an explanation. He just fixed the mower. I finished the job and was grateful I had not been killed.

⟞⊹ ⊹⟝

One of the boys who came around wasn't very nice to Randy, bullying him all the time.

"Mother, Harry hit me again," Randy would complain. "I can't ride my bike without him chasing me. What can I do?" This situation continued for a period. Harry was my age but taller than I was and perhaps thirty pounds heavier. He was a big boy.

"Mike, the next time Harry hits Randy, I want you to whip him. Do you understand me? You beat him up!" Mother demanded.

"All right, Mother, I'll take care of it," I said.

The very next day Randy came running to the house. "Harry punched me again, just now!" he said. I jumped on my bicycle and rode to the end of the driveway where Harry was standing.

"Why did you hit Randy?" I asked, but before he could respond, I struck. With one swift left hook, I sent Harry to his knees. It was a perfect punch that landed on his nose and upper lip. Blood gushed from both, and water poured from Harry's eyes—not because he was crying, but from the pain.

"Don't you ever hit my brother again. Do you understand me, Harry?" I said as I stood over him.

"Yes, now leave me alone, you bully!" He got up and headed home to attend to his injuries. After that, Randy had no more problems from Harry.

⊨⊣ ⊢⊨

One afternoon Daddy confronted me over an issue, and just as he had always done in the past, he approached me in a manner suggesting a whipping or beating was fast approaching. Without thinking, I took a defensive posture and glared at Daddy as if to say, "Do you want to fight me?" It was a stance I had used successfully against opponents in Oakley that had many times stopped a fight before it began. At the age of fourteen, I was now almost as big as Daddy, who was only five feet seven inches tall and wore a size seven shoe. He halted his advance in disbelief. Silently, I stood there holding my ground. I also was in shock about what I had just done but realized it was too late to back down. I waited for Daddy's response, unsure of what was going to happen next.

"No boy of mine should ever think he can whip me! That'll never happen! Do you understand me, son?" he said as he stomped off.

"John, you've raised some tough boys. Maybe too hard. They might be able to whip you!" Mother said. With that, the whippings and beatings inflicted on me by Daddy came to an end. At the time, I didn't understand they had ended. Instead, what unfolded in my relationship with Daddy for the next four years, my high school years, was an uneasy tension, a standoff. For the most part, Mother's whippings ended too, although sometimes she was prone to regress, treating her teenage sons like children. From that time forward, I no longer called my father Daddy but merely Dad. I made the change to emphasize the fact I had grown up.

—≒+ +≒—

During the summer while we lived in the Edgewood parsonage, I began to read the newspaper. Throughout my life, we always had maintained a subscription to the *Asheville Citizen-Times*, but it was only now that I became interested in reading it. For many years, I had been following current events on TV. Reading the newspaper was a natural evolution. My attention stemmed from the growing importance of the Vietnam War, but as I read about it, I also became engaged in all the other current events. I couldn't get enough, reading the newspaper daily from cover to cover.

The Vietnam War had escalated over the past two years, from the time Congress passed the Gulf of Tonkin Resolution on August 7, 1964, in response to sea battles between North Vietnamese naval vessels and the US destroyers *USS Maddox* and *USS Turner*.

The resolution authorized President Johnson to assist the American allies in Southeast Asia by whatever means possible, including the use of conventional armed forces. From the time of the resolution's passage, the Vietnam War had grown rapidly. It had also engendered opposition by university students and by many involved with the civil rights movement, including Martin Luther King Jr. Antiwar activists had held many demonstrations. My support of the war centered on the idea of *containment*, a policy that asserted that the best way to stall the spread of Communism was through military, economic, and diplomatic strategies and by enhancing America's security and influence abroad. Containment was also intended to prevent a domino effect of one country after another in a region of the world falling under Communism's influence.

Repelling North Vietnam's aggression against South Vietnam seemed to fit this policy correctly. I was in complete agreement with what President Johnson was trying to accomplish. My support for the Vietnam War remained steady throughout my high school years, even as the opposition to the war grew, but eventually it waned after I entered college.

In August 1966, I entered Enka High School as a freshman. It was all-white and located about one mile from the parsonage. In the mornings, Johnny and I stood in the aisle for the short ride to the school, since we were the last stop and the bus was full. Likewise, in the afternoons, we stood again, giving those with longer distances to travel the opportunity to sit.

I loved everything about Enka High School. It was a modern facility with bright lights, shiny linoleum floors, and top-notch lockers. Every student was assigned one, even first-year students. I bought a combination lock just for its use. I was excited about changing classes, getting to know all my new classmates, and being a part of such a beautiful place. My satisfaction showed in my report cards, too. I had mostly As and Bs while taking English, algebra, Latin, health, and physical education.

Johnny and I attended the pep rallies and all the football and basketball games. We quickly settled into the school we believed was to be ours for the next four years. Campus life was grand. At Enka High School, I saw, for the first time, a girl wearing a miniskirt. Emily Stanton was the homecoming queen and girlfriend of Richard Donnelly, the captain of the varsity basketball team. She was beautiful and looked very fine in her miniskirt and long, straight blond hair. I was awestruck. She was bolder than most of the other girls at school, although there were others who followed her example. Mostly, the girls wore dresses or skirts that were longer, while the boys wore dress slacks and button-down shirts.

I didn't believe life could get any better than Enka High School. Then suddenly during the Christmas break, it all ended without warning. "Young'uns, I have an announcement to make," Dad said on a Saturday morning. "I've been called to pastor Mount Hope Baptist Church for the second time. We'll be moving the week after Christmas. I'll be making the announcement tomorrow morning at church."

I was devastated. "No, how can you leave a church after only six months? That's not right," I protested. My objections fell on deaf ears.

"I've made the decision, and it's final. All of you get ready to move. We're going back to Franklin."

I was so distraught that I didn't sleep that night. On Sunday morning, when I got up for breakfast, I fainted straight away, landing on the dining room floor and walloping my mouth. I was out cold. Mother and Dad revived me. At church that morning, things were dreadful. As Dad made the announcement, many in the congregation gasped in disbelief.

"Preacher Willis, what did we do to drive you away so soon?" someone asked.

"Nothing, nothing at all. I'm just obeying the voice of the Lord. A man of God must always listen to the master," he replied. I didn't want to return to Mount Hope, Franklin, and country living. My heart was in the city, in Asheville. I didn't believe anything good could come from the move.

CHAPTER 27

RETURN TO MOUNT HOPE

We returned to Mount Hope a few days after Christmas 1966, which allowed us to settle into the parsonage before school started back in January. There had been virtually no change since our departure four and a half years earlier. The church was the same, the parsonage was the same, and Cartoogechaye was the same. I felt like I had traveled back in time.

Attendance at Mount Hope Baptist Church had remained steady at around sixty in Sunday school and one hundred for Sunday morning worship. The same families attended, and all the activities were the same. Dad's salary was $100 per week, up from the weekly salary of $60 he had previously earned at Mount Hope, but considerably less than what he had made at both Oakley and Edgewood. He had taken a step back and had returned to a small rural church, a decision I didn't understand.

At the Mount Hope parsonage, Johnny, Randy, Phillip, and I got the larger bedroom that had previously belonged to the girls, and Deborah and Dawn got the bedroom that had been ours during the first stay.

The home now had a crudely made sidewalk and front door stoop, while concrete had replaced the dirt floor in the basement. The six-foot drop-off at the kitchen door was still there. A propane furnace had replaced the coal-burning stove in the living room, but we still opened the windows to cool the house. Another modern feature was a clothes dryer we brought with us. We had gotten it while we lived in Oakley. Also, the parsonage now had a private telephone line, which replaced the eight-party line that had been there during our first stay. Offsetting these modern advances was a return to some old ways such as having to burn trash again in a fifty-five-gallon steel drum and having to look out at night into pitch darkness because there were no streetlights.

Cartoogechaye Creek was still a prominent feature of the landscape as it continued to meander through the valley, and all the old fishing holes were intact. The trout had patiently waited for us to return to throw in a line, a pastime that had ended once we moved to Oakley. The old logging trails still weaved their way through the woods imploring me to revisit all the places where I once had been. Our most prominent neighbors were still Bob and Cecil Parker, who had continued to run their dairy farm with the assistance of Neil, Bob's son. They had also begun raising beef cattle in our absence, and these cows now roamed the field west of the parsonage that had grown corn during our first stay.

Arrowood Glade was still a place where we went swimming and picnicking, although the Lyndon B. Johnson Job Corps Civilian Conservation Center had been built there during our time away. "When you're at Arrowood swimming, be sure and watch out for all those hoodlums the federal government has brought in there to train. Most are just good-for-nothing juvenile delinquents," Mother said of the Job Corps trainees.

Kiser's Store still stood less than a quarter mile east, and Cartoogechaye Elementary School was still half a mile to the west. An unaltered way of life greeted me on my return to Mount Hope, a fate I feared. I didn't want to be back. I had changed too much.

⇥ ⇤

After the first of the year, Johnny and I enrolled at Franklin High School. We rode the school bus into town along US Highway 64 every morning and took the same route in the afternoon, a five-mile trip each way. The high school was integrated, which was a surprise to me, given the school's rural status. Matthew Wilson, who was in my homeroom, was the first African American student with whom I shared a classroom. Many addressed him as "Mattchew," mimicking the black southern dialect common to the area. I always pronounced his name correctly, believing it was derogatory for whites to use such language when speaking to African Americans, even though Matthew seemed to take it good-naturedly.

Dress at the school was more conservative than at Enka High School. Except for the cheerleading outfits, there were no miniskirts when I arrived. Still, by the time I graduated in 1970, many of the girls were wearing them, six inches above the knee. The girls wore dresses or skirts, while the boys wore dress pants and button-down shirts. Some of the agricultural boys wore blue jeans.

Franklin High School was old and much worn. The main building was a brick, two-story, rectangular, flat-roof facility heated by a coal-burning boiler and cooled by push-out windows. It was dimly lit and had tile flooring. The main entrance and school offices were in the southern portion of the building. The cafeteria was located on that end too, on the bottom floor, while the library was located there also, just above it. There were four other buildings on the campus—an older building that had previously been an elementary school but now was used to house some high school classes, a gymnasium, an annex building attached to the gym, and an agricultural building. Also, by my senior year, a new fine arts building and auditorium had been built. The campus housed approximately nine hundred students. There were no lockers like we had at Enka High School. Instead, I got an open shelf within a wooden, partitioned bookcase-style structure that was in the main hallway. Hooks were underneath these cubbyholes and served as a place to hang coats. It was an open area that meant nothing was secure. Still, it served as a place to store my books between classes.

The school and its accommodations were very inferior to those at Enka. The condition of the facilities, glum and needing repair, reflected my mood upon enrolling at Franklin High School. I entered the second half of my first year of high school year depressed and in anguish. Emotionally, I could barely function. My mind was in a fog. It seemed death was preferable to life.

Since the school didn't offer Latin, I had two study halls, one in the morning and the other in the afternoon. I sat withdrawn during these periods, barely able to interact with my new classmates. In my other classes, I just went through the motions, trying to make it to the end of the day. The days dragged into weeks as my anxiety grew. I just couldn't adjust to life at Franklin High School. I found no consolation at home either, and Cartoogechaye Creek and the woods, which had once provided solace, seemed now to be empty places for me. I couldn't be comforted. It was an emotional upheaval from which I emerged only after a lengthy period.

The situation was made worse in the spring when I tried out for the school's baseball team. From Oakley onward, baseball had been my passion. After Little League, I had played Babe Ruth baseball. I now looked forward to making the high school team, and I did make it, briefly. The eighteen-man roster came out, and I was on it. After a few weeks of practice, Coach Raby announced that to save money on uniforms and equipment, the roster was to be trimmed to sixteen. Frank Pangle and I were cut from the team, another devastating blow that sent me further into misery.

My grades during this period didn't suffer, as I buried my despair in studying. By the end of the year, I had As and a few Bs. I maintained these grades throughout my high school years.

The end of the school year made me wonder what kind of summer break I would have. Dad went back to his familiar routine of holding a revival in the spring, which I attended along with the entire family. It coincided with the Six-Day War in the Middle East, June 5 to June 10, 1967. The occasion of the war set off a spectacular week of revival meetings in which Dad proclaimed the end of time was near. The fact that Israel was to celebrate its twentieth year as a sovereign state lent credence to this fundamentalist interpretation of the Bible.

"Get ready children. Jesus is coming soon!" Dad preached to the entire congregation every evening. He included a detailed explanation as to how these events were to unfold. Dad's exhortations fueled both fear and excitement, a fervor that took weeks to cool off afterward.

When the revival ended, I returned to the question "What am I to do with myself this summer?" For the past five years, I had not had to ask that question since all those other summers had had more than enough activity. This quandary only fueled my gloominess.

On television, I saw Salem cigarette commercials that glamorized this menthol brand and made me want to try them. The ads depicted scenes of people smoking near water and having an excellent time. I thought cigarette smoking might help my depressed mood. Having not smoked a cigarette since I was three years old and having smoked corn silk only once at Cartoogechaye Elementary School, I decided it was time to give it a real try. I walked down to Kiser's Store, where I bought the green-and-white-colored pack from Bud Kiser. I didn't fear him telling Mother or Dad since many boys my age bought them there. Besides, Bud was happy to get the sale. Just as in the commercials, I returned and found some water to sit beside, the baptizing hole at Cartoogechaye Creek, on the east bank next to Patton Road.

I opened the pack and lit a cigarette. I immediately began coughing and hacking as I drew the smoke into my lungs. *Maybe I need to give this time. Force myself to use up the entire thing!* I thought. With every puff, the coughing and hacking got worse, not better. When I finally finished the cigarette, I thought, *What am I going to do with this pack of cigarettes? Where am I going to hide them? Mother and Dad will be mad if they know I'm smoking. Maybe smoking isn't for me.* I sat by the creek contemplating what to do. I looked at the pack of Salems. I then looked out over Cartoogechaye Creek and tossed the pack of cigarettes into the water.

Then I turned my attention to Cartoogechaye Creek and the woods, places where I had not wanted to venture since returning. I took my fishing pole, which had been long unused, and fished the creek. I had forgotten how sitting at the old fishing holes had brought me comfort, how the sun brought inner warmth and strength, how the sound of the water rushing by had been a healing balm for my troubled soul. I drank in all these experiences once again. I hiked the woods to all the old places I had once visited. I sat in isolated enclaves that once had been regular stops on my romps through the woods. Now I sat in respect, taking in all that was around me, communing with nature—something I had not done for many years. As I sat quietly, the birds sang, the crickets chirped, the frogs croaked. A gentle breeze rustled the leaves. The sun above the trees created patterns interspersed among the shadows of the leaves. All that I experienced helped mend my broken soul.

With my brother-in-law, Jim, I ventured out to other nearby trout streams. As we went fishing at Wayah Creek, I decided to give tobacco another try. This time it was chewing tobacco. The sweet smell of Jim's Beech-Nut was irresistible. As I watched him put the brown leaf tobacco between his cheek and gum, I wanted to try it.

"Jim, let me have some of that chewing tobacco," I said.

"Okay, but be sure not to swallow any of it. Just spit it out."

I put a wad of tobacco into my mouth but immediately gulped some juice as the taste quickly activated my saliva glands. We got our fishing gear and headed toward the trout stream. Jim went ahead of me and had already disappeared when my head began to swim. I spat the tobacco out. I got dizzy just seeing the motion of the water. The tobacco already had made me sick. I struggled to return to the car, where I waited for Jim to return. I finally vomited.

Upon his return three hours later, Jim was surprised to find me lying in the front seat of the car. I had not even put a hook into the water. "I told you not to swallow the juice!" Jim said after I told him what had happened. It was the first and last time I ever chewed tobacco.

Television began to occupy more of my day. When Dad pastored Oakley Baptist Chruch, I had watched very few programs consistently since my evenings had many other activities. But here, there wasn't anything else to do. My interest in rock music waned in Franklin, for a time. It seemed like all the songs and groups reminded me of my years in Asheville—especially the Beatles. Music had left my life.

Dark Shadows was an afternoon soap opera I liked, but it was different from other soaps. The program featured ghosts, vampires, werewolves, zombies, monsters, witches, time travel (both into the past and into the future), and a parallel universe. It was a show I rushed home from school to see.

Additionally, from the time of the first Super Bowl on January 15, 1967, I became a fan of professional football. I also became a fan of college football and basketball. We were finally able to watch many of these programs in color, as Dad traded in the old square-box, black-and-white RCA TV set that had been in our home for twelve years for a brand-new RCA color set. We got the new television during the time after the presidential election of 1968. I watched Richard M. Nixon elected in black and white but watched his inauguration in color.

Dad continued his interest in professional boxing, and he still didn't like Muhammad Ali, the champion. He had supported Ali's opponent in every title defense since Ali had beaten Sonny Liston to get the title belt. Dad was glad when the boxing federation suspended Muhammad Ali's boxing license and stripped him of his title in 1967 for refusing to be inducted into the US Armed Forces.

"That Muhammad Ali is just a Communist sympathizer. He deserves what he got," Dad said. Dad was happy with Joe Frazier, who eventually became the undisputed world champion.

I also practiced shooting to ready myself for hunting season, and in the process, renewed my proficiency with a twelve-gauge shotgun, a .410 shotgun, and a .22 rifle. Johnny and I had already developed our skills years earlier before our move to Oakley. That fall I put my talent to use hunting birds, squirrels, and rabbits. I could accurately shoot birds and rabbits with the twelve gauge. Squirrels were so easy to shoot that I switched from the twelve gauge, at first using the .410 and then changing again to the .22. I soon learned I didn't like to hunt. I simply couldn't justify it, since I didn't like to eat the game. The wild taste was too much for me. I believed it was okay for others to hunt if they ate the meat, but my hunting days quickly came to an end.

At the end of the summer, it was time to return to Franklin High School for my sophomore year. I was still suffering from depression, but the season had allowed me to begin mending.

CHAPTER 28
FRANKLIN HIGH SCHOOL

My sophomore year at Franklin High School started out better than had my freshman year. During the summer months, I had finally came to terms with our return to Mount Hope. I still wasn't happy but had accepted the situation as something unalterable. I plunged into my schoolwork, taking geometry, Spanish, English, biology, and civics. I was pleasant to the girls but kept a safe distance. Around the boys, I was more talkative, but overall, I was somewhat quiet, shy, and reserved to everyone. For the most part, I tried to get along and not draw attention to myself. Bobby Peak soon learned my calm exterior masked a toughness honed from my harsh upbringing at home, and my fighting in the Cartoogechaye, Oakley, and Edgewood communities.

One day in Mr. McKee's English class, the two of us squared off. I had not expected a fight but found myself in one. Mr. McKee had left the room, and it was during his absence that the fight took place. As had been my strategy, which I had developed from years of fighting, I sought a quick and decisive strike, one quick punch precisely delivered. Because I was in a classroom, I didn't want to draw blood, so I aimed my punch for Bobby's chin. As I swung the left hook, Bobby raised his chin ever so slightly. Whap! I hit Bobby right in his Adam's apple. He went flying through two rows of seats, landing on the floor. Bobby grabbed his throat and gasped for air. For a second I thought maybe I had killed him. Terrified, I went to help Bobby up from the floor and apologized as he got back to his feet. Finally, he could breathe and swallow again.

We realigned all the desks scattered during the brief melee, and to my surprise, none of my classmates reported the incident to Mr. McKee upon his return. After the fight, Ellen Mashburn said, "Mike, you're both a nice and sometimes mean boy!" This altercation served as a wake-up call for me. After it, I decided I must put fighting behind me. It wasn't appropriate behavior for a high school student. It was the last fight I ever had. As word spread through the student body, I came to realize just how infrequent a classroom fight was at Franklin High School. No one could remember it happening before. Most fights occurred behind the agricultural building, after school. Word of the fight also served another purpose, a warning to other potential opponents that I wasn't a pushover.

During my sophomore year, in Mrs. Perry's civics class, I decided, after lengthy consideration, to pursue a college education. Just as my eighth-grade teacher, Mrs. Williams, had encouraged me, I had enrolled in all the college preparatory classes since coming to high school. But, for me, it still had been an open question as to whether I was going or not. In thinking about the possibility, I had developed a vague notion that, if I went to college, I might want to study forestry. This idea had come from my love of the woods. On the other hand, I couldn't see spending the rest of my life in a forest since the city life from my years in Asheville had become too ingrained in me.

While I was in civics class, my future became clear. Public service had always held my interest; that was my calling. From the age of eight and the presidential election of 1960, I had been captivated by government and politics. This interest had started me watching the news on television and reading the newspaper from cover to cover when I turned fourteen. As we watched a film on the threat of Communism to our society and the world, I made the decision. *I'll go to college. I want to help protect our democracy. I'll do something worthwhile with my life. Maybe I can make a difference,* I concluded. I had no idea how to get into college.

In January 1968, I traded my study hall period for an opportunity to take drivers' education. I looked forward to getting my license and the new freedom it would bring. At first, I drove Dad's 1956 Dodge Custom Royal around the circular drive at Mount Hope Baptist Church over and over for practice. It had an automatic transmission. Later, Mr. Ramsey, the drivers' education teacher, took groups of four out in the student-driver car to get real road experience.

At the City Restaurant, we pulled off the road, and I took the steering wheel. It was my turn to drive. As I pulled out, Mr. Ramsey told me to put on the blinker and turn left. I activated the left signal, just as he instructed, but when I pulled out, I turned right onto the highway. It was an embarrassing moment, as my classmates got a good laugh. The incident had revealed a small handicap. I couldn't tell left from right without the use of a crutch. My crutch was the writing callus on my left middle finger, which I had to touch with my left index finger to get my orientation. That day, because of my nervousness, I forgot to use the crutch, which resulted in my going the wrong direction. I thought it was too complicated to explain this handicap to my laughing classmates and Mr. Ramsey.

As time drew near for me to get my license, Dad saw a vehicle crisis approaching since Johnny had gotten his driver's license the previous year. To remedy the problem, he bought a vehicle for Johnny and me to share, a green 1963 Corvair convertible. The Corvair gave us the freedom we needed. Johnny and I began driving to school, a status reserved for only a select number of students. When it got warm enough, we put the top down and cruised through Franklin on Friday and Saturday nights like many of our other classmates. We circled the City Restaurant, traveled west on Main Street, up Town Hill, through Franklin, and out to the Sunset Restaurant along Harrison Avenue, where we turned around. We then headed back east on Palmer Street toward the City Restaurant, where we began our journey. We cruised in this manner all evening long, sometimes stopping in the parking lot of the City Restaurant to visit with friends or along the route where others had parked to watch everyone else cruise. Life was good.

In the spring, after my sixteenth birthday, I passed my driver's test and obtained my license. After that, Johnny and I argued about who was to drive the Corvair. "I'm the oldest. When we're together, I'll drive!" Johnny insisted.

Johnny usually got his way. Still, I had many opportunities to drive. The Corvair had a manual transmission that I had learned to use competently but not when stopped on a hill, a situation I tried to avoid. The inevitable soon happened. While traveling up Town Hill into downtown Franklin, a traffic jam developed, resulting in slow moving, start-and-stop traffic all the way up. With each stop, I feared the Corvair would roll back into the car behind me. As we inched up Town Hill, I stalled several times before finally reaching level ground. It was a good lesson. By the time I got to the top of the incline, I had mastered the art of clutching on a hill.

Having our driver's licenses and our shared car allowed Johnny and me to get involved in more school activities. We drove to the football and basketball games in the fall and winter months and got involved in other social activities throughout the rest of the year.

Next to Franklin High School was the Tom Thumb Inn, where we put a quarter in the jukebox and listened to the latest rock hits while we had hamburgers or hot dogs and a milkshake or

Coke. Perry's Drug Store was the most popular student gathering place downtown. Loretta, Isabella, and Louise were always friendly and provided delightful service. From Perry's soda fountain, we ordered the store's famous orangeades, chocolate drinks, strawberry milkshakes, or cherry Cokes. We also perused the stacks of 45 rpm records, looked through the comic book section, and checked out the latest selections from the model-car rack. Down at Angel's Drug Store, we ordered ice cream or cherry Cokes from the pretty women behind the counter wearing bright-red lipstick. At Carolina Pharmacy, we ordered hot dogs at the snack bar, the best in town. Bower's Department Store also had a snack bar in the back, where we bought hamburgers, the cheapest available anywhere.

In the colder months, we saw movies at the Macon Theater, located in downtown Franklin. It had a balcony where only the bravest girl sat with her date. Many parents forbade their daughters from sitting there because of its notorious reputation. In the warmer months, Vernon Stiles, owner of the Macon Theater, shut it down because the building had no air conditioning and opened the Franklin Drive-In Theater for the summer.

My classmates referred to the drive-in as the "Passion Pit," since there were stories of the conception of many Maconians there. They also called it the "Skeeter Feeder" because the location was low-lying and swampy, attracting mosquitoes that moviegoers had to fight off each night. You had to get to the drive-in early enough to drive from space to space to find a speaker that worked.

Johnny began to date, something I wanted to do also but was terrified to try. For some reason, every time I thought about asking a girl for a date, the same anxiety came over me that I had experienced with Denise Lingelbach at Edgewood. When talking and being friends, I communicated quite well with a girl, but if I thought about asking her out, I panicked. Despite my fear of dating, the freedom of having a license and a car to drive improved my mood and helped ease my depression. The decision to go to college also brightened my life, as it gave me hope for the future. It seemed I had finally turned the corner.

━✦ ✦━

On March 31, 1968, President Johnson announced he was pulling out of his presidential reelection bid to concentrate on the war in Vietnam, which had become very unpopular with many Americans, particularly young people. American's unease with the war had been growing from the beginning but intensified when the Tet Offensive began on January 31, 1968. The Viet Cong and the North Vietnamese Army pushed into South Vietnam and proved their capability of conducting warfare, undermining the United States' position that they were weak forces.

Thus, more and more people began to question whether the war was worthwhile. Johnson's departure from the campaign was also attributable to the ongoing turmoil in America expressed by the growing counterculture, which included the hippie movement, new left activism, and the emergence of the Black Power movement. Further, the long hot summers in the years following Johnson's election in 1964 resulted in significant race riots in many major American cities. These riots had produced fear, not just in the communities where they occurred but also throughout the entire country, including my hometown.

Tensions among classes, generations, and races all played into the president's unpopularity, which ultimately led to his decision not to run for reelection. I found myself anguished by all the upheaval. I supported the war. I didn't like the hippie movement. I believed the leftists were misguided, and I thought the Black Power movement was responsible for much of the rioting. The times seemed confusing and dangerous. These events and Dad's unrelenting Biblical pronouncements that the end of time was upon us made it feel like it was.

"Do we not hear of wars and rumors of wars?" Dad preached. "Are not nations rising against nations and kingdoms against kingdoms? In America, the black nation has risen against the white nation, and the white nation has risen against the black nation. Israel is under attack by her enemies. Those in Judea will soon flee to the mountains. We are in a period of great distress, unequaled from the beginning of the world until now. It will never be equaled again because all these signs mean Jesus will soon split the eastern sky and return to take his children home!"

Just after Johnson's announcement, during the week of April 1 to April 6, 1968, Dad began the annual spring revival at Mount Hope Baptist Church. Harold Townsend was the guest preacher. He lived in Knoxville and drove back and forth each night to the meetings. On the evening of April 4, Reverend Townsend came into the church, very excited.

"Brothers and sisters, on my way from Knoxville, I heard news on the radio that was music to my ears. Martin 'Lucifer' King was assassinated today in Memphis, Tennessee! Praise the Lord! Hallelujah! That black troublemaker finally got what he deserved! God has saved America! I pulled over, stopped, got out, and danced a jig all the way around my car, over and over. People passing must have wondered what was wrong with me, but I didn't care. I was praising God! It's the best news I've heard in my lifetime," he said.

Most of the congregation agreed with Harold Townsend, shouting "Amen," "Hallelujah," and "Preach it, brother." A few sat quietly in disbelief.

Mother agreed with Reverend Townsend. "I'm glad that black bastard is dead!" she said at home after the church meeting.

Dad remained quiet during the service since most of the people in attendance agreed with his good friend, Harold Townsend.

At home, he said, "I didn't agree with King on many things, but this shooting was wrong. It can only bring more trouble." It did. Fierce riots broke out across America as word spread of King's assassination. I was shocked by the callousness of people's reactions. I was stunned that Harold Townsend believed God was pleased by such a criminal act. I was upset with Mother's harsh remarks, and I was disappointed that Dad had not spoken out against the killing that evening. The riots that followed troubled me, but King's assassination proved to be a defining moment in my life.

"Will I be like Harold Townsend, Mother, and all those who shouted with delight? Will I remain quiet like Dad? Will I be just another southern racist?" I asked.

In his last speech spoken the night before the assassination, about a bomb threat that had been made against his plane that day, Martin Luther King Jr. had sounded prophetic about his life and the events to come. Like everyone, Dr. King told those assembled he did not know what the future held—his life was in God's hands. But, regardless, he'd already been to the mountaintop and had looked over and seen the promised land, and whether he got to be with them or not, they as a people would get to the promised land.

Hearing these words, I said, "No! From now on, I will support and work for equal rights and justice for all Americans, regardless of the color of their skin."

The country had not had time to recover from King's assassination when on June 5, 1968, an assassin shot Senator Robert F. Kennedy in Los Angeles. It happened just after he won the California primary election for the Democratic nomination for president of the United States. On June 6, the next day, he died from his wounds. News of his assassination shook the nation. All the networks extensively covered the aftermath, funeral mass, and slow-moving train ride bearing Kennedy's remains to Washington, DC. His family buried him near his older brother, President John F. Kennedy.

I sat glued to the television in stunned disbelief, just as I had watched in 1963 during the time of President Kennedy's assassination. I was as sickened by this tragedy as I had been of that of Martin Luther King Jr., fearing what might happen next. I had believed Kennedy would win the Democratic nomination and defeat the Republican candidate, Richard M. Nixon.

Robert Kennedy's death changed what I thought to be the inevitable. The bloody riots that occurred at the Democratic Convention held from August 26 to August 29 in Chicago were a continuation of the unsettling events of the spring and summer. After the convention, I was confident Richard M. Nixon would win the election.

On November 5, Nixon faced and narrowly defeated Vice President Hubert H. Humphrey. Segregationist George C. Wallace Jr., a third-party candidate, was also on the ballot. He carried five southern states. Dad supported Nixon, but Mother was noncommittal. The day after the election, Mother, observing Nixon's win said, "I voted for Wallace! I can't stand Nixon, that son of a bitch! I've never voted for him." Mother's racism had remained unaltered.

In the summer of 1968, I began my first job working for Richard Burnett—who owned a body shop—painting automobiles and fixing wrecked vehicles. Richard, a young father of a small son and daughter, worked hard to provide for his family. They attended Mount Hope Baptist Church. I told him, "I'll be glad to work. I've decided to go to college, so I need to start saving some money. A job would be great." The next day I began working for $1.60 an hour. I worked eight hours a day, stopping only for a thirty-minute break to eat the lunch that Richard's wife cooked. We sat at their dinner table along with their children. The body shop was next to the house.

The job went well for the first few weeks, or at least I thought it did. One Friday Richard said, "Mike, next week I don't have enough work for you. I hope you understand."

"Yes, I do, but if you need me later, just let me know."

By the Wednesday night church service, Richard said, "Suddenly, my business picked up this week. I need you to come back."

The next day I returned. When it was time for our lunch break, Richard had gone on ahead of me, leaving me alone with his young son, Ricky. Once Richard was gone, the boy blurted out, "Daddy had you come back because he couldn't find anybody else. He said you're too slow. You need to speed up!" After saying this, Ricky put his hand over his mouth and ran off toward the house.

I went on to the house for lunch as though nothing had happened. Nothing else was said. The boy had not told me anything I didn't already know. I realized I was very slow. My perfectionism made me that way, and regardless of how hard I tried, I couldn't work any faster. I worked the rest of the summer for Richard, but the experience made me realize just how important a college degree was for my future. It was clear I couldn't rely on manual labor for a livelihood.

In addition to working for Richard Burnett, I was also recruited by Mrs. Slagle to mow her lawn. She was the sixth-grade teacher at Cartoogechaye Elementary School and was alleged to be the meanest educator there. Because of her reputation, Mrs. Slagle could find no one to do her mowing. I agreed because I wanted the money, and I wasn't afraid of her. We were living in Oakley during my sixth-grade year, and I had no history with her. Mrs. Slagle paid me seven dollars for a job that took seven hours to complete. Every other week, I also trimmed between her blueberries, which took an additional hour. For this work, she paid me an extra dollar.

I had to bring the mower from home and supply the gasoline, but Mrs. Slagle served me lunch and all the lemonade I could drink. It felt odd sitting at the dinner table on Saturday afternoon with Mrs. Slagle, an old maid, and her old-maid sister who lived there too. I was willing to do about anything to earn money for college.

Before the end of the summer and the beginning of my junior year at Franklin High School, Dad sat me down in his study at the Mount Hope parsonage to tell me some bad news.

"Son, have you noticed the moles on your mother's arms and legs and the one she's kept a bandage on because it keeps running and won't heal up?"

"Yes, I've seen them. Mother just had some taken off by the doctor," I replied.

"It's skin cancer, a very deadly form called melanoma. The doctor says your mother only has six months to a year to live. Since you're one of the older children, I'm telling you, but I'll not be telling the younger ones. I want you to do all you can around here not to cause trouble or to upset your mother."

"Six months to a year. How can that be?" I said in disbelief.

"That's what the doctor said. Melanoma is a skin cancer that gets into the bloodstream, and when it does, it's too late. It's one of the fastest-killing cancers around," he said.

"Who else knows?" I asked, still trying to comprehend what Dad was telling me.

"I've already called Elaine and Gloria, and I'll tell Johnny when he gets home. The others don't need to know for now. Your mother doesn't want to talk about it, so don't be asking her any questions. She doesn't even know I've told you. She didn't want any of you to know, but I've decided it's best to tell you anyway."

I left Dad's study in a state of emotional paralysis. My mind had numbed, as a terrible feeling of hopelessness and emptiness swept over me. Even though Mother and I had never been close and I had never felt her love, I was unable to sleep or eat for days. I couldn't cry, but sorrow swept over me every time I looked at her. Of all the emotions I had ever felt, this was the worst. Life as I had known it was coming to an end. It was a mixed feeling. How could one live without a mother? Who was going to rear my younger siblings? What did the future now hold? These thoughts and many other fears filled my mind in the days and months that followed. Severe anxiety flooded my life. I could barely function. Over the next year, I waited for the inevitable to happen.

CHAPTER 29

ANN PERRY

During this time of emotional distress, Ann Perry came into my life. In August 1968, I returned to Franklin High School for my junior year. I quickly settled into a routine of attending English, history, chemistry, second-year Spanish, and second-year Algebra. I threw myself into my schoolwork. It was the best way for me to tune out all the pain at home.

In the summer, I had seen *The Graduate* at the Franklin Drive-In Theater. The movie was still fresh as I returned to school that fall. I couldn't forget one song from the film. It wasn't the more popular "Mrs. Robinson" but another Simon and Garfunkel song that was also featured—"Scarborough Fair."

The song had put me into a romantic mood. Because of its love narrative, I longed for the companionship of a girl. It was a newer rendition of an old Scottish ballad that dated back to medieval times, having its origins in 1253, when King Henry III of England stipulated by a royal charter that a forty-five-day fair was to be held each year in Scarborough in North Yorkshire. Merchants came from all over England, Norway, Denmark, the Baltic, and the Byzantine Empire. The huge event brought large crowds of buyers, sellers, and pleasure-seekers.

The fair continued until 1788. From the Scarborough Fair, the ballad eventually emerged. As it was passed down from generation to generation, dozens of versions were adapted, modified, and rewritten as the song spread. Simon and Garfunkel's lyrics were a shortened version. It tells the tale of a young man who asks his former lover to fulfill a series of impossible tasks, concluding he will take her back if she completes them.

In some versions, the song is a duet, with the woman giving her lover a series of equally impossible tasks, promising to become his true love if he is successful. The refrain, which enumerates various herbs, is common to English folk songs, having no meaning except to provide the rhyme. In their version, Simon and Garfunkel also conveyed an antiwar theme, but I preferred to concentrate on the love theme.

"Scarborough Fair" set the stage for my relationship with Ann Perry, whom I got to know in study hall. I knew who she was, but I had never talked to her. She was a cheerleader, cute, and liked by all the students. Since Ann was a senior, I had never had a class with her. I was surprised to find her in my study hall. Ann had dark-brown shoulder-length hair and a lovely complexion and was very shapely. She was a fashionable dresser, always looking her best. Ann also had beautiful handwriting. I always had admired Ann, even before I got to know her.

Ann was very active at Franklin High School. She had been a junior varsity cheerleader before spending the next three years on the varsity squad, being named co-captain her senior year. In her junior and senior years, Ann was on the homecoming court. Additionally, she was active in the Spanish Club, serving as secretary her junior year and vice president her senior year. In fact, Ann had acquired the nickname "Spain" from a trip the Spanish Club had taken to that country the previous year. She was also in the Monogram Club, serving as vice president her senior year. Ann was secretary-treasurer of her sophomore class and treasurer of her junior class. As a member of the National Honor Society, she was also very smart.

In contrast, I participated in very few school activities until the guidance counselor said that to get into college, I needed to get involved in some school groups. After this warning, I joined the Junior-Senior Program Committee, Pep Club, Radio Club, and the Spanish Club, at Ann's urging. Also, in my senior year, I was elected to the student council.

A girl of Ann's quality was what I was looking for in a girlfriend. Still, the idea of asking her out struck terror in my heart. There wasn't one boy at Franklin High School whom I feared, but I was panic-stricken by Ann Perry. On the first day in study hall, Ann put me at ease. She came and sat right behind me and, to my pleasure, immediately struck up a conversation. From the very beginning, for both of us, study hall wasn't so much about studying as it was a time of fun and sharing. I needed this diversion. It was the only time during the day I didn't feel the heavy burden of home, the darkest days I had ever known.

At first, it was just fun being with Ann. I didn't immediately fall in love with her. I was cautious because of my fear of asking a girl out, but there was another obstacle also. Ann had a boyfriend, Charlie Leatherman, who was on the varsity football team. This fact told me to keep my emotions in check. I didn't think I could compete with such an admired, athletic guy. Instead, I tried to be satisfied with just being Ann's friend.

There were differences in our backgrounds. Ann's father was James Perry, a pharmacist, and co-owner of Perry's Drug Store in downtown Franklin. Her family lived in the town in a big house, and they were Methodists. They were prominent members of Franklin's social class. By contrast, I was the son of a Baptist preacher living out in the country in a parsonage. My home was five miles from town in Cartoogechaye. Many saw me as just another country boy and not within Ann's social order. Still, I found these differences were offset by how well we got along.

"Ann, you're a senior this year. Are you seventeen or eighteen?" I asked one day.

"I'm sixteen."

"Sixteen! Then how is it that you're a senior?" I asked.

"I skipped a grade in elementary school because I was so far ahead of my classmates."

"Wow! You must be smart."

"Not really, I'm not so good with history. Mike, can you help me?" she asked.

"History is one of my best subjects. I'll be glad to help," I promised. From that day forward, I tutored Ann in history every time she asked.

"When's your birthday?" I asked her one day.

"March 27."

"That's very close to mine, February 6. Just think, you'd be in my junior class if you hadn't been moved up a grade," I said.

"That's true, but instead, I'll be off to college next year."

"What will you study?" I asked.

"I may study education and become a teacher."

"You're smart, so you'll make a great teacher," I said.

"What about you, Mike, are you going to college?"

"Yes, to study political science and then work in government and maybe go into politics."

"You'll be successful. You're excellent with history, so government and politics should fit your interests too," Ann said. Other than this conversation, I didn't talk to Ann about politics since I didn't know her political leanings, if she had any, and I didn't want it to be an obstacle in our friendship. I also excluded religion from our talks, concluding that differences in either politics or religion could be detrimental to our budding relationship.

I thought about telling Ann about Mother's sickness but couldn't bring myself to speak of it, preferring instead the trouble-free conversations we had. Talking about dark issues wasn't what I needed. My hour with Ann each day was joyful and pleasant. My friendship with her breathed life back into me. Our conversations made me feel normal and happy.

I felt peaceful and at ease with Ann. I came to study hall each day with great excitement, knowing I was going to hear her voice, see into her eyes, and experience the beautiful person she was. I eagerly anticipated our time together and was disappointed on the days she wasn't there due to sickness or for some other reason.

Ann enjoyed life, and she liked to laugh. She was a bit mischievous too. We took pleasure in teasing the substitute teachers who occasionally occupied the classroom. Our regular study hall teacher, Mrs. Crawford, was very lenient with us, never interrupting or dissuading our conversations.

Ann and I had a great time. I had not felt so at home at Franklin High School before. Because of Ann, I looked forward to coming to school each day. By Christmas break, I had fallen deeply in love with her—my first real love. My heart was aglow whenever I was with Ann. It was an intense emotion. During the holidays I decided to ask her out. It was the only way to know if she felt the same about me. I had many doubts and fears about trying. I didn't think my effort would succeed. I reasoned that because Ann had a boyfriend, she would say no. Also, I thought, *What outcome will my asking have on our friendship the rest of the school year, if she says no? It would be very awkward afterward. I couldn't endure the rejection. What am I to do? If I don't even try, I could regret it for the rest of my life.* I returned to school after Christmas pondering these ideas.

In study hall, my friendship with Ann continued as it had before. She had no idea I was deeply in love with her. This gorgeous creature had stolen my heart, and she didn't even know it.

For all her popularity, Ann Perry was somewhat quiet and a bit shy when she was in a group. Still, she was a very open and objective person who loved life. She seemed to welcome challenges and was goal oriented. Underlying her quiet persona was a natural leader who was a very responsible, forceful, and self-reliant individual. Still, Ann had a gentleness and softness I admired. All these attributes are what made me love her. I also liked her straightforwardness, honesty, and generosity.

When I saw her in the hallway between classes, Ann sometimes wore Charlie Leatherman's letter jacket, which was a great discouragement to me, because it reminded me that she belonged to someone else. I noticed Ann never wore the jacket to study hall, though, which made me imagine that perhaps she took it off to avoid offending me. This notion was encouraging and made me more determined to get up enough bravery to ask her out. *Is what I feel for Ann mutual, or is it simply a hopeless, one-sided fantasy?* I asked myself. *I'll only know if I ask.*

After Christmas break, in January 1969, the basketball season was fully underway. I attended the events with a newly acquired interest since it meant I got to see Ann cheer at the games. Earlier, during football and the first part of the basketball season, I had not yet fallen in love with Ann, and my interest wasn't as great. Now, I couldn't wait to get to these events.

As Johnny, Randy, and I drove to the sporting contests, we listened to rock and roll. I now heard the music with renewed interest, since my thoughts of Ann had put music back into my life. Several of the top tunes during these months became fixed in my heart and permanently identified with Ann Perry. These songs included "Build Me Up, Buttercup" by the Foundations, "This Magic Moment" by Jay and the Americans, and "You've Made Me So Very Happy" by Blood, Sweat & Tears.

I imagined being with Ann all the time. Throughout the winter and into the spring of 1969, I vowed to ask her out. Each week started the same. I came to study hall, having practiced what I was going to say. I squirmed and fidgeted while Ann and I talked, trying to get enough courage, but at the end of the class, I left without asking her out.

Finally, by the middle of May, I came to the realization I was never going to ask her for a date. *It's too late now,* I reasoned. *The school year is almost over, and Ann will be going to college in the fall.* I decided just to enjoy the time I had left with her. The final day of school arrived, and it was time to say good-bye since Ann was graduating, along with the rest of the Franklin High School class of 1969.

"Ann, I've enjoyed getting to know you this year. You've become a good friend. I hope you have a good summer and enjoy college in the fall," I said.

"Thank you, Mike. I've enjoyed getting to know you too. You've been a sweet boy. Best of luck to you always." With these words, we went our separate ways. I never got over Ann Perry.

In July 1969, on the "Johnny Cash Show," Bob Dylan and Johnny Cash sang a duet of an old song Bob Dylan had first recorded in 1963 on his album *The Free-Wheelin' Bob Dylan.* The song was "Girl from the North Country." The singer asks if you (the listener) are traveling in the north country fair where the wind hits heavy on the borderline to remember him to one who lives there, since she was once his true love. The singer continues to build the scene of snowstorms, freezing rivers, and summer's end; of a need for his lover to have a warm coat in the howling winds; and of her long, flowing hair by which he remembers her most. He concludes by questioning whether she remembers him at all. I wondered the same about Ann.

CHAPTER 30

MOVING ON

After school had ended, a critical issue for me was getting past Ann Perry. I had big plans for college, and I needed to figure out how to get there. Finding summer work was a priority in this quest. I continued mowing Mrs. Slagle's lawn for a dollar an hour on Saturdays. Also, Coach Raby and Coach Pattillo recruited me to work in their tomato field, pulling weeds. Their large truck arrived very early each morning, before the sun came up, to transport me to the field. By the time it arrived, the truck already was filled with other boys from the Cartoogechaye community, all riding in the back. We worked all day, taking only a short break for lunch. We packed our meals at home and brought them with us. The group of boys sat under the shade trees near Cartoogechaye Creek during the noon break. Some of us waded into the stream to cool off.

The coaches provided plenty of water in coolers and encouraged us to drink often to avoid dehydration. Weeding tomato plants was the hardest work I ever did. The only way to weed them effectively was to crawl on your hands and knees. By the end of the day, my hands and knees were sore and bleeding, and every joint in my body ached. The next morning when the truck returned, I was so sore I could hardly move. Such was the life of a tomato-field weed puller. We got eighty-five cents an hour, which was the minimum wage for farm workers. Once the tomatoes ripened, I was asked to help with the harvest. I agreed since it appeared this work was less physical than weed pulling, which it was. I soon learned that I wasn't suited for tomato picking, though.

"Okay, boys, do you see this tomato?" Coach Raby asked as he held it up. "To know if it's ready for picking, you have to look at the bottom. If it's ready, you'll see just the slightest shade of pink. That's how you'll know to pick it. Now that's easy enough, isn't it?" The only problem for me was I couldn't see any pink at all. Every tomato looked the same—green. This fact didn't keep me from picking them, though. I guessed at it all day long. The next morning I was up early and waiting for the truck to arrive, but to my surprise, as it approached, it passed by without stopping. Coach Raby waved at me as he sped onward. It was his way of saying my tomato-picking services were no longer needed.

I also worked as a short-order cook and cashier at the Franklin Drive-In Theater on Friday and Saturday nights. The owner, Vernon Stiles, had first hired Randy, who then recruited me. It was great fun working at the drive-in. I arrived before the sun set to precook hamburgers, get the hot dogs roasting, and make fresh popcorn. Cars began arriving just before dusk, and by nightfall the drive-in was full. The business started out fast and continued briskly throughout the evening. All the concession workers were so busy that breaks were rare. Sometimes I drank a Coke as I worked, just to get through the evening. I tried to put my cup in a spot no one would bother. Still, more than once, my drink was sold to a customer by one of the other workers. The only fringe benefit to working at the Franklin Drive-In Theater was getting in to see the movies free when I wasn't working. In fact, anyone in the family could see them for free, if they were with Randy or me. Many times during the week I drove our 1963 Corvair there, top down, and watched movies all evening long. It was great fun.

⇒+ +⇐

On Sunday, July 20, 1969, I eagerly watched on television, along with millions of other Americans, as the Apollo 11 lunar module, *Eagle*, landed on the moon in the Sea of Tranquility. I was so excited about the upcoming event that on Saturday, the day before, I had left the Franklin Golf Course swimming pool early to watch as Apollo 11 made a forty-minute television transmission after entering lunar orbit. As the *Eagle* made its descent to the surface of the moon on that Sunday, the excitement and anticipation were almost too much to endure. Our family watched with trepidation, as we didn't know whether the lunar lander was to land or crash.

I was awestruck as Commander Neil Armstrong said, "Houston, Tranquility Base here. The *Eagle* has landed." It was the fulfillment of a goal to reach the moon before the end of the 1960s and before the Soviet Union got there, established in 1961 by President John F. Kennedy.

Achieving the objective had not come without a sacrifice, as three astronauts were killed in an accident just a few weeks after our return to Mount Hope. It happened on January 27, 1967, on Launch Pad 34 at Cape Canaveral in a simulated launch of what would have been the first manned mission of the Apollo program. Still, we had done it. America had reached the moon first, beating the Soviets, and making history.

Everyone was proud of this monumental achievement and eagerly awaited the planned first moonwalk later that night. Church began at seven o'clock that evening and ended on its regular schedule. Most of the members quickly dispersed afterward, as they didn't want to miss the moonwalk, which was to be broadcast live on television.

"I'd like to see that moon walk, but I don't have a television set," Old Man Crawford said to Dad.

"Come on over to the parsonage. You can watch it with us," Dad said. Mr. and Mrs. Crawford came to watch, along with a few others from the church. At 10:56 p.m. Eastern Daylight Time, Commander Neil Armstrong became the first human to set foot on another celestial body.

"That's one small step for man, one giant leap for mankind," Armstrong said as he placed his foot onto the surface of the moon. Buzz Aldrin, the lunar module pilot, soon followed Neil Armstrong to the lunar surface. I snapped four pictures with the Kodak camera I had gotten for Christmas in 1967, hoping at least one of them would capture the image on television of the unfurling of the American flag.

After watching the scene from the moon for a while, Old Man Crawford said, "I don't believe for one minute they are walking on the moon. They've made it all up to try to fool us. I think they're somewhere in Arizona, in the desert, or some other place like that!"

"I believe they're on the moon, just like you see it. The government couldn't pull off such a fraud," I said. Everyone else agreed with me.

"Just you wait. You'll see that all this has been nothing but one big lie," Old Man Crawford insisted.

In August I returned to Franklin High School for my senior year and continued my studies, taking English, history, advanced chemistry, government, and typing. I took typing since it was a skill that I believed would help me in college. Most of the students in the class were sophomores, including my brother, Randy. It was the only class we ever had together.

As school began, I was perplexed and haunted by questions about Mother's melanoma, since I was afraid to ask Dad about it. *What is the situation with Mother? A year has passed since Dad told me about her cancer. He said she only had six months to a year to live, but after more than a year, there is no sign of sickness. Did he lie?* I wondered. After wrestling with this issue for a period, I finally asked anyway.

"Son, according to the doctor, your mother's melanoma is in remission. They don't know how long it will last. It could be weeks or months or years; they just don't know," Dad said.

"Her remission could last for weeks or months or years? That's so uncertain," I said.

"Yes, that's true, but we can be thankful for now. I've prayed for God's will in the matter," he replied. This new information took lots of stress off my life since I had been waiting for the worst outcome for more than a year. Although I knew there was no certainty about it, I chose to believe Mother would live for years. This belief allowed me to cope with her illness, regardless of the eventual outcome.

At school, I set out to discover how to get into college. Mrs. Whitmire assisted me since she was my guidance counselor. She said, "Mike, you'll have to get your parents to fill out all these financial aid forms. You also need to make up your mind on which colleges you'd like to attend. You need to go ahead and get those applications sent off before November."

At home, I showed the financial aid forms to Mother and Dad. "I don't know how to fill those complicated things out. Give them to your mother," Dad said.

"I don't have time since I started that new sewing job at the mill. Besides, I'm like your daddy. I don't know how to fill them out either. I don't know what to tell you," Mother said.

It was true Mother had begun a new job at Bluebell, a textile mill, the first job she had ever had. She had taken the job despite the melanoma. A coworker picked Mother up each morning and brought her home every afternoon since Mother didn't drive. Mother had taken the job, she said, to have some spending money. As for Dad, I only thought he didn't care. I read and studied all the financial aid forms, becoming familiar with everything that was needed.

"Dad, I'll need your last year's tax return. I can fill these forms out once I have that," I said. He found the tax return in his study and gave it to me. I filled out the financial aid forms being careful not to miss anything.

"Now that my financial aid forms are complete, I can apply to some colleges," I told them. I had chosen three universities that interested me—Western Carolina University (a regional school), Wake Forest University, and the University of North Carolina at Chapel Hill. I reasoned Western Carolina University was my first choice since I could commute from home, making it the most economical. I applied there first.

"Mother, can you and Dad pay the application fee?" I asked.

"My word, how much money is this college idea going to cost us?"

"It'll be the only money I'll need," I said. Western Carolina University was the only school to which I applied. I never again asked Mother and Dad to help with college expenses. After applying, I waited for a response. In a few months, I got an acceptance letter from Western Carolina University. I was on my way to college, being fully qualified for the Basic Educational Opportunity Grant due to our family income and the number of dependents at home. Throughout my college years, I also received the maximum amount available from the National Defense Student Loan program. These two sources, along with summer employment and a little help from some of my family members, provided the means for me to complete college. Still, I had to finish high school first.

In Mrs. Simpson's English class, we studied more than just English. We also debated about the Vietnam War. She was completely against the war and wanted American military forces withdrawn immediately. I argued that the war was necessary. We had to contain the threat of Communism wherever it existed, and withdrawing from Vietnam would show American weakness. Our regular debates on the issue made me consider joining the marines and volunteering for service in Vietnam. *If I serve, the GI Bill could help pay for college once I'm out,* I reasoned. *On the other hand, if I don't go to college now, I may never have the opportunity later.*

This underlying debate went on in my head for a lengthy period until I finally decided it was best to take the Class II-S student deferment and go to Western Carolina University. I thought if I didn't go to college right out of high school, I might forever miss the opportunity. The idea of getting killed in Vietnam never occurred to me. While I disagreed with Mrs. Simpson about Vietnam, she had my respect. She was one of only a few high school teachers who ever challenged me to think for myself. And in time, after entering college, I came to view the war as she did.

Mr. Reese, my typing teacher, was on the other end of the spectrum. He was a very troubled individual who seemed to take pleasure in making his students miserable. Mr. Reese dispensed zeroes for the slightest infraction. Everyone in the classroom was unhappy because of this teacher's attitude, which was also adversely affecting our grades. One day while we were waiting for Mr. Reese to come to class, a discussion ensued about how badly he was mistreating us. "But what can we do about it? He's the teacher," someone said.

"Being a teacher doesn't give him the right to treat us so dreadfully and to give us bad grades that we don't deserve!" another person said.

"I know what to do, but it will take all of us together to pull it off," I said.

"What is it?" several said simultaneously.

"Let's stage a typing strike! Let's refuse to type until Mr. Reese listens to all our grievances!" I said.

"Yes, that's an excellent idea! Are we all in agreement?" someone else said.

"Yes!" the entire class yelled.

"Listen, here's how we'll do it," I said. "When Mr. Reese presses his stopwatch and tells us to start our exam, we sit with our hands in our laps. No one is to strike a key. Is that understood?"

"Okay!" everyone said. Shortly after that, Mr. Reese entered the room, and, as was his custom, the first thing he did was to begin the daily typing test.

"Now, students, we will start today's test on three: one, two, three." We all sat with our hands in our laps except for Linda, who started banging away on her typewriter. "Linda, stop!" Mr. Reese yelled. "We all must be a little hard of hearing today. We'll try this one more time. Now students, again on three: one, two, three." Again, Linda was the only one to start banging on her typewriter. The rest kept our hands in our laps. "Just what is going on with this class?" Mr. Reese said.

"We want to discuss our complaints with you before we type again. We want to address your rudeness and unfair grading," I said. My statement got the discussion going as the other class members proceeded to say how unhappy they were with Mr. Reese's behavior. To his credit, Mr. Reese listened, and in the days that followed, adjusted, but not that day.

"Everyone who participated in the typing strike gets a zero for today's work, and that includes everyone but Linda," Mr. Reese said. "Mike, as the ringleader, I want you to report to the principal's office right now!" I got up and walked down the hallway to Mr. Frazier's. There I saw Assistant Principal Stott, who was also my government teacher.

"What are you doing here?" Mr. Stott asked.

"Mr. Reese sent me down here because he said I was causing a disturbance in his class, but Mr. Stott, I've been at Franklin High School since I was a freshman. Have you ever known me to cause any trouble?" I said.

"Go on back to class, and be careful not to upset Mr. Reese again," Mr. Stott advised.

"Thank you, Mr. Stott. I'm very disturbed Mr. Reese has spoiled my reputation. After all, I'm a senior, and this is the first time I've ever been to the principal's office," I said as I left.

Other than the unreported fight I had in my sophomore year, I had a clean reputation at Franklin High School. In fact, I was a model student who didn't drink or do drugs and was never in a compromising situation.

Ironically, my classmates gave me the nickname "Devil," not because I lived up to the name but because I was the opposite of it. Besides, Keith Corbin had the nickname "Red" in honor of his red hair, and another name had to be chosen for me, even though I was red haired too. My classmates might have had a different opinion of me if they had witnessed Johnny and me alone at the parsonage one evening. Johnny had gotten a regular part-time job at the A & P Supermarket in Franklin, saved his money, and bought a 1960 Ford Starliner, so he didn't have to share a car with Randy and me. He had purchased and installed a Hurst shifter for the manual transmission, a status symbol around the high school. Hurst shifters were known for their high performance. Johnny souped up the engine and installed a loud muffler. You could hear him coming or going for a quarter of a mile.

One evening while Johnny and I were alone at the parsonage (an unusual situation because the house was almost always full of family), we were watching television when Johnny said, "Mike, I hear something outside. Someone's here!"

"I don't hear anything," I said and kept watching television.

Johnny went to the window and peeked out. "Somebody is in my car! I can still hear the noise," he said.

By now, Johnny had my attention. "What can we do?" Johnny asked.

Taking the loaded twelve-gauge shotgun from the closet, I said, "We can use this. We'll open the door and shoot up in the air. If a burglar is there, the blast will scare him off."

"That's a good plan!" Johnny said.

"Here, take the shotgun and do it!" I said.

Johnny looked at the shotgun and then at the door and said, "It's your idea. You do it."

"But it's your car!" I said.

"Aw, come on. You've got the shotgun; you go first," he said.

"Okay, big chicken, open the door for me." Johnny opened the door, and I stepped out into the darkness, not knowing what to expect but having the shotgun already pointed in the air. I fired it over the top of Johnny's car. I immediately saw a shadowy figure exiting. We could hear the clicking of his shoes on the asphalt as he raced east along the road. We waited, and once we were certain there was no one else, Johnny and I headed over to inspect his car. We found the Hurst shifter dangling on the manual transmission but still attached. We had thwarted the attempted theft.

Toward the end of the school year and graduation, Al Cabe and I were discussing in our government class the fact that neither one of us had ever played hooky from school. We believed this was an unfortunate situation for both of us that we had to rectify. We planned to skip school the next day, opting to hike to the Cullasaja Falls. Al knew the route through the Nantahala Forest that would take us there from below the falls.

"Mr. Stott, we've decided to play hooky tomorrow since neither Al nor I have ever done it. You won't hold it against us, will you?" I asked.

"I didn't hear what you just said, but have a splendid time," he said.

Early the next morning, Al and I headed out with our fishing poles. It took all day to hike to the falls, fish for native brown trout, release our catch back into the water, and return home. It was a beautiful day.

⊶ ⊷

On June 2, 1970, I graduated from Franklin High School, along with Johnny and the entire senior class. We were all excited about our accomplishment. After graduation, there was no waiting around. I was off to stay with my sister Elaine and Jack Barnett, my brother-in-law, in Asheville, where I was to spend the summer working for the Asheville Steel Company. It was a summer job that Elaine had arranged for me with her employer. This work was just what I needed, a good-paying summer job to help me with my college expenses in the fall. I was paid $1.85 an hour—twenty cents over the minimum wage. As I packed my belongings and put them into Elaine and Jack's car, Mother became emotional. She shed some tears as she wished me good-bye for the summer. It was the first time I had ever seen her display any emotion toward me at all.

CHAPTER 31

A YEAR LIKE NO OTHER

In the fall of 1970, I returned home to start my freshman year at Western Carolina University. It was to be a year like no other. Beginning in September, I commuted to school each day, about a thirty-mile drive each way, in a red 1964 Corvair Dad had bought to replace the green 1963 model that Randy had wrecked.

To save on gasoline and car expenses, I carpooled to the university each day with Al Cabe and a couple of other college students. We met just east of Franklin on the highway, where three of us left our vehicles and then rode with the fourth, whoever was designated to drive for the week. Each took a turn, which meant we only had to drive to school once a month. We got to Western in time for the person who had the earliest class to make it and stayed until the person with the latest class finished in the afternoon. I took advantage of the in-between times to study at the student center. I also found lunch at one of the university cafeterias.

I was frightened of failing and spent every spare moment studying. Because of this trepidation, it didn't matter if I was at home or school. I could study anywhere. I usually got home by midafternoon, took a short break from my studies, visited with the family, and then ate supper. In the evening, I returned to my studies in my bedroom, until going to bed.

I noticed there was a lot of new tension between Mother and Dad, but because of my worries about starting college, I had not paid much attention to it. One day when I arrived home, Mother said, "Your Daddy is lazy! We've got bills to pay. I'm working like a dog at the mill. And your Daddy sleeps all morning after I'm gone. He won't turn his hand to do a damn thing around here. John goes to Canton to see his parents now more than he's ever gone. He's just a momma's boy who has never grown up. What grown man has to spend all his time with his mother?" Mother went on, "Preaching is a lazy man's profession. Your Daddy found the perfect job when he started preaching. It allows him to do nothing and then be out all hours of the night. He's just purely and simply lazy, and I'm tired of it!"

On another afternoon, Mother made a very odd request. "Mike, will you drive past Babs Neely's and see if your Daddy's car is there?" Babs still served as the church secretary, the same position she had held the first time Dad pastored Mount Hope Baptist Church.

"I sure will, but why?"

"Don't ask me why. I have my suspicions. Just go and check," Mother replied.

I drove up Wayah Road for a quarter mile to where Babs's house stood on the right. Dad's yellow Volkswagen Beetle, which he had recently purchased, was parked there. I went on up the road, turned around, and went back to the parsonage.

"Yes, Mother, his car is there," I said. "What's going on?"

"I don't know. It's something I'm keeping my eye on."

Another day Mother said, "Mike, I want you to go and see if Babs's car is still at Ruth Hunter's." Dad had taken Dawn there for her piano lessons. Babs's daughter had lessons there that ended just as Dawn's began.

"I'll go," I said, but this time I didn't ask any questions. I drove the two miles to Mrs. Hunter's house and saw Dad and Babs outside talking. Back home I said, "Yes, Mother, I saw Babs and Dad talking."

"That just burns me up. I'm mad as hell! Don't say anything to your Daddy about this. Do you understand?" Mother warned.

"Yes, Mother. I wouldn't know what to say to him anyway."

My spying on Dad at Mother's request continued until Christmas. On most of these undercover operations, I found Dad was with Babs. Spying on Dad didn't interrupt my school studies too much. By the end of fall, I had successfully completed my first quarter. I was happy to have survived.

Not having to study during the Christmas break allowed me to observe more of what was happening between Mother and Dad. The tension had escalated. For the most part, it was low-key but constant. One afternoon, Mack Neely, Babs's husband, drove up to the parsonage. Upon seeing him arrive, Dad quickly went outside to talk. I overheard Mack say, "I'm going to beat your ass, you son of a bitch! I'll expose you to the whole church unless you resign." Mack got out of his car, strode over to Dad with his fists raised, and was trying to hit him.

"Hold on, Mack, there's nothing to it. You've misunderstood," Dad said.

Mack took a swing at Dad, just grazing the side of his head, and drove off. Mother was as mad as I had ever seen her.

"Did that asshole hit you?" Mother asked.

"Dad, what's going on? Why was Mack trying to fight you?" I asked.

"He's saying I'm having an affair with Babs, but there is nothing to it. Nothing to it at all. It's all a big misunderstanding on his part," Dad said. "Hopefully, he'll get over it." For the rest of the Christmas season, Dad acted strangely. Every time the telephone rang, he jumped to answer it. Sometimes Dad talked in a quiet tone. On other occasions, he only said "yes" or "no" several times before hanging up. The tension between Mother and Dad continued to grow.

Just after Christmas, on January 10, 1971, Grandmother Willis died suddenly of a stroke. She was seventy-nine years old. Dad was devastated by the loss of his mother, who had been in excellent health up until her death. The week after Grandmother's funeral, Dad brought Granddaddy home to live with us. Dad put him in the study, where a bed was already set up for visiting preachers. This unexpected development made Mother angry.

"You can bring your daddy here, but you'll have to take care of him. I'm working, and I won't quit!"

"I'll take care of him myself," Dad said. This arrangement lasted for less than two weeks. During the day Dad stayed home and tended to Granddaddy, but as soon as Mother came home, Dad was out the door and gone, leaving Mother to care for him.

"That asshole still thinks I'll quit my job, but it's not going to happen," Mother told me.

One evening it was late, and Dad had not gotten home to help Granddaddy get ready for bed. Mother came to my bedroom, where I was studying, since the 1971 winter quarter had commenced at Western. I was hard at my schoolwork once again.

"Mike, I hate to ask you to help, but your Daddy's not home, and your Granddaddy wants to go to bed. I can't help him undress. Will you do it?" she asked.

"Yes, I'll help, but where's Dad? He said he'd be home to take care of him."

"I don't know, but this is going to stop." I helped Granddaddy get ready and into his bed. Later that evening after Dad came home, I heard Mother arguing with him in their bedroom. Within a few days, Aunt Naomi arrived to take Granddaddy to live with her.

⇌ ⇋

The news came suddenly and without warning on the next Friday afternoon. Mother received a call from a neighbor after arriving home from work. "Mrs. Willis, I hate to be the bearer of bad news, but did you know your husband and Babs Neely were seen leaving the A & P parking lot together? Babs got out of her car, put bags into his, and off they went.

I called Mack Neely, and he came by and picked up his car. "I'm sorry, but it looks like they've left town together," he said.

Mother's face turned pale. She sat down with her face in her hands before telling me what she had just heard. Then she began to sob. I was shocked and didn't know what to say. While all the signs had been there for the past several months, I still hadn't thought Dad was having an affair with Babs. I believed him when he said the events that had occurred were a mix-up and there was nothing to them.

Mother's sobbing turned to wailing, as she couldn't be comforted. She was in a state of shock and confusion. Finally, she gathered herself enough to call my older sisters, Elaine and Gloria, and a few of her closest friends. News of what had happened spread like wildfire among the sixteen thousand residents of Macon County, a community that had grown only slightly throughout the years. At Mount Hope, on Sunday, none of our family members attended church services. We were too upset, confused, and embarrassed to go. Even though it wasn't our act, we all felt the disgrace and shame of what had transpired. The deacons of Mount Hope improvised with men from the church taking charge of the services that day.

On Monday morning, I carpooled to Western as usual. I knew all three of my friends had already heard the news, but we made the entire ride in silence. I said nothing to them. I felt too much shame. They said nothing to me.

The church met that week for a business session to consider its options.

"Mike, I want you to sneak through the back of the church and listen," Mother said.

"I'll do it, Mother." I entered through the back door of the educational wing of the church, went upstairs, and stood near the sanctuary, where I could hear the proceedings from behind a closed door.

"Ladies and gentlemen, we have a crisis here at Mount Hope unlike any we've ever faced before," said one of the deacons.

"What do we need to do?" someone asked.

"First, we have to take care of Mildred Willis and the children. We can't ask them to leave the parsonage now. We haven't even officially heard from John Willis to know his intent. We need to let them stay for now until all this can get sorted out," someone said.

"What about money? How is Mildred going to live without money?" another person asked.

"I vote that we pay Mildred Preacher Willis's salary and let her and the children stay in the parsonage until this matter gets resolved," someone motioned. The motion was seconded and approved unanimously.

Back at the parsonage, I relayed this news to Mother just before a deacon stopped by to tell her of the decision. She was greatly relieved.

After Dad left, Mother had been unable to continue working. She had quit her job at Bluebell. For the next several weeks, we heard nothing and knew nothing, and neither did the Neely family.

Elaine and Gloria came to comfort and offer support to Mother, but no one could calm her. Every time the telephone rang, Mother jumped to answer it, hoping it was Dad.

After getting home from college in the afternoon, I would watch the cars as they passed along the highway, hoping to spot Dad's yellow Volkswagen Beetle. Mother looked too. Since I could do nothing about what was happening, I concentrated on my schoolwork. It was the only way for me to escape the misery of the situation. When I was studying, it seemed as if I was in a different world. After a few weeks, Babs returned home, and I went to talk to her.

Babs said, "John brought me home. He said he couldn't live with what he'd done. We were going to live in Michigan, where I have family members, but he ended up bringing me back."

"Did Dad say where he was going?"

"No, he dropped me off and left without saying. I've been in love with John since the first time he came to Mount Hope, and he loves me. We've been seeing each other all these years. That's the reason he came back the second time. I worked hard to get him to come back. I had missed him so very much. Mike, I'm sorry— please forgive me!" she said.

Not knowing anything else to say, I replied, "Babs, I forgive you."

She broke down in tears. "Thank you. Thank you, Mike. You'll never know what this means to me."

After Babs's return, we still heard nothing from Dad. Mother remained distraught.

At Western, the winter quarter ended, and I had achieved an excellent grade point average despite the emotional upheaval at home.

We spent many weeks waiting, not knowing if Dad was dead or alive. Finally, he called Mother one evening. When she heard his voice on the telephone, the relief on her face was overwhelming. I knew I had to help her with whatever decision she needed to make. Earlier I had offered to quit college and get a job to help support Mother and my younger siblings. This offer only made her cry. My older siblings had also offered to help, but Mother was emotionally paralyzed and could make no decisions.

"What did Dad say?" I asked Mother after the telephone conversation.

"He's in Cleveland, Tennessee. He went there after dropping Babs off at home. He wants to meet me in Murphy this Saturday to talk things over. He wants us to get back together. Will you drive me over there?

"Yes, Mother, I'll do whatever you ask." That Saturday I sat in the car as Mother and Dad met in a restaurant in Murphy, North Carolina, had lunch, and talked. Afterward, Dad came out and greeted me briefly before leaving. On the return trip, I asked, "Mother, what are you going to do?"

"I don't have a choice. I've got to go back to him. I still have four children to raise. We'll move to Cleveland at the end of the school year in June," she replied.

"If that's your decision, I'll do all I can to get you moved."

After the meeting with Mother, Dad began calling her every evening as they made plans for the move to Tennessee. Mother was greatly relieved, and it showed. For the first time since Dad had departed, she laughed. Mother returned to Murphy to see Dad on several occasions after that first visit. She warned each of us to tell no one of the impending relocation. Mother didn't want to upset the members of Mount Hope.

During this period, Dad finally sent a long-overdue letter to the Mount Hope Baptist Church congregation, officially resigning as the pastor. The plans to move might have gone unnoticed if it had not been for a newspaper article in the *Cleveland Daily Banner* announcing John R. Willis Jr. as pastor of Tasso Baptist Church in Bradley County, Tennessee, the county where Cleveland was situated.

Someone from Cartoogechaye was passing through Cleveland on his or her way home from Chattanooga and bought a copy of the local newspaper while stopping to eat. In it was a picture of Dad, along with the announcement. This person brought the paper home and showed it throughout the community.

News of Dad's resurfacing in Cleveland, Tennessee, and the fact he was already serving as pastor of another church spread through Macon County like lightning. A deacon called Mother to ask if she knew.

"Yes, I've talked to John, and I plan to move to Cleveland once the school year is over. Will the church allow me to stay in the parsonage until then?" Mother asked.

"I don't know, Mildred. We'll need to take the matter to the church."

Mount Hope held another business meeting to address the latest issue. Some felt betrayed. They thought Mother had deceived the church. Others sympathized with her and said she had no choice in the matter and the family should stay until June. The latter opinion prevailed.

"Mildred, the church voted to let you stay and to keep paying you John's salary until school lets out in June," a deacon told her.

"Thank you. I appreciate the kindness of the church," Mother said.

The 1971 spring quarter ended at Western Carolina University about the same time the Macon County Public Schools dismissed in June. I finished the grading period very strongly. Even though I had experienced great conflict in my home life, my academic career was beginning to flourish.

After school had ended, I helped Mother with the task of moving the household to Cleveland. Randy and our two brothers-in-law, Jim and Jack, helped. Johnny had already moved to Cleveland to take a new job, living with Dad until the rest of the family arrived. Dad didn't return to Mount Hope to assist us, electing instead to meet the rented truck once we arrived in Cleveland.

⇥ ⇤

That summer I didn't stay with the rest of the family in Cleveland. I was too upset and moved in with Gloria and Jim and their children, Jimmy and Carol. They lived in the Sugarfork community of Macon County, where Jim had become the pastor of Sugarfork Baptist Church.

Gloria and Jim had moved to Franklin earlier. My reason for staying in Franklin was that Western had arranged a summer job for me at the Macon County Recreation Park as part of the university's student work-study program. While this job, in fact, kept me in Franklin, it also served as good reason not to move to Cleveland.

At the recreation park, I worked for minimum wage, $1.65 per hour, mowing grass and doing maintenance work. The unpleasantness of the year was still very raw. I preferred to work at the park in obscurity, avoiding anyone I knew from Mount Hope or the community as much as possible. Personally, I still felt the shame of Dad's transgression, making it hard for me to face friends or acquaintances.

It was at the recreation park that Ann Perry briefly reappeared in my life. I had not seen her since that final day in study hall in 1969.

The Macon County Recreation Park had been open for only a few years, and the park's new pool was a big attraction to the locals. Ann had come home to enjoy her summer break from college at the end of her sophomore year, and the pool was the perfect place for her. She came on a regular basis.

Upon her arrival, Ann always wore a sorority T-shirt over her bathing suit. I was startled the first day I saw her. I hid out, away from the pool, to prevent her from seeing me. I couldn't bear the thought of talking to her. *What does she know about Dad and Babs and all the trouble from Mount Hope?* I asked myself. *What could I possibly say? No, I won't do it. I won't talk to Ann Perry.*

I didn't need to work around the pool, which made it easy to avoid Ann. Still, on occasion, she saw me from a distance and waved. I waved back but never went over. I always wondered what she thought of my unfriendly behavior. Still, at the time it didn't matter; I simply couldn't bring myself even to say hello.

Sometimes I observed Ann from a distance, on a hillside overlooking the pool. I fondly remembered the daily talks we had once had in high school. *It'd be nice to be back there with Ann, to talk like we once did,* I mused. I quickly dismissed this idle thought. *Life has changed. You can't go back—just forget it.* Summer ended, and Ann went back to college. I returned to Western. It was the last time I ever saw her, but I thought of her often.

CHAPTER 32

FAREWELL TO MOUNT HOPE

At the end of the summer, I bade farewell to Mount Hope Baptist Church and Franklin. My many years there had been mostly bitter. I looked forward to returning to Western Carolina University for the 1971 fall quarter and my sophomore year of college. I moved into a dormitory on campus. I had no choice since Mother and Dad had moved away.

≔ ≕

In January 1972, Mother's melanoma returned with a vengeance. It metastasized first to her bladder and then to her brain. Over the course of a ten-month period, she had many surgeries and fought valiantly, but in the end, cancer took her. Most weekends I left my college studies and headed to Cleveland to visit. I drove 129 miles each way. As the end grew nearer, the emotional toll that Mother's sickness and impending death exacted on my siblings and me was beyond description.

On Friday, October 27, 1972, the first quarter of my junior year at Western, I was called out of my international politics class and told I needed to leave immediately; Mother would not live through the day. I thanked the messenger and returned to my seat. My head was swirling. I couldn't think. I couldn't hear the professor. Slowly I gathered myself, made my way to my off-campus residence, collected my belongings, and headed to Cleveland in the old maroon 1964 Ford Fairlane I had bought to replace the 1964 Corvair after its engine blew up. It was a three-hour trip. I got to the hospital in the early evening. I was the last sibling to arrive. My mother died within thirty minutes of my arrival. It seemed as if she was waiting for me to get there. She was forty-four years old. We held a visitation in Cleveland, where all of Dad's new church members, friends, and fellow pastors paid their last respects. A large crowd gathered.

The following night, a second visitation occurred in Canton, Mother's hometown. The crowd was crushing. We held the funeral on the third day at Edgewood Baptist Church. It was standing room only. We buried Mother in the church cemetery following the service. Dad believed it appropriate to bury Mother there. He said Edgewood was the only church where she had been happy.

I continued my studies. In 1974, I graduated with honors from Western Carolina University with a bachelor of arts degree, completing a double major in political science and history. I fulfilled my goal of a college education. I overcame all the obstacles and headed toward a better life. I immediately went on to graduate school. In 1976, I completed a master's degree in public administration at the University of Tennessee at Knoxville. Following the completion of my education, I settled in Cleveland, where I began a lifelong career in local government management, hospital administration, and politics.

I applied all the lessons learned from my growing up years in every area of my career. While working in the local county government, I was passionate about helping those in need and advocated for policies and actions that best benefited everyone in our community. While working at the county hospital, I became zealous about providing the best healthcare possible to all our citizens, including the indigent. In politics, as chairman of one of the local political parties, I found a platform to help elect individuals locally, regionally, and statewide who shared my philosophy to use government for good purposes and to represent all the people dutifully. The hardships I endured and the toughness I developed in my early years more than prepared me for the rough-and-tumble world of this work.

Beyond my job, I became a strong advocate of volunteerism working with the local chapters of the United Way, the American Heart Association, the American Cancer Society, the Kiwanis Club, and other such organizations to help improve the lives of people in the community.

Personally, I have used the lessons of my youth as a guide and as a reminder that honesty and integrity are the most important values in life. These guiding principles have allowed me to maintain fulfilling and loving relationships with my family while also cultivating respectful associations in the community and with longtime friends. I do not take any of these relationships for granted, for it is with them I find my greatest satisfaction.

⊨⊣ ⊢⊨

For the next twenty years, Dad pastored various churches in southeast Tennessee. The news of what had happened at the Mount Hope Baptist Church never made its way to Cleveland. He remarried in the summer of 1974. She was a member of his church. For the rest of his life, Dad denied he and Babs had ever had an affair. He maintained they had only been friends and that he had merely taken her to see her family in Michigan—nothing more. Dad's constant denials about Babs and the past, including the abuse of his children, resulted in our relationship remaining strained. The standoff with Dad, begun in my childhood, continued throughout the rest of his life.

While attending the 1992 Southern Baptist Convention in Indianapolis, Indiana, Dad collapsed on the floor from heart disease. He died of complications a month later, on July 5, 1992, at an Indianapolis hospital. He was sixty-nine years old.

We held a visitation in Cleveland, where a large crowd gathered, one of the largest I ever witnessed. The visitation was followed by a funeral the next day at Cedar Springs Baptist Church, where Dad served as pastor at the time of his death. It was standing room only. A funeral caravan next traveled to Edgewood Baptist Church. Dad's body was to have lain in repose at the church before his burial, but when we arrived, the local pastors had organized a second funeral service in which many preachers eulogized Dad as a great man of God. The church was packed. We buried Dad next to Mother in the church cemetery.

In August 1980, Johnny's wife, Joan, my sister-in-law, delivered the news casually while we were talking. "Mike, I've meant to tell you. Do you remember Ann Perry from high school?" she asked. Joan didn't know I had once been in love with Ann. I had never told anyone.

"Yes, I remember her. Why?" I said.

"She died of breast cancer. They buried her a while back in Franklin. She'd been sick for a long time."

"You remember, she went with Charlie Leatherman all through high school," Johnny said.

"Yes, I remember that too. Ann and I had study hall together her senior year, when I was a junior. We became splendid friends.

I'm sorry to hear the news. Ann was a lovely person," I said, as I tried to hide my surprise and sorrow. "Was she married?"

"Yes, but she didn't marry anyone from Franklin," Joan said.

"So, she never married Charlie Leatherman!" I stated.

"No, she was teaching school in Georgia," Joan said.

"Did she have any children?" I asked.

"No, she had no children," Joan replied.

"It's a shame. Ann was one of the finest girls I ever knew."

"She battled cancer for a long time," Joan said.

"I'm sorry she had to suffer, that her life was cut so short. She had a lot to offer. Some things are just not fair!" I said.

The news of Ann's death was devastating. I was upset and grief stricken, even though I had not seen her for years or even tried to keep up with her. Back at home, I kept thinking, *How dreadful! Ann was young. She was only twenty-eight, too young to die!* Twenty-eight myself and still unmarried, I tried to shake the news off, but her death continued to distress me. I thought about returning to Franklin to visit her grave. I rejected this idea at first, but I couldn't get past the troublesome urge to make the visit. *Why visit? I didn't keep in touch. I never told Ann I loved her. I don't have any reason to go.* Still, I couldn't let it go. Finally, I decided to make the trip.

It was hot, still summertime. The sun was high in the blue sky when I arrived. A slight haze was in the air from the summer heat. The wind was calm. It was a typical summer day in the mountains. Woodlawn Cemetery was one of Franklin's largest. Upon my arrival, I had no trouble finding the grave. I went straight to Ann's gravesite, even though I had no idea where to begin looking.

I stood at the foot of her grave. The marker read: "Ann Perry Thomas, March 27, 1952–August 4, 1980." I thought, *There was so much more to Ann's life than what's on this marker. She was a beautiful girl and talented.*

Time passed. The only sounds I heard were the birds chirping in the nearby trees. I wanted to know what it was that had made me make the visit. As I lingered, it became apparent. "Ann, you breathed strength into me during a tough time of my life. You helped me feel normal during a very dark period. That's the reason I'm here today, to thank you. It's the least I can do. It's the only thing I can do," I said.

There was no one else in the cemetery; I was all alone. I sat down at the foot of Ann's grave. Simon and Garfunkel's song "Scarborough Fair" began playing in my heart.

Back at home, as I slept, I dreamed I was back at Woodlawn Cemetery, still sitting at the foot of Ann's grave. A bright figure appeared to me dressed in white, a large masculine form that hovered above the ground. The brilliance of his presence made me shade my eyes as I looked at him.

"Are you going to Scarborough Fair?" I asked.

He looked at me but didn't speak.

"Remember me to one who lives there. Ann once was a true love of mine." The figure never spoke as it was engulfed in a brilliant light and vanished. I awoke from the dream.

Some time later, in the winter, I made a second trip to Ann's grave. Another song was calling me back. The sun was shining brightly on that crisp, cold day as a bitter breeze rattled the bare limbs of the nearby trees. As I arrived, there was a single white, billowy cloud floating across an otherwise crystal-clear blue sky. I thought the sight was unusual. I couldn't ever remember seeing a single cloud floating so lazily while the wind was blowing so sharply. I stood at Ann's grave just as I had done before. The strange cloud momentarily returned my thoughts to the sky. I gazed upward for a second look, but the cloud had vanished, exposing a waxing gibbous moon.

It was a beautiful sight to see, the moon rising from the east just above the horizon in the midafternoon, over the distant mountains. Again, I was alone in the cemetery. My attention returned to Ann's grave as I sat down at the foot of it on the frozen ground. This time Bob Dylan's "Girl from the North Country" began playing in my heart. I wondered if Ann had ever remembered me at all. I returned home. In time, I overcame the sorrowfulness of Ann Perry's death, but I never forgot Ann. How could I? I once had loved her very deeply.

EPILOGUE

Throughout my life, the images of what I have written have sometimes played over and over like a movie in my mind. At other times, the story appears as if it is an old stuck phonograph record playing on a turntable. It gets to a scratch in the vinyl and never gets past it, repeating that portion of the song in an unending circular path. I had hoped that writing this book would finally make the film in my head finish playing and the stuck vinyl record stop—and to some extent, they have. But I only exchanged these images for new ones—the pages of my book, which now flip constantly in my mind. I have concluded that I will just have to live with these memories in whatever way they choose to come. After all, the walls of my past still talk.

Writing this book has allowed me to see my parents in a new way, to assess them in the light of my experiences in this world, a half century removed. While I will never be able to fully understand their motives and actions and the choices they made, I have learned that every human being makes mistakes, and that given an opportunity to correct them, most would. For that reason, I have developed greater forbearance for my parents, John and Mildred Willis, and have chosen to dedicate myself to the positive things they taught me. Dad imparted racial tolerance and acceptance. Mother trained me to be a fighter, and though her negative words might have brought about the opposite, they inspired me to succeed. Both taught me to respect those with disabilities, and each instilled in me toughness, which turned out to be a crucial attribute throughout my life.

I also attribute my perseverance to my parents—that is, a belief in myself and confidence to keep at it.

Anyone who experienced what I did would have an excuse for giving up, for losing his or her diligence. After all, hardship can be the death knell of success. Still, I believed in myself. And where did I find this reliance? I honed it in my alone times in the woods and mountains of western North Carolina, in the cornfields, and at Cartoogechaye Creek while immersed in the wonders of nature.

There are scars I have had to live with. Notwithstanding my optimistic view, I have experienced anxiety throughout much of my life, eventually diagnosed as generalized anxiety disorder (GAD). It most likely developed during my abusive childhood. GAD is more than normal stress; it is chronic and exaggerated worry and tension. Unable to relax, a person with this condition often feels restless, keyed up, or on edge; is fatigued; has difficulty concentrating; and sometimes his or her mind goes blank. He or she also experiences irritability, muscle tension, and sleep disturbance. I experienced all these symptoms. Nothing seemed to provoke it.

A person with GAD anticipates disaster and worries about many things, the source of which is difficult to pinpoint. The older I got, the more these symptoms plagued me, which finally resulted in my seeking help. For years now, I have successfully battled the disorder with medication. I feel like an entirely different person.

After writing this book, I have also concluded something else. When I began, I viewed my life from an "otherworldly" perspective. I believed I was among the people of Appalachia but not of them. I was a character out of place, a person not of the mountains, and a soul no one understood. But this assessment was incorrect. Now I know that much of me never left Appalachia. The things I experienced, the lessons I learned, and the outcome of my life have all been shaped by my experiences there. It is evident my life is intricately interwoven with the Blue Ridge Mountains. We cannot be separated.

ABOUT THE AUTHOR

Michael K. Willis was born and raised in the Appalachian region of the Blue Ridge Mountains in western North Carolina.

Willis received his bachelor's degree in political science and history from Western Carolina University and his master's degree in public administration from the University of Tennessee at Knoxville. He currently lives in Asheville, North Carolina.

Made in the USA
Columbia, SC
19 August 2017